VOLUME 544　　　　　　　　　　　　　　　　　MARCH 1996

THE ANNALS

of The American Academy *of* Political
and Social Science

ALAN W. HESTON, *Editor*
NEIL A. WEINER, *Assistant Editor*

IMPACTS OF CHANGING EMPLOYMENT:
IF THE GOOD JOBS GO AWAY

Special Editor of this Volume

ARTHUR B. SHOSTAK
*Department of Psychology,
Sociology and
Anthropology
Drexel University
Philadelphia
Pennsylvania*

Weeks-Townsend Memorial Library
Union College
Barbourville, KY 40906

 SAGE Periodicals Press *THOUSAND OAKS LONDON NEW DELHI*

The American Academy of Political and Social Science

3937 Chestnut Street   Philadelphia, Pennsylvania 19104

Board of Directors

ELMER B. STAATS	ANTHONY J. SCIRICA
MARVIN E. WOLFGANG	FREDERICK HELDRING
RICHARD D. LAMBERT	LYNN A. CURTIS
LLOYD N. CUTLER	MARY ANN MEYERS
HENRY W. SAWYER, III	SARA MILLER McCUNE

Officers

President
MARVIN E. WOLFGANG

Vice President
RICHARD D. LAMBERT, *First Vice President*

Secretary	*Treasurer*	*Counsel*
ANTHONY J. SCIRICA	ELMER B. STAATS	HENRY W. SAWYER, III

Assistant to the President
MARY E. PARKER

Editors, THE ANNALS

ALAN W. HESTON, *Editor*   RICHARD D. LAMBERT, *Editor Emeritus*
ERICA GINSBURG, *Managing Editor*   NEIL A. WEINER, *Assistant Editor*

Origin and Purpose. The Academy was organized December 14, 1889, to promote the progress of political and social science, especially through publications and meetings. The Academy does not take sides in controverted questions, but seeks to gather and present reliable information to assist the public in forming an intelligent and accurate judgment.

Meetings. The Academy occasionally holds a meeting in the spring extending over two days.

Publications. THE ANNALS is the bimonthly publication of The Academy. Each issue contains articles on some prominent social or political problem, written at the invitation of the editors. Also, monographs are published from time to time, numbers of which are distributed to pertinent professional organizations. These volumes constitute important reference works on the topics with which they deal, and they are extensively cited by authorities throughout the United States and abroad. The papers presented at the meetings of The Academy are included in THE ANNALS.

Membership. Each member of The Academy receives THE ANNALS and may attend the meetings of The Academy. Membership is open only to individuals. Annual dues: $51.00 for the regular paperbound edition (clothbound, $74.00). Add $12.00 per year for membership outside the U.S.A. Members may also purchase single issues of THE ANNALS for $15.00 each (clothbound, $19.00). Add $2.00 for shipping and handling on all prepaid orders.

Subscriptions. THE ANNALS (ISSN 0002-7162) is published six times annually—in January, March, May, July, September, and November. Institutions may subscribe to THE ANNALS at the annual rate: $197.00 (clothbound, $229.00). Add $12.00 per year for subscriptions outside the U.S.A. Institutional rates for single issues: $34.00 each (clothbound, $40.00).

Second class postage paid at Thousand Oaks, California, and additional offices.

Single issues of THE ANNALS may be obtained by individuals who are not members of The Academy for $18.00 each (clothbound, $28.00). Add $2.00 for shipping and handling on all prepaid orders. Single issues of THE ANNALS have proven to be excellent supplementary texts for classroom use. Direct inquiries regarding adoptions to THE ANNALS c/o Sage Publications (address below).

All correspondence concerning membership in The Academy, dues renewals, inquiries about membership status, and/or purchase of single issues of THE ANNALS should be sent to THE ANNALS c/o Sage Publications, Inc., 2455 Teller Road, Thousand Oaks, CA 91320. Telephone: (805) 499-0721; FAX/Order line: (805) 499-0871. *Please note that orders under $30 must be prepaid.* Sage affiliates in London and India will assist institutional subscribers abroad with regard to orders, claims, and inquiries for both subscriptions and single issues.

Printed on recycled, acid-free paper

THE ANNALS
© 1996 *by* The American Academy *of* Political *and* Social Science

All rights reserved. No part of this volume may be reproduced or utilized in any form or by any means, electronic or mechanical, including photocopying, recording or by any information storage and retrieval system, without permission in writing from the publisher. All inquiries for reproduction or permission should be sent to Sage Publications, 2455 Teller Road, Thousand Oaks, CA 91320.

Editorial Office: 3937 Chestnut Street, Philadelphia, PA 19104.

For information about membership* (individuals only) and subscriptions (institutions), address:

SAGE PUBLICATIONS, INC.
2455 Teller Road
Thousand Oaks, CA 91320

From India and South Asia, write to:	*From the UK, Europe, the Middle East and Africa, write to:*
SAGE PUBLICATIONS INDIA Pvt. Ltd P.O. Box 4215 New Delhi 110 048 INDIA	SAGE PUBLICATIONS LTD 6 Bonhill Street London EC2A 4PU UNITED KINGDOM

SAGE Production Staff: ERIC LAW, SHEILA BERG, DORIS HUS, and ROSE TYLAK

**Please note that members of The Academy receive THE ANNALS with their membership.*

Library of Congress Catalog Card Number 95-69941
International Standard Serial Number ISSN 0002-7162
International Standard Book Number ISBN 0-7619-0138-8 (Vol. 544, 1996 paper)
International Standard Book Number ISBN 0-7619-0137-X (Vol. 544, 1996 cloth)
Manufactured in the United States of America. First printing, March 1996.

The articles appearing in THE ANNALS are indexed in *Academic Index, Book Review Index, Combined Retrospective Index Sets, Current Contents, General Periodicals Index, Public Affairs Information Service Bulletin, Pro-Views,* and *Social Sciences Index.* They are also abstracted and indexed in *ABC Pol Sci, America: History and Life, Automatic Subject Citation Alert, Book Review Digest, Family Resources Database, Higher Education Abstracts, Historical Abstracts, Human Resources Abstracts, International Political Science Abstracts, Managing Abstracts, Periodica Islamica, Sage Urban Studies Abstracts, Social Planning/Policy & Development Abstracts, Social Sciences Citation Index, Social Work Research & Abstracts, Sociological Abstracts, United States Political Science Documents,* and/or *Work Related Abstracts,* and are available on microfilm from University Microfilms, Ann Arbor, Michigan.

Information about membership rates, institutional subscriptions, and back issue prices may be found on the facing page.

Advertising. Current rates and specifications may be obtained by writing to THE ANNALS Advertising and Promotion Manager at the Thousand Oaks office (address above).

Claims. Claims for undelivered copies must be made no later than twelve months following month of publication. The publisher will supply missing copies when losses have been sustained in transit and when the reserve stock will permit.

Change of Address. Six weeks' advance notice must be given when notifying of change of address to ensure proper identification. Please specify name of journal. Send address changes to: THE ANNALS, c/o Sage Publications, Inc., 2455 Teller Road, Thousand Oaks, CA 91320.

THE ANNALS

of The American Academy *of* Political *and* Social Science

ALAN W. HESTON, *Editor*
NEIL A. WEINER, *Assistant Editor*

──────────── FORTHCOMING ────────────

**CHALLENGES IN RISK ASSESSMENT
AND RISK MANAGEMENT**
Special Editors: Howard Kunreuther and Paul Slovic
Volume 545   May 1996

THE MEDIA AND POLITICS
Special Editor: Kathleen Hall Jamieson
Volume 546   July 1996

THE FUTURE OF HONG KONG
Special Editor: Max J. Skidmore
Volume 547   September 1996

See page 2 for information on Academy membership and
purchase of single volumes of **The Annals.**

CONTENTS

PREFACE . . . . *Arthur B. Shostak*   8

DEFINING THE CHALLENGE

A NEW SOCIAL CONTRACT . . . . *Jeremy Rifkin*   16
JOBS: NEW CHALLENGES, NEW RESPONSES . . . . *Sumner M. Rosen*   27
HUMAN CAPITAL DEVELOPMENT:
   AMERICA'S GREATEST CHALLENGE . . . . *Theodore Hershberg*   43

REFINING THE CHALLENGE

HIGH TECHNOLOGY AND WORK TOMORROW . . . . *Stanley Aronowitz and William DiFazio*   52

SERVICE WORKERS: HUMAN RESOURCES
   OR LABOR COSTS? . . . . *Barbara A. Gutek*   68

ASSESSING ONGOING REFORMS

THE GERMAN APPRENTICESHIP SYSTEM:
   LESSONS FOR AUSTIN, TEXAS . . . . *Robert W. Glover*   83
THE END OF HAWAII'S PLANTATIONS:
   BACK TO THE FUTURE? . . . . *Lawrence W. Boyd, Jr.*   95
DISLOCATION POLICIES IN THE USA:
   WHAT SHOULD WE BE DOING? . . . . *Ross Koppel and Alice Hoffman*   111
DISLOCATION POLICIES IN WESTERN EUROPE:
   PAST, PRESENT, AND FUTURE . . . . *Thomas Samuel Eberle*   127
EMPLOYMENT FLEXIBILITY AND
   JOBLESSNESS IN LOW-GROWTH,
   RESTRUCTURED JAPAN . . . . *Koji Taira and Solomon B. Levine*   140

LOOKING BEYOND

REWORKING WORK: TOUGH TIMES AHEAD . . . . *Joseph F. Coates*   154
COMPUTERS DON'T KILL JOBS,
   PEOPLE DO: TECHNOLOGY AND
   POWER IN THE WORKPLACE . . . . *Charley Richardson*   167
PERFORMING WORK WITHOUT DOING JOBS . . . . *Daniel Marschall*   180
THE EMPLOYMENT OF NEW ENDS: PLANNING
   FOR PERMANENT UNEMPLOYMENT . . . . *David Macarov*   191
EPILOGUE . . . . *Arthur B. Shostak*   203
BOOK DEPARTMENT   206
INDEX   241

BOOK DEPARTMENT CONTENTS

INTERNATIONAL RELATIONS AND POLITICS

ADAMS, JAMES. *Sellout: Aldrich Ames and the Corruption of the CIA.* Herbert Foerstel 206

KOLKO, GABRIEL. *Century of War: Politics, Conflicts, and Society since 1914.* Mary Beth Emmerichs 207

MLYN, ERIC. *The State, Society, and Limited Nuclear War.* Leonard A. Cole 208

MÜLLER, HARALD, DAVID FISCHER, and WOLFGANG KÖTTER. *Nuclear Non-Proliferation and Global Order.* Eric Waldman 208

AFRICA, ASIA, AND LATIN AMERICA

GOLDMAN, MERLE. *Sowing the Seeds of Democracy in China: Political Reform in the Deng Xiaoping Era;* LIN, JING. *The Opening of the Chinese Mind: Democratic Changes in China since 1978.* Richard Baum 210

HOSTON, GERMAINE A. *The State, Identity, and the National Question in China and Japan.* Hilary Conroy with George C. C. Chang 212

MACKERRAS, COLIN. *China's Minorities: Integration and Modernization in the Twentieth Century.* Wayne Patterson 214

RUBIN, BARNETT R. *The Fragmentation of Afghanistan: State Formation and Collapse in the International System;* RAIS, RASUL BAKHSH. *War without Winners: Afghanistan's Uncertain Transition after the Cold War.* Robert Nichols 214

UNITED STATES

ALESINA, ALBERTO and HOWARD ROSENTHAL. *Partisan Politics, Divided Government, and the Economy.* Bryan D. Jones 216

BERG, JOHN C. *Unequal Struggle: Class, Gender, Race, and Power in the U.S. Congress.* Anne Sisson Runyan 217

EISENSTEIN, ZILLAH R. *The Color of Gender: Reimaging Democracy;* MANN, CORAMAE RICHEY. *Unequal Justice: A Question of Color.* Katy J. Harriger 218

ELLIS, RICHARD J. *Presidential Lightning Rods: The Politics of Blame Avoidance.* Rhonda Kinney 219

ELSHTAIN, JEAN BETHKE. *Democracy on Trial;* KRASNO, JONATHAN S. *Challengers, Competition, and Reelection: Comparing Senate and House Elections.* Eric M. Uslaner 220

HART, VIVIEN. *Bound by Our Constitution: Women, Workers, and the Minimum Wage.* Nancy Breen 223

McDONALD, FORREST. *The American Presidency: An Intellectual History.* Harry W. Reynolds, Jr. 223

PECORELLA, ROBERT F. *Community Power in a Postreform City: Politics in New York City.* Jeffrey M. Berry................................. 225

REDISH, MARTIN H. *The Constitution as Political Structure.* Howard Gillman 226

WEED, CLYDE P. *The Nemesis of Reform: The Republican Party during the New Deal.* John Frendreis 227

SOCIOLOGY

HADDAD, YVONNE Y. and JANE IDLEMAN SMITH. *Mission to America: Five Islamic Sectarian Communities in North America.* Robert J. Young 227

KEATING, W. DENNIS. *The Suburban Racial Dilemma: Housing and Neighborhoods.* Elisabeth Lasch-Quinn 228

McMAHON, CHRISTOPHER. *Authority and Democracy: A General Theory of Government and Management.* Mark E. Rush 229

TORRES, ANDRÉS. *Between Melting Pot and Mosaic: African Americans and Puerto Ricans in the New York Political Economy.* Barbara Schmitter Heisler 231

WHITE, MERRY. *The Material Child: Coming of Age in Japan and America.* Jean E. Brooks 232

ECONOMICS

GRAVELLE, JANE G. *The Economic Effects of Taxing Capital Income.* Bernard P. Herber 232

HECKSCHER, CHARLES. *White Collar Blues.* Alexander M. Thompson III 233

VIETOR, RICHARD H. K. *Contrived Competition: Regulation and Deregulation in America.* David Gabel 234

PREFACE

Throughout my nearly four decades now as an industrial sociologist, I have been preoccupied with an ironic and far-reaching question: what if paid employment was to steadily disappear? What would become of the men and women for whom such employment, especially good jobs, was a central organizing element in their lives? Above all, what could we dare to do now to alleviate the worse possible consequences of such a development?

This is hardly an armchair or ivory-tower line of speculation. Over the past twenty years I have been privileged to teach courses twice a year, for a week each time, at the AFL-CIO George Meany Center for Labor Studies in Silver Spring, Maryland. My adult students, all labor activists, regularly share aloud in class their ongoing and generally harrowing experiences with corporate downsizing, the upgrading of worker productivity, the arrival of ever better automation, and other dazzling sources of the relentless loss of jobs. The oldest among them report that the range and pace of job loss is greater than anything they have ever known, and the youngest sigh with recognition of the troubles they anticipate ahead.

Similarly, in my years of consulting coast to coast with school districts eager to improve their school-to-work connection, I am increasingly meeting educators who no longer trust that they can guide youngsters into tomorrow's world of work, so hazy and uncertain is the picture. Parents are even more troubled as confidence ebbs in the likelihood that there will always be enough good jobs, or even enough poor jobs, for their offspring. Pollsters tell of the sagging faith youngsters have in their ability to improve on the standard of living earned by their folks.

Traveling overseas, I found in my interviews recently with Swedish labor leaders much anxiety stirred by an unprecedented level of joblessness in a country with one of the highest levels of unionization in the free world. Western Europe, including Germany, is likewise troubled, and the former Soviet Union and China both confront a growing unemployment problem, one compounded by the hunger to catch up with advanced postindustrial nations even while somehow ensuring enough employees a regular payroll and hope for even better times.

As far-fetched as the possibility of rapid job loss may sound to currently well-off Americans, anxiety about this is actually well taken, given the rapid pace with which agricultural work in advanced nations shrank in the first half of the twentieth century and the steady erosion of manufacturing jobs in these same countries in the second half.

Now, to compound the matter, we verge on an entirely new workplace existence, one we can extrapolate cautiously from steadily emerging partnerships of human workers with awesomely smart equipment. The latter, once voice activated, voice responsive, and capable of "reasoning," may replace more and more employees, even as automatic teller machines have sharply reduced the number of bank clerks.

Thoughtful forecasts of when such powerful machinery might match and even exceed human intelligence move the fateful date ever closer (the decade of 2020 is commonly cited). After such a switching point in history, it is unclear who then will be the senior partner and who the junior. Farsighted parties are already troubled by the related specter of massive and continued job loss to imaginative applications of artificial intelligence.

As the contributors to this issue of *The Annals* explain, the worst-case scenario does not have to prove a self-fulfilling prophecy. The 17 writers I have been fortunate enough to assemble believe we can still adapt proactive measures likely to keep mankind in the saddle and keep machines from riding our backs (as Emerson feared)—provided, that is, that we act swiftly and surely in our best interest. They help define that interest, assess ongoing reforms, call for bold new responses, highlight the central matter of power holding, and in other valuable ways, buoy our confidence that the future does not just happen to us but is deliberately made in the present.

In part 1, "Defining the Challenge," writer and public policy expert Jeremy Rifkin, easily the best-known contemporary American commentator on the subject, helps frame the volume's entire discussion. He has no doubt that current unemployment statistics hide a "darker reality," one he lays bare with vexing details. Rifkin challenges market optimists and other Pollyannas who forecast an endless supply of job openings, as he expects millions instead to soon lose their jobs permanently to high-technology innovations.

What is necessary is creation of a new social contract, one that should emerge from what Rifkin calls "high-tech populism" for the Information Age. It would include winning a thirty-hour workweek by the year 2005, a feat whose accomplishment he diagrams. It would also refocus attention on the Third Sector, our nonprofit community, "the last best hope for both restoring the work life of the country and creating a new political vision that can move our society into a postmarket era." Anticipating legitimate questions about how we might pay the wages of millions seeking jobs in a vastly expanded Third Sector, Rifkin highlights several plausible sources of payroll funds.

Thoroughly versed in the intricacies of the subject, Rifkin's advocacy of economic justice as humane politics warrants careful consideration, especially against the backdrop of his fear that the steady loss of good jobs heightens the chances of worldwide upheaval.

Sharpening the focus, economist Sumner M. Rosen underlines the centrality of the labor market in our lives. He explains many reasons for the ominous failure of national economic and manpower policy, much of the blame for which he assigns to the hold ideological conservatism has on many mainstream economists and policy analysts. Rosen urges attention instead to several "weighty arguments" in support of serious efforts to reduce unemployment. He offers several pragmatic reform ideas and emphasizes the urgency of promoting "retention where possible, retraining where appropriate, reemployment when needed, and opportunities for new entrants to the labor force."

Closing out this introductory material is a related but distinctive perspective offered by Theodore Hershberg, a professor of public policy and history. He calls attention to our urgent need to upgrade our human capital: our education, skill levels, and problem-solving abilities. We are mistaken, he warns, to get drawn into competing in the global market on the basis of wages rather than skills. We ought instead to engage in a national debate over the key ends to work for in our schools, and set high national standards for human capital development, the "greatest challenge facing America."

In part 2, "Refining the Challenge," the general picture sketched in part 1 is explored in greater detail and, in some instances, challenged by scholars often less sanguine about our ability to rise to the challenge.

Techno-optimists, or those who herald the arrival of a cornucopia of highly skilled, well-paid jobs, come in for sharp criticism from Professors Stanley Aronowitz and William DiFazio. The two have completed rare field research into the actual work experience of engineers, architects, and draftsmen confronted by new design technologies. Hershberg notwithstanding, they find skill no longer central to the labor process, a change that substantially undermines worker bargaining power and indispensability.

With knowledge now the emergent center of production, a continued shift to worker-displacing smart automation appears a good likelihood. Aronowitz and DiFazio scoff at the utopian fantasies of the techno-optimists and warn instead of dystopian possibilities we cannot ignore.

A shift away from skill in the service sector of the labor force is clarified by Professor Barbara A. Gutek. She maintains that this fast-growing sector is actually divided between a shrinking bloc in old-fashioned relationships with client/customers (much as a law office partner might have with long-standing clients) and a rapidly growing bloc who provide only a cursory and impersonal encounter (much as a paralegal might offer a customer at a drop-in legal office).

Employees in the latter situation, Gutek contends, are likely candidates for near-future replacement by smart equipment, such as home-based software and Internet downloading services. She worries aloud about an attendant loss to society in the ethic of caring and in millions of jobs for workers with no other place to go. Refusing to mistake a trend for a law, Gutek urges reforms that can protect against an inordinate loss of old-fashioned service jobs and ensure care and quality in the provision of all types of services.

In part 3, "Assessing Ongoing Reforms," attention shifts to the strengths and weaknesses of present-day responses to job loss, the better to measure the adequacy of our thinking and actions in the matter.

National media understandably focus on congressional bills, acts, and programs. Unfortunately, overlooked are relatively small-scale labor market reform efforts quietly testing and improving critical components of our response to the extraordinary changes under way at work.

Research scientist Robert W. Glover focuses on an ongoing project in Austin, Texas, a pathbreaking effort to adapt to one American city the widely acclaimed German apprenticeship system. Austin offers lessons in how elected officials and area business leaders can upgrade their contribution to urban school-to-work efforts. As well, it reminds us of the importance of scanning the globe for field-tested reforms worth custom-tailoring to the American work scene.

Austin's young and vulnerable project may falter, but its goal will long remain critical: we *must* rapidly and significantly improve our school-to-work system if young Americans are to have a fair chance in tomorrow's workforce, whether it is expanding or contracting.

State-level experiments, much like those of progressive cities like Austin, also escape the attention frequently owed. Labor economist Lawrence W. Boyd offers a revealing study of the ongoing response in Hawaii to the closing of massive sugar plantations. He analyzes the social, political, and economic consequences of the efforts of federal and state governments, labor unions, displaced workers, and community activists as they try to counter the rapid loss of jobs in agriculture and the vagaries of the tourism market.

Although still quite young, the Hawaiian approach already offers some valuable lessons for the 49 other states. A unique synthesis of both "unconscious" and systematic planning, richly suffused with aloha values (caring for others), the Hawaiian multifaceted response to sudden large-scale disruption in the local labor market stirs fresh hope, an emotion all too rare where official response to job churning is concerned.

Absence of hope, in turn, can be traced in part to the uneven, if not dismal, record of national job-training efforts since the end of World War II. Researchers Ross Koppel and Alice Hoffman interviewed almost 500 displaced steelworkers about their recent experiences in a leading federal training program. They learned much that can only disappoint citizens who want to believe the federal government equal to the job loss challenge. Indeed, "workers who believed the experts, who took training, and who sought new jobs are far worse off than their stubborn and less trained colleagues." Little wonder, accordingly, that the researchers contend such programs "may not be a solution at all."

Which is not to give up entirely (albeit some in Congress who determine appropriations for job retraining legislate as if they have). Koppel and Hoffman recommend pragmatic reforms in current training approaches well worth national attention and adaptation, even as they remain skeptical about the chances of implementation, given the current deficit-reduction preoccupation of national policymakers.

We next look overseas at Western Europe and Japan, two major sources of experimentation trials and ensuing lessons for America. Not surprisingly, the news is mixed. On the one hand, innovations in meeting the job-change challenge are under way. But on the other, gains are few and far between.

Thomas Samuel Eberle analyzes the Swiss and German reactions to unprecedented mass job loss. He explains the details of a novel reform, a negotiated four-day workweek in automobile plants, now getting worldwide attention. He links its uneven existence to a revealing tension that persists between modernization and the traditional culture. His article makes plain the complexity of something as seemingly straightforward as a shorter workweek, and it reminds us of the need to probe deeply any innovation to really grasp its significance.

Similarly, Koji Taira and Solomon B. Levine get beneath superficial media treatment of the modern Japanese economy and explain what is and is not happening to the venerable lifetime-employment-security feature of that economy. Their careful and knowledgeable treatment of the subtleties of the Japanese labor scene goes far to correct any pro-security illusions we might have entertained about it.

In the closing section, part 4, "Looking Beyond," the essays push the border of the subject. Each offers more speculation than is common earlier in the volume, a tack consistent with the writer's notion—encouraged by this editor—that only thinking "out of the box" will really prove equal to the challenge.

Futurist Joseph F. Coates begins by exposing the weaknesses of the conventional economic framework. He sheds fresh light on the emerging situation, and details it through the year 2005. Coates declines to join others in attempting to solve the unemployment problem; instead, he advances some cogent reform ideas of his own. Three goals are championed: "to improve productivity; . . . to broadly distribute benefits of that productivity; and . . . respectable work for all through most of their lives."

Labor educator Charley Richardson takes a different tack. More than other contributors, he focuses intently on those who make decisions about which technologies come into and dominate the workplace. He insists that such people can be forced to make decisions far more attuned with general well-being than tolerated today. The critical matter is who is to have power, those currently wrecking havoc with our labor force or those who agree with the values earlier espoused by Rifkin, Rosen, Hershberg, and their compatriots in this volume.

Skeptical regarding the chances of mainstream reforms (such as a shorter workweek or Third Sector job creation) in the current budget-cutting climate, Richardson contends that it all comes back to the question of power. He has no confidence in reform ideas that essentially leave the current power distribution unchanged and actually buttress it by pacifying an otherwise pained and therefore problematic workforce. Power is the key, and in a cogent and hard-hitting way, he advances several ideas for achieving its redistribution. Richardson insists that unless and until workers and their unions wrestle more power from those now dictating work technologies, our national drift into hard times is assured.

All the more fascinating, therefore, is the most imaginative essay in the entire volume. Written by labor intellectual Daniel Marschall, it is a creative exercise in backcasting, a method used by futurists that highlights the scene some years ahead and proceeds to trace back to the present the path by which we might have gotten there.

Marschall's work world is the brightest defined by any contributor. It is a scene in which workers are proving equal to radical twenty-first-century work changes, thanks in large part to extraordinary improvements in American labor unions and related national programs. Power has clearly been redistributed, though not by the militant means and class warfare many readers will probably have associated with the Richardson advocacy.

Whether or not this refreshingly original backcasting is finally convincing, and regardless of one's persuasion regarding the near future of trade unionism, readers will find the many intriguing and novel reform ideas Marschall packs into his speculative piece quite rewarding.

It only remains now to close by exploring a taboo topic, one that has the power to responsibly turn the entire discussion upside down and inside out.

It is just possible that what we have taken throughout as a dire danger is actually a bright opportunity! We may be on the verge of finally freeing ourselves from an activity many barely accommodate, so spirit-damaging and soul-bruising is most work nowadays. We may be about to employ smart equipment so imaginatively as to free ourselves for far more exciting, rewarding, and empowering lives than humans have ever known.

This unorthodox possibility has long intrigued professor emeritus David Macarov, and his unusual argument against the pro-work stance of other contributors usefully reminds us how much remains for study in this many-sided and convoluted matter.

Macarov actually condemns the popular goal of full employment as a fata morgana, a beautiful mirage constantly beckoning an onlooker to destruction. He explains why he is convinced we cannot ever again significantly reduce unemployment. Indeed, he insists that "efforts to achieve full employment not only end in frustration, but inevitably lead to personal degradation, societal corruption, economic disaster, and global danger."

Macarov would have us adopt a new work-deflating and leisure-advancing paradigm, "one in which something other than work will be the overriding and controlling value, and in which the distribution of technologically derived wealth will not be based upon individual work activities or records." He offers several ideas about how to get there from here and rebuts several of the obvious criticisms that his provocative ideas attract.

APOLOGIA

Naturally, had space permitted, the volume would extend far beyond its present coverage to include articles on South American and African responses to the challenge of the employment-unemployment ratio and the related question of the distribution of good and bad jobs. Attention is owed the shift toward shorter hours being negotiated in Europe, the fraying of the Social Safety Net in New Zealand, the remarkable success of the Israelis in integrating a 25 percent overnight gain in population—Russian Jews—into their workforce, the discovery of virtual slavery in work sites in Brazil and other developing countries, and the emergence of a vast army of rootless migratory workers around the globe.

As well, I would have liked to have drawn on the relevant writings of specialists who take issue with various contributors, for example, futurist Charles Handy, who condemns the Marcarov vision of a leisure-centered future as a vision of hell, not of heaven. In its place, he details a plan for creating a "portfolio" approach to work, one that might put work "back into the heart of life" and make it "perhaps, the best of the four-letter words."[1] Similarly, futurists Richard Carlson and Bruce Goldman contend that "wild-eyed projections of massive job loss among the middle class could not be farther from the truth."[2]

Finally, I wish space limitations had allowed me to include some off-the-wall material on how futures topics like nanotechnology, biological engineering, solar power, fusion power, space stations, and the like, bear on our current speculation about the shape and character of jobs and work tomorrow.

Unfortunately, broader geographic coverage, engaging arguments, and future possibilities will all have to wait for another *Annals* volume dedicated to the jobs challenge, one for which this issue can serve as a thoughtful and wide-ranging foundation.

SUMMARY

As is often true with many-sided social questions, controversy and differences in emphasis divide the volume's contributors in illuminating ways.

Some worry that a shift from human skills to machine knowledge is getting away from us (Aronowitz and DiFazio; Gutek), while others insist that pragmatic reform options are numerous and still promising (Rosen; Coates; Taira and Levine). Some would have us focus especially on upgrading human capital (Hershberg and Glover), while others emphasize massive job-creation efforts (Rifkin, Rosen, and Eberle). Some laud progressive government responses to the present-day job loss crisis (Boyd), while others rue the many weaknesses of such efforts (Koppel and Hoffman). Most take the conventional scene for granted, while at least one calls for substantial revision (Richardson). Almost all agree that the ready availability of good jobs should remain one of our highest priorities (just after keeping the peace), though even here a thoughtful dissent is offered (Macarov).

1. Charles Handy, *The Age of Unreason* (Boston: Harvard Business School Press, 1990), p. 181.
2. Richard Carlson and Bruce Goldman, *Fast Forward: Where Technology, Demographics, and History Will Take America and the World in the Next Thirty Years* (New York: HarperBusiness, 1994), p. 121.

Given the concern the volume's contributors have with the prospect of an almost workless world in a mere half-century, it would seem advisable to advance on both fronts simultaneously, that is, to promote job-centered reforms (and power redistribution ideas) in the short run, even as we nurture leisure-centered reforms (and power redistribution ideas) for use in decades further out. The stakes are so high that it would seem wise to promote both seemingly contradictory programs at one and the same time, a paradox befitting the subject's rich complexity.

The paradox melts away, however, when we remind ourselves of the legitimacy of expectations for fresh opportunities in an almost workless world, one even Aldous Huxley might judge a caring, rather than a brave, new world.

ARTHUR B. SHOSTAK

A New Social Contract

By JEREMY RIFKIN

ABSTRACT: We are in the early stages of a long-term shift from mass labor to highly skilled elite labor, accompanied by increasing automation in the production of goods and the delivery of services. Workerless factories and virtual companies loom on the horizon. While the emerging knowledge sector and new markets abroad will create some new jobs, these will be too few to absorb the millions of workers displaced by new technologies in the manufacturing and service sectors. Although unemployment is still relatively low, it can be expected to climb steadily and inexorably as the global economy catapults into the Information Age over the course of the next half century. Every nation will have to grapple with the question of what to do with the millions of people whose labor is needed less, or not at all, in an ever more automated global economy.

Jeremy Rifkin is the author of The End of Work: The Decline of the Global Labor Force and the Dawn of the Post-Market Era. *He has a B.S. in economics from the Wharton School at the University of Pennsylvania and an M.A. in international affairs from the Fletcher School of Law and Diplomacy at Tufts University. He is the president and founder of the Washington, D.C.-based Foundation on Economic Trends. Rifkin has been influential in shaping public policy in the United States and around the world.*

IMMEDIATELY following the 1994 elections that swept the Republicans into power in the U.S. Congress for the first time since 1952, pollsters asked voters—in focus groups—why they switched their party allegiance so abruptly. To their surprise, they found that the real issue fueling voter unrest had little to do with either the Republican Contract with America or President Clinton's New Covenant for America. Rather, voters were registering a far deeper fear, one that was little talked about during the campaign. Millions of Americans sense that an enormous shift is taking place in the economy, and they are beginning to worry that there may not be a place for them in the new high-technology Information Age. Talk of balancing budgets, imposing term limits on Congress, and ending unfunded mandates does little to address the underlying concerns of a workforce plagued by declining real wages, dead-end jobs, part-time temporary employment, and long-term structural unemployment.

The concern over diminishing jobs in a changing economy is being voiced with increasing frequency in Congress and in state legislatures as the politicians turn their attention to the welfare issue. While there is general agreement among the leaders of both political parties that welfare benefits must be limited in duration and that all able-bodied people must be retrained for jobs, neither Republicans nor Democrats have bothered to ask the more fundamental question, What jobs?

We are long overdue for a political debate in our country—and, indeed, around the world—over how best to address the profound changes taking place in the nature of work as we make the transition into the Information Age. That debate should include a discussion of alternative ways of defining human worth now that the commodity value of most people's labor is diminishing in an ever more automated global marketplace.

THE DAWN OF A
NEW ECONOMIC ERA

After years of wishful forecasts and false starts, the new computer and communications technologies are finally making their long-anticipated impact on the workplace and the economy, throwing the world community into the grip of a powerful new economic revolution. Information Age technologies are already eliminating entire employment categories. Many jobs will never come back. Blue-collar workers, secretaries, receptionists, clerical workers, sales clerks, bank tellers, telephone operators, librarians, wholesalers, and middle managers are just a few of the many occupations destined for virtual extinction.

Although government reports claim that unemployment in the United States is slightly down, they conceal a darker reality. Millions of American workers have been displaced by new technologies and corporate reengineering and are now working at low-wage, dead-end jobs, or as temporary employees without benefits. Millions of others have become so discouraged that they are no longer looking for work and therefore go uncounted in the official unemployment figures. More than 15 percent of the American people are currently living below the poverty level.

Earlier industrial technologies replaced the physical power of human labor, substituting machines for body and brawn. The new computer-based technologies, however, promise a replacement of the human mind, substituting thinking machines for human beings across the entire gamut of economic activity. The implications are profound and far-reaching. To begin with, more than 75 percent of the labor force in most industrial nations engages in work that is little more than simple repetitive tasks. Automated machinery, robots, and increasingly sophisticated computers can perform many, if not most, of these jobs. In the United States alone, that means that in the years ahead more than 90 million jobs in a labor force of 124 million are potentially vulnerable to replacement by machines. With current surveys showing that less than 5 percent of companies around the world have even begun to make the transition to the new machine culture, massive unemployment of a kind never before experienced seems all but inevitable in the coming decades.

Of course, market optimists continue to argue that the new technologies of the Information Age will pave the way for an array of new products and services that will create even more jobs. After a debate on the Cable News Network more than a year ago, Dr. Laura Tyson—then president of the Council of Economic Advisors and currently the president of the White House Economic Council—accused me of shortsightedness and reminded me that the invention of the automobile eliminated thousands of jobs in the buggy industry but created even more jobs in the fledgling auto industry. It is true that the Information Age will create many new products and services, some with nearly universal market potential. Unlike the past, however, when mass labor was required to produce these goods, in the future they will be churned out in nearly workerless factories and be marketed by nearly virtual companies.

Most defenders of the trickle-down theory of technology continue to hold out hope that the expansion of markets and the prospect of a global trading economy will keep enough people employed, at least in the United States, for the foreseeable future. Murray Weidenbaum, president of the Council of Economic Advisors under President Reagan, and now director of the Center for Business at Washington University in St. Louis, argues that new markets, especially in Asia, will provide sufficient purchasing power to keep Americans employed in the coming century. Unfortunately, Weidenbaum and others fail to take into account the fact that companies all over the world will be competing for these same new markets, reducing the job-creating potential in the United States in the years ahead. Equally important, virtually every country in the world is creating a two-tier society in the wake of the dramatic changes occurring in the nature of work. The question is whether one-fifth of the world's population—those gainfully employed in the emerging knowledge sector—have sufficient purchasing power to absorb the dramatic increases in production arising from the new Information Age economy.

The reality is that the world is polarizing into two potentially irreconcilable forces: on one side, an information elite that controls and manages the high-tech global economy and, on the other, a growing number of permanently displaced workers who have few prospects and little hope of meaningful employment in an increasingly automated world. While the knowledge sector and new markets abroad will create some new jobs, these will be far too few to absorb the millions of people displaced by the new technologies of the high-tech revolution.

Up to now, the politicians in both the Democratic and Republican parties have steadfastly refused to address what is likely to be the seminal economic and social issue of the next several decades: what to do with the millions of people whose labor is needed less, or not at all, in an ever more automated global economy. Instead, they have gushed over the great technological breakthroughs that are driving us ever faster into the world of cyberspace and have issued breathless pronouncements on the wonders that await us along the information superhighway.

While both Newt Gingrich and President Clinton have embraced the Information Age, extolling the virtues of cyberspace and virtual reality, the Left's response has been to continue to fight a rearguard action, targeting ideological issues and concerns of a bygone industrial era. In this respect, the Left's current profile bears a striking likeness to the populists of the turn of the century who fought to maintain an agrarian culture that was quickly being subsumed by the forces of urbanization and industrialization.

In the meantime, few intellectuals and even fewer activists are giving serious attention to the critical issues raised by the Information Age, especially the question of how to ensure that the dramatic productivity gains of the new high-tech global economy will be shared broadly by every segment of the population. A fair and equitable distribution of the productivity gains would require a dramatic shortening of the workweek in countries around the world and a concerted effort by central governments to provide alternative employment in the Third Sector, or social economy, for those workers whose labor is no longer needed in the marketplace. If, however, the dramatic productivity gains of the high-tech revolution are not shared, but rather used primarily to enhance corporate profit to the exclusive benefit of stockholders, top corporate managers, and the emerging elite of high-tech knowledge workers, chances are that the growing gap between the haves and the have-nots of the world will lead to social and political upheaval on a global scale.

What is required now is a bold new social vision and a broad-based political movement that can speak directly to the challenges facing us in the new economic era. We need a high-tech populism for the Information Age.

THE 30-HOUR WORKWEEK

To begin with, serious attention ought to be focused on shortening the workweek to 30 hours by the year 2005. We need to remind the business community and the politicians that the new technologies were supposed to free us for greater leisure, not longer unemployment lines. In the Industrial Era, when new technologies boosted productivity and reduced labor requirements, working people organized and demanded their right to share in the gains with shorter workweeks and better pay and benefits.

Today, reformers around the world are beginning to call for a 30-hour workweek to bring schedules in line with the new productive potential of Information Age technologies. In France and Germany, mainstream politicians as well as business and labor leaders have joined together in support of a radically reduced workweek. The 30-hour week will likely be introduced in parts of Europe within the next three to five years.

Still, in the United States, the argument persists that fewer hours at existing pay could put companies at a competitive disadvantage globally. One way to address the concern is to extend generous tax credits for shifting to a shorter workweek and hiring additional workers. The size of the tax credit could be determined by the number of workers hired and the total amount of the increased payroll. The loss of revenue up front, some argue, would likely be made up for later by the taxable revenue generated by an increase in workers bringing home a paycheck. The Clinton administration has already floated the idea of providing tax credits to companies that hire welfare recipients, setting a precedent for a broader initiative that would cover the bulk of the workforce. Finally, the government might consider granting additional tax credits to those companies willing to also include a profit-sharing plan along with a reduction of the workweek to allow workers to participate even more fully in the productivity gains.

The American people should consider setting a goal of reaching a 30-hour workweek by the year 2005. The 30-hour workweek is likely to enjoy widespread support among working Americans harried by the stress of long work schedules. While many Americans have lost their jobs or are working only part-time as temps, those still holding on to a full-time job are being forced to work even longer hours. Many companies prefer to employ a smaller workforce at longer hours rather than a larger one at shorter hours, to save the costs of providing additional benefits, including health care and pensions. Even with the payment of time and a half for over time, companies still pay out less than they would if they had to pay for benefit packages for a larger workforce.

A 6-hour workday would mean that most parents would leave for work when their children left for school each morning and arrive home in the afternoon when their children came home. The 30-hour workweek is a powerful vision and could unite a number of diverse constituencies. For parenting organizations, women's groups, and religious organizations that have decried the loss of parental supervision in the home and the disintegration of the American family, the 30-hour workweek is an idea whose time has come. For organized labor, whose power has been steadily eroding for several decades, the 6-hour day offers a last opportunity to regain a foothold in the emerging Information Age. Working together, these powerful constituencies could mount an effective grassroots campaign for the steady reduction of work hours in American society.

THIRD SECTOR POLITICS

While the demand for a 30-hour workweek ought to be the rallying cry of a new high-tech populist movement, it should be accompanied by a new vision of a postmarket era. We need to begin to ponder the unthinkable—to imagine new ways of living in the Information Age.

With the need for mass labor diminishing in an ever more automated global economy, new opportunities for engaging human labor become possible. Unfortunately, we have become so used to thinking of ourselves almost exclusively as producers and consumers that the very idea of creating a revolutionary new context for human activity seems almost fanciful. Yet we are at that very moment in world history where machine technology can begin to substitute for human toil in the production of goods and delivery of services. Large numbers of people are being freed from the production process. Whether that emancipation from the marketplace leads to chronic unemployment, the increasing polarization of rich and poor, and class warfare on a global scale or to a renaissance of the human spirit and a transformation of consciousness depends, to a great extent, on whether a new political movement can combine the demand for economic justice with a call for a new way of living in the world.

The first question to ask is what to do with the increasing numbers of people whose labor is simply not needed in the marketplace, even with a reduced workweek. It is unrealistic to believe that the local, state, and federal governments will continue to act as employers of last resort, as they have for the past half-century. In the wake of mounting debts and deficits, government, at every level, can be expected to downsize and diminish in the years ahead. With both the marketplace and government playing a reduced role in the work lives of millions of Americans, the Third Sector, or nonprofit community, becomes the last best hope for both restoring the work life of the country and creating a new political vision that can move our society into a postmarket era.

For more than 200 years, Third Sector activity has shaped the American experience. While historians are quick to credit the market and government sectors with America's greatness, the civil society has played an equally aggressive role in defining the American way of life. The nation's first schools and colleges, its hospitals, social service organizations, fraternal orders, women's clubs, youth organizations, civil rights groups, social justice organizations, conservation and environmental protection groups, animal welfare organizations, theaters, orchestras, art galleries, libraries, museums, civic associations, community development organizations, neighborhood advisory councils, volunteer fire departments, and civilian security patrols are all creatures of the Third Sector.

Third Sector organizations serve many functions. They are the incubators of new ideas and forums to air social grievances. Community associations integrate streams of immigrants into the American experience. They are places where the poor and the helpless can find a helping hand. Nonprofit organizations like museums, libraries, and historical societies help preserve traditions and open doors to new kinds of intellectual experiences. The Third Sector is where many people first learn how to practice the art of democratic participation. It is where companionship is sought and friendships are formed. The independent sector provides a place and time for exploring the spiritual dimension. Religious and therapeutic organizations allow millions of Americans to leave behind the secular concerns of daily life. Finally, the Third Sector is where people relax and play and more fully experience the pleasures of life and nature.

The American people ought to consider making a direct investment in expanded job creation in the nonprofit sector, as an alternative to welfare, for the increasing number of jobless who find themselves locked out of the new high-tech global marketplace. State and local governments could provide an income voucher for those permanently unemployed Americans willing to be retrained and placed in community-building jobs in the Third Sector. The government could also award grants to nonprofit organizations to help them recruit and train the poor for jobs in their organizations.

An income voucher would allow millions of unemployed Americans, working through thousands of neighborhood organizations, the opportunity to help themselves. Providing a social wage in return for community-service work would also benefit both business and government. Reduced unemployment means more people could afford to buy goods and services, which would spur more businesses to open up in poor neighborhoods, creating additional jobs. Greater employment would also generate more taxes for the local, state, and federal governments. A rise in employment would also cut the crime rate and thereby lower the cost of maintaining law and order.

Providing income vouchers directly to individuals who are able to secure a job in a nonprofit neighborhood organization is a far less costly and more effective way of addressing the problem of structural unemployment than setting up expensive government programs and the bureaucratic machinery to administer them. By making the individual qualify and compete for a job in the nonprofit sector, we retain much of the incentive normally associated with employment in the marketplace. Then, too, nonprofit organizations are, more often than not, organic creations born in the neighborhoods they serve and therefore generally more attuned to the needs of local communities than are government-administered public programs. For all of these reasons, a reemergent civil society seems a likely successor to more government in addressing the very real and pressing needs of the millions of Americans left by the wayside along the information superhighway.

The Third Sector cuts a wide swath through society. Nonprofit activities run the gamut from social services to health care, education and research, the arts, religion, and advocacy. The sector is made up of millions of volunteers as well as paid employees. There are currently more than 1.4 million nonprofit organizations in the United States, with total combined assets of more than $500 billion. A study conducted by Yale economist Gabriel Rudney in the 1980s estimated that the expenditures of America's nonprofit and voluntary organizations exceeded the gross domestic product (GDP) of all but seven nations in the world. The nonprofit sector already contributes more than 6 percent of the GDP and is responsible for 10.5 percent of total national employment. More people are employed in Third Sector organizations than work in the construction, electronics, transportation, or textile and apparel industries.

Today, nonprofit and voluntary organizations are serving millions of Americans in every neighborhood and community of the country. Their reach and scope often eclipse both the private and public sectors, touching and affecting the lives of every American, often more profoundly than the forces of the marketplace or the agencies and bureaucracies of government.

Although nonprofit and voluntary organizations exist in most other countries, nowhere are they as well developed as in the United States. Americans have often turned to nonprofit and voluntary organizations as a refuge—a place where personal relationships can be nurtured, status can be achieved, and a sense of community can be created. Max Lerner, the economist and educator, once observed that through their affiliations with civic organizations, Americans hope to overcome their sense of personal isolation and alienation and become part of a real community. This is a primordial need that cannot be filled by either the forces of the market or the dictates of government. Lerner writes, "It is in them [civic associations] . . . that the sense of community comes closest to being achieved."[1]

The Third Sector incorporates many of the necessary elements for a compelling alternative vision to the utilitarian ethos of the marketplace. Nonetheless, the spirit of the social economy has not yet gelled into a powerful countervailing worldview capable of setting the agenda for a nation. This is due, in large part, to the extraordinary hold that the values of the marketplace have had over the affairs of the nation.

The market vision, wedded to a materialistic cornucopia, glorifies production principles and efficiency standards as the primary means of advancing happiness. As long as people's primary identification is with the market economy, the values of expanded production and unlimited consumption will continue to influence personal behavior. People will continue to think of themselves, first

1. Max Lerner, "The Joiners," in *America's Voluntary Spirit*, ed. Brian O'Connell (Washington, DC: Foundation Center, 1983), p. 86.

and foremost, as consumers of goods and services.

The Third Sector vision offers a much needed antidote to the materialism that has so dominated twentieth-century industrial thinking. While workers in the private sector are motivated by material gain and view security in terms of increased consumption, Third Sector participants are motivated by service to others and view security in terms of strengthened personal relationships and a sense of grounding in the larger community.

The Third Sector's role is likely to increase significantly in the years ahead for the simple reason that many of the tasks performed in this sector involve intimate social skills that are not easily reducible to computerization. Ironically, what we have come to think of as high-status skills in the marketplace—even professional jobs requiring years of training—are often reducible, at least in part, to digitization and automation. Already, sophisticated information technologies and robotics are replacing many of the conventional tasks of engineers, architects, managers, accountants, lawyers, and even physicians. On the other hand, many of the skills we have traditionally relegated to the bottom of the economic pyramid and treated as low-status occupations are far too complicated and complex to be replaced by computers and robotization. An adult care worker managing a day care center and nurturing twenty children is far too complex to be subsumed by the new technologies. In the coming decades, we are likely to witness a profound shift in what we regard as meaningful work as market skills become more automated and intimate people skills in the Third Sector become more valued.

FINANCING A SOCIAL INCOME

Paying for a social income and for reeducation and training programs to prepare men and women for a career of community service in the Third Sector would require significant government funds. Some of the money could come from savings brought about by gradually replacing many of the current welfare programs with direct payments to persons performing community-service work. Government funds could also be freed up by discontinuing costly subsidies to corporations that have outgrown their domestic commitments and now operate in countries around the world. The federal government provided transnational corporations with tens of billions in subsidies in 1993 in the form of direct payments and tax breaks.

Additional monies could be raised by cutting unnecessary defense programs. Despite the fact that the Cold War is over, the federal government continues to maintain a bloated defense budget. While Congress has scaled down defense appropriations in recent years, military expenditures are expected to run at about 89 percent of Cold War spending between 1994 and 1998. In a 1992 report, the Congressional Budget Office concluded that defense spending could be cut by a rate of 7 percent a year over a five-year period without compromising the nation's military preparedness or undermining national security.[2]

Perhaps the most equitable and far-reaching approach to raising the needed funds would be to enact a value-added tax (VAT) on all high-tech goods and services. While the VAT is a new and untried idea in the United States, it has been adopted by more than 59 countries, including virtually every major European nation. By enacting a VAT of between 5 and 7 percent on all high-tech goods and services, the federal government could generate billions of dollars of additional revenue—more than what would be required to finance a social wage for those willing to work in the Third Sector.

Vested interests as well as the new Republican majority in Congress and in many of the state legislatures are likely to resist the idea of providing an income voucher in return for community service. Yet the alternative of leaving the problem of long-term technological unemployment unattended is even more onerous. A growing underclass of permanently unemployable Americans could lead to widespread social unrest, increased violence, escalating crime and incarceration, and the further disintegration of American society. Eventually, society will have to ask whether it makes more sense to spend approximately $30,000 per head to keep millions of people in jail each year, or use those same funds for job retraining and income vouchers so that people can find meaningful work in nonprofit organizations in the Third Sector, servicing their neighborhoods and restoring their communities.

In the debate over how best to divide up the benefits of productivity advances brought on by the new high-tech global economy, we must ultimately grapple with an elementary question of economic justice. Put simply, does every member of society, even the poorest among us, have a right to participate in and benefit from the productivity gains of the information and communication technology revolutions? If the answer is yes, then some form of compensation will have to be made to the increasing number of unemployed whose labor will be needed less, or not at all, in the new high-tech automated world of the twenty-first century.

By shortening the workweek to 30 hours and providing an income voucher for permanently unemployed people in return for retraining and service in the Third Sector, we can begin to address some of the many structural issues facing a society in transition to an automated future. These twin demands are powerful lightning rods for a new high-tech political movement in the coming Information Age.

Interestingly enough, the nation's schools are already beginning to prepare the next generation for a life split between work in the marketplace and service in the Third Sector. While schools are teaching children how to access the information superhighway and find their way in cyberspace, they are also introducing mandatory community service work in nonprofit organizations as a require-

---

2. U.S., Congressional Budget Office, *Reducing the Deficit: Spending and Revenue Options* (Washington, DC: Government Printing Office, 1992), pp. 11-13.

ment for graduation. Twenty years from now, those same children may find themselves working a few hours each day in the marketplace and spending the remainder of their day engaged in civic and social endeavors in their local neighborhoods and communities.

There has been quite a bit of discussion in recent years about the pressing need for a new, more humane politics. The transition to a global trading economy and the increasing automation of production and services over the next four to five decades raises the fundamental question of how millions of people will find meaning in their lives now that the commodity value of their labor is needed less, or not at all, in the capitalist marketplace. Redirecting—even partially—the energies, talents, and resources of millions of people toward meaningful work in the Third Sector provides a clear and achievable vision, one that can give concrete substance to a new politics in the coming century.

Jobs: New Challenges, New Responses

By SUMNER M. ROSEN

ABSTRACT: Labor markets are central to economic life. They shape the organization of work and the lives of those who work or need work. Recent experience confirms a systemic tilt in favor of employers' needs and interests at the expense of earnings, job security, and opportunities for new entrants to the labor force. Conservative ideology has been effectively linked to employers' interests. The result has been that public policies of demonstrated effectiveness in assuring a better balance in labor markets have been weakened. Changing labor market conditions will require renewal and redesign of these tested remedies and development of new measures adequate to respond to new conditions in the global economy and in labor markets. Among these the most important will be reduced working time, limits on freedom to invest or disinvest capital, stronger community-based power to share in the decision-making process and in the distribution of costs and benefits, and a new synthesis of paid work, work that is important to society, and leisure. These are specified and discussed.

Sumner M. Rosen taught graduate courses in social policy at Columbia University until his retirement in 1993. He held union positions in research and education and has consulted with unions in the United States and other countries. He was a fellow at the International Labor Organization in 1994. His publications deal with industrial relations, unions and society, labor market policy, and other topics. He has been a visiting scholar at the Center for the Study of Human Rights at Columbia University and the New York State School of Industrial and Labor Relations at Cornell University.

AT every contract negotiation, in every hiring decision, during every working day, the labor market is a silent, ubiquitous presence. Labor shortages and scarcities, or their opposite, shape the decision-making process and the quality of employee-management relationships. Sometimes the process is visible, even dramatic, as when new contracts are being negotiated or when employers consider their response to changes in markets or technology or other factors. It is central and pervasive even when not consciously acknowledged.

In the mid-1970s, when negotiations were in process about legislation intended to strengthen the 1946 Employment Act, George Meany, president of the American Federation of Labor and Congress of Industrial Organizations, captured the heart of the matter when he said, reflecting a lifetime of collective bargaining, that the length of the list of demands inside the plant depended directly on the length of the line outside. The matter could not be put more concisely or cogently.

The focus of this article is on these questions:

1. What explains the failure of U.S. economic policy to restore and sustain maximum levels of employment in the period that began with the election of Richard M. Nixon as president in 1968?

2. What changes are needed in public policies and in the intellectual foundations on which policymakers rely in order to revise and extend the labor market measures needed to promote economic efficiency and social equity through more buoyant and equitable labor market conditions?

3. How have new forces at work in the economy and in labor markets affected the prospects for shrinking the gaps in opportunity and reward between the several groups that work or seek work, gaps most evident in terms of race, gender, ethnicity, and geography?

THE UNITED STATES IN THE GLOBAL CONTEXT

In the late twentieth century, levels of unemployment and underemployment have reached massive proportions, estimated in 1995 at 820 million worldwide, equal to one-third of the global labor force; this included 35 million in the advanced industrial economies.[1] Yet even in a global employment crisis, official unemployment rates varied widely, from 2.8 percent in Japan and 3.8 percent in Switzerland to 12.2 percent in France in 1995.

While the effects of economic change are largely shaped by broad economic forces, the distribution of the benefits or burdens largely depends on the domestic policies and institutional arrangements of individual countries. These in turn embody the balance of social and political forces, generally representing the interests of labor and capital. They take form in the structural arrangements that are shaped and driven by the political system, the priorities of economic and social policies, negotiating structures, and systems of representation within the workplace.

1. International Labour Office, *World Employment 1995* (Geneva: International Labour Office, 1995).

Viewed in comparative perspective, the United States operates at or near one end of a spectrum among Western nations that ranges from laissez-faire to social democracy.[2] Among the Western economies in recent decades, the United States has focused less than most on employment as a central concern of public policy.

THE ROOTS OF U.S. AMBIVALENCE

Division and conflict were visible even during the early postwar years, when the issue of jobs was a central focus of public policy and economic debate. Widespread concern that the end of the war might see an end to war-induced prosperity and a return of high levels of unemployment generated extensive discussion and debate around the drafting of federal legislation that would for the first time mandate government action to prevent large-scale unemployment.

What first took shape in the Senate as a "full employment" bill was steadily reshaped into the innocuous Employment Act of 1946, omitting both legislative mandates and effective instruments in the hands of the national executive.[3] Efforts to strengthen the law in the mid-1970s produced some improvement but included so many loopholes that the revised legislation has had little impact on either policy or public awareness.[4]

In the mid-1990s, new efforts were under way, though in a political climate that was hostile despite the reality of ever greater numbers of unemployed and underemployed in a context of slow economic growth, stagnant earnings, increasing job insecurity, and drastically eroded union effectiveness.[5]

As levels of unemployment increased together with major structural changes in the domestic economy, mainstream economists and policy analysts advanced explanations of why levels of unemployment well above those of the first two postwar decades had become the norm. Some cited a changing labor force. Their contention was that as the proportion of women, young people, minority-group members, and immigrants increased, lower levels of skill, education, and productivity left increasing numbers unable to find jobs in an increasingly competitive economy, creating a quasi-permanent surplus of the unemployable or those able to secure and hold only low-paid jobs in labor-intensive sectors like garment manufacturing, fast food, warehouse, and similar work.

Other mainstream economists and policy analysts argued that rigid rules imposed by unions hampered

---

2. Comparisons are harder to make with Japan and the other Asian tigers—South Korea, Taiwan, Singapore, Hong Kong—where the central state has played a leading, often controlling role in economic management as well as labor market policy and labor-management relations.

3. Stephen Bailey, *Congress Makes a Law* (New York: Vintage, 1964).

4. Helen Ginsburg, *Full Employment and Public Policy: The United States and Sweden* (Lexington, MA: D.C. Heath, Lexington Books, 1983), pp. 63-84.

5. David Dembo and Ward Morehouse, *The Underbelly of the U.S. Economy: Joblessness and the Pauperization of Work in America* (New York: Council on International and Public Affairs, 1995).

flexibility and employers' ability to adapt to changing markets, technology, and other forces.

By the early 1970s, the focus of national economic policy had been shifted from full employment to control of inflation. This reached a dramatic peak when the Federal Reserve Board imposed drastic reductions on the money supply in order to end the inflationary spiral of the latter half of the decade. Unemployment rose to levels not experienced since the end of the Great Depression. The lack of significant public or political outcry appeared to ratify the shift. In the country's politics, the era of primary focus on jobs and employment had ended.

Since then unemployment levels have remained consistently well above those of the first three postwar decades, when officially measured unemployment seldom reached 5 percent even at the trough of the business cycle. By contrast, in the post-1975 era, this rate seldom fell below 5 percent even at the peak of the cycle. In the 1992 presidential campaign, the Democratic rhetoric stressed economic growth but lacked specific focus on the job issue, which appeared to have lost its political and popular appeal.

IDEOLOGY IN THE SADDLE

When World War II ended, the U.S. economy was the most modern and productive in the world. Whatever the credibility now of the arguments cited earlier—a question we consider later—they do not explain the strength of the opposition that successfully watered down the early drafts of the Employment Act. Our review of the compromises that were made in the postwar years supports the conclusion that even when there were no serious barriers to the establishment and maintenance of high levels of employment, strong opposition effectively blocked adoption of policies and programs that would effectively promote that goal. The explanation then—as now—is at root one of ideological conservatism that opposed then, as it does now, the deployment by a strong central government of the arsenal of fiscal and monetary instruments that constitute Keynes's policy tool kit intended to ensure a balance between the number of job seekers and the number of jobs available.[6]

WHAT ECONOMISTS TEACH: SCIENCE OR SOMETHING ELSE?

Economists and policy analysts who argue that slack labor markets are inevitable rely on a body of work that stems from A. W. Phillips's analysis of long-term relationships between wages and unemployment levels in the British economy.[7]

Milton Friedman and other modern conservative economists adapted this analysis to derive what came to be known as the natural non-inflation-accelerating rate of unemployment (NAIRU). They argued that efforts to reduce unemployment below this rate would prove unsustainable because of the inevitable and politically

---

6. William Beveridge, *Full Employment in a Free Society* (London: Allen & Unwin, 1944).

7. A. W. Phillips, "The Relation between Unemployment and the Rate of Change of Money Wages in the United Kingdom, 1862-1957," *Economica*, 25:283-99 (Nov. 1958).

unacceptable increase in the rate of inflation that it would cause. William Vickrey, a former president of the American Economics Association, called NAIRU "one of the most vicious euphemisms ever coined."[8]

Robert Eisner, also a former president of the economics association, has cautioned against reliance on the models of self-perpetuating and accelerating inflation used to justify current levels of unemployment. He urges more energetic and effective policies to reduce unemployment, arguing that inflation rates would not increase, and might well decrease to stable rates of unemployment as low as 2.8 to 3.8 percent, over a three- to five-year period. He concludes that "we have no sound basis for deliberately raising unemployment. On the contrary, we ought to be trying to reduce it, not only by supply-side measures, but by ensuring that the economy is not starved for adequate aggregate demand or productivity-increasing public investment."[9]

Robert Lekachman cited the historical record to argue that "between 1968 and 1973 the Phillips curve hypothesis received as fair a test as the imperfect politics of parliamentary democracy are ever likely to allow. By that test it ignominiously failed."[10]

Garth Mangum and colleagues cite Utah's record of rapid job growth and low unemployment with little inflationary effect in the 1988-94 period to caution against reliance on any national policymaking model in an economy with enormous differences in demographics, occupational distribution, and other determinants of economic process and outcomes. They write:

The Utah experience argues for first examining the experience of other low unemployment states, then, assuming similar results, taking some risks in returning to the quest, which, after all, is still a legal requirement: the pursuit of maximum employment, production, and purchasing power.[11]

The most recent edition of the preeminent economics textbook provides a graphic illustration of variation in the NAIRU over recent decades that is so wide and unpredictable as to cast doubt on its value for either prediction or policy.[12]

Economics has acquired influence in both popular understanding and policymaking, but economists are no more immune than other social scientists to the tendency to lend the weight of their judgments to the prevailing distribution of power and influence. Their judgments and conclusions about how low unemployment can go need to be treated skeptically, with due attention to the likelihood that they will reflect, even if not explicitly, the views and interests of those with a material or intellectual stake in the outcome. This places them in a position well short of scientific certainty.

---

8. William Vickrey, "Today's Task for Economists," *Challenge—The Magazine of Economic Affairs*, 36(2):10 (Mar.-Apr. 1993).

9. Robert Eisner, "Our NAIRU Limit: The Governing Myth of Economic Policy," *American Prospect*, pp. 58-63 (Spring 1995).

10. Robert Lekachman, *Economists at Bay* (New York: McGraw-Hill, 1976), p. 51.

11. Mangum et al., unpublished memorandum, University of Utah, 1995.

12. Paul A. Samuelson and William D. Nordhaus, *Economics*, 15th ed. (New York: McGraw-Hill, 1995), p. 588.

NONECONOMIC CRITERIA

Weighty arguments in support of serious efforts to reduce unemployment have their roots in work in theology and principles of morality, human rights, public health, and ecological sustainability. Each is summarized here.

In its important pastoral letter in the mid-1980s, the U.S. Conference of Catholic Bishops argued that "full employment is the foundation of a just society" and that "work with adequate pay for all who seek it is the primary means for achieving justice in our society." Supporting arguments were drawn from biblical passages and a century of social analysis in the work of popes and theologians, as well as modern studies of effects and costs of unemployment with respect to human dignity and self-esteem, family stability, race and gender discrimination, youths and their prospects, as well as the costs to society at large. Other religious bodies have made similar statements.[13]

Human rights advocates argue that access to employment is a universal right that merits legislative embodiment and judicial enforcement. A series of human rights declarations and covenants have invested employment rights with the mantle of international law and treaties binding on nations that ratify them.

They include the United Nations Charter, the Universal Declaration of Human Rights (1948), and the International Covenant on Economic, Social and Cultural Rights (1976). Covenants that do not directly address the issue of employment are also relevant because of the demonstrable negative effects of unemployment on the condition of women (the Convention on the Elimination of All Forms of Discrimination against Women [1981]) and racial minorities (the International Convention on the Elimination of All Forms of Racial Discrimination [1969]).

Conventions of the International Labor Organization (ILO) articulate rights and principles that have achieved international recognition as central to the advancement of social justice in modern economic life. Among them are the Philadelphia Declaration, adopted in 1944 to mark the twenty-fifth anniversary of the founding of the ILO, and the ILO's statement calling for full employment for the 1995 Social Summit of the United Nations in Copenhagen. Their cumulative weight has not yet been sufficiently felt in the domain of economic policy within the United States, but the future should incorporate the results of advocacy and teaching.[14]

M. Harvey Brenner has studied the effects of unemployment on health, medical and mental, for many years and in many places. His findings and conclusions are compelling and persuasive: unemployment is a more powerful factor in explaining

---

13. U.S. Conference of Catholic Bishops, *Economic Justice for All* (Washington, DC: U.S. Conference of Catholic Bishops, 1986), paras. 136, 73.

14. Philip Harvey, "Employment as a Human Right," in *Sociology and the Public Agenda*, ed. W. J. Wilson (Thousand Oaks, CA: Sage, 1993); idem, *Securing the Right to Employment: Social Welfare Policy and the Unemployed in the United States* (Princeton, NJ: Princeton University Press, 1989).

and predicting a wide range of hazards to health than virtually any other. The range of effects include mental hospital admissions, homicide and suicide rates, alcoholism, and cardiovascular illness and death, among others.[15] When, at a 1994 conference, Brenner was asked about the threats to health posed by inflation, he replied that he had never been able to find any. A resolution adopted by the American Public Health Association in 1995 calls for public policies to address problems of unemployment and underemployment as hazards to public health.

The ecological imperative is relevant because it includes the conservation of community and human bonds; they need to be protected against the destructive effects of rapid economic change executed without regard to the livelihoods at stake and the risks posed to society by erosion or elimination of the basis of livelihood. While popular opinion often poses jobs and environmental protection in opposition to one another, more careful analysis supports the view that, as in conversion from military to civilian use, ecological values are fully consistent with steady job creation.[16]

The analysis developed here is intended to demonstrate that the consensus on which conservatives rely in opposition to any serious effort to achieve lower levels of unemployment is insecure in its conceptual roots and vulnerable when a wider perspective is brought to bear than that encompassed by mainstream economics.

We turn next to an assessment of the record in relationship to criteria of equity and efficiency, and to discussion of the programs and policies that would improve how labor markets work and, in the process, reduce or eliminate the imbalances and inequities that now characterize relationships between the two sides of the labor market, employers and workers.

THE REALITIES OF U.S. LABOR MARKETS

The official measures of employment and underemployment omit more than they reveal. People are counted as employed if they worked even one hour during the survey week. Those who are not working because of illness, vacation, or labor-management disputes are counted as employed whether or not they are paid. To be counted as unemployed one must have looked for work during the prior four weeks; workers who have stopped looking because they have become discouraged are counted as such but are not included among the unemployed.

Other changes made beginning in 1967 narrowed the definition of unemployment, and reduced the percentage reported as unemployed, by (1) excluding people absent from work because of a strike or because they were looking for another job, (2) excluding people 14 or 15 years old without regard to their need for paid work, and (3) including the armed forces stationed in the United States as part of the labor force—the de-

---

15. M. Harvey Brenner, "Health and the National Economy," in *Human Capital and Development*, ed. P. C. Huang (Greenwich, CT: JAI Press, 1993).

16. Herman E. Daly and John B. Cobb, Jr., *For the Common Good: Redirecting the Economy toward Community, the Environment, and a Sustainable Future* (Boston: Beacon Press, 1989), pp. 309-14.

nominator in calculating the unemployment rate.

Recalculation of the jobless rate taking account of these and other limitations yields, for 1994, 15.9 million as the total number, twice the official total of 8.0 million, and a jobless rate of 12.5 percent, more than double the official rate of 6.1 percent.[17] This translates into large-scale and long-lasting differences in labor market experience across lines of race, gender, ethnicity, age, and geography.

In early 1995, when the official unemployment rate was 5.4 percent, the rate for Hispanic workers was 8.9 percent and for black workers, 10.1 percent. In 1993, 20.5 million people experienced one or more spells of unemployment. Of all workers, 22.2 percent worked part-time; 14.3 percent of men worked part-time; 31.1 percent of women did. Among full-time workers—those who work 35 or more hours per week—11 percent worked fewer than 40 weeks in the year.

Job displacement was especially high for black and Hispanic workers in manufacturing. Fewer of the displaced black workers found new jobs (58 percent) than did similarly displaced white workers (70 percent), and more of them lost health coverage that had been provided in their previous jobs, compared to white workers. Fewer blacks and Hispanics than whites are actually in the labor force as measured by the employment-population ratio.

These disparities understate the gravity of the problem of joblessness, especially among blacks and acutely among young black men. In some cities, the labor force participation rates for these young men is less than one in four. Combined with a high unemployment rate, the percent of jobless black young men in New York in 1988—a "prosperity" year—exceeded 90 percent![18]

William Julius Wilson's recent work on labor markets in Chicago documents drastic declines in employment and employment opportunities for black men, the consequence primarily of the restructuring of the city's economy and the large-scale exodus of industry and decline of opportunities for industrial work. One of the most striking and sobering findings is that in "both inner-city Chicago and at the national level, black men born during or just after World War II were more than 2.5 times more likely to marry after their child's conception, regardless of economic and educational status, than men born during the late 1950s who became fathers at a similar age."[19]

Other dimensions of unequal opportunity, reward, and security across the lines of race, gender, and ethnicity are less dramatic but equally sobering reminders of the pervasive

17. Dembo and Morehouse, *Underbelly of the U.S. Economy*.

18. U.S., Department of Labor, Bureau of Labor Statistics, various reports, press releases; Governor's Advisory Committee for Black Affairs, Labor and Employment Subcommittee, *Improving the Labor Market Status of Black New Yorkers* (Albany, NY: Governor's Advisory Committee for Black Affairs, 1988), p. 9.

19. William Julius Wilson, "Race, Class, and Poverty in Urban America: A Comparative Perspective" (Rosenberg/Humphrey Presidential Lecture, City College of New York, 30 Apr. 1992), p. 14.

and largely unreported dimensions of inequality that are accentuated by continuing conditions of slackness in labor markets. It is, for example, plausible to connect the disaffection and cynicism of middle-aged white working-class men, as seen in the rapid growth of militias and other expressions of alienation and disillusionment, with the shrinkage of industrial employment in Michigan and other older industrial states.

The second major limitation in the official data is the failure to count the number of those underemployed and the effects of steady decline in the number of good jobs. This includes involuntary part-time work and working below the level of training, skill, and experience that workers would expect in a balanced economy. There is an important difference between, on the one hand, short-run reliance on such jobs in times of layoff or cyclical decline, and, on the other, a permanent reduction in the number of good jobs that the economy provides.

Evidence is strong that in the post-1965 period there has been such a reduction, shifting more people, many permanently, out of the core and into the periphery of the labor market. They are especially vulnerable to intermittent unemployment and chronic job insecurity.

Between 1987 and 1992, a total of 5.6 million workers who had been with one employer for three years or more lost their jobs; in the 1980s, the *Fortune* 500 reduced employment by 3.4 million. This wave of corporate downsizing accelerated and widened in the 1989-92 economic decline but, contrary to experience in earlier business cycles, did not stop or reverse direction when the level of economic activity began to rise; it continued virtually without letup.

While corporate profits increased 11 percent in 1994, following a 13 percent increase in 1993, corporations reduced employment by 516,069 jobs in 1994, close to the level of 552,292 in 1991, a recession year.[20] Company after company, including those with large profits, continued to cut.

Multiple motivations are at work: reduce union strength, increase control of work, strengthen ability to compete, and so on. One of the most compelling is the desire to lower what economists and accountants call the break-even point, that level of production that enables a company to earn a profit even when market demand declines, as it does in periods of recession. In 1995, Caterpillar, Harley-Davidson, Sun Microsystems, and the big three automakers were all systematically reducing employment levels in anticipation of a post-1995 recession.[21]

The result is that manufacturing employment, which rebounded after previous recessions, continued to decline after 1991. As good jobs shrink in number, the secondary labor market grows and the periphery becomes the only destination for increasing numbers of workers. None of this is

20. Matt Murray, "Thanks, Goodbye: Amid Record Profits, Companies Continue to Lay Off Employees; Eliminating Salaries Boosts Earnings but Also Adds Anxiety and Disloyalty; Ms. Cromer's Clenched Teeth," *Wall Street Journal*, 4 May 1995.

21. James Sterngold, "Facing the Next Recession without Fear," *New York Times*, 4 May 1995.

captured in employment or labor force data. The heralded restoration of the productivity of U.S. industry after the recession of the late 1980s was largely achieved by reducing employment levels.

The burdens of downsizing are disproportionately felt by the less skilled, minorities, women, and older workers. For example, while the mean duration of unemployment for all workers in 1990 was 12 weeks, it was 18 weeks for workers aged 55 and above. Older workers, like blacks and many women, are more likely than others to give up the search for work and join the ranks of the discouraged unemployed.[22] The effects of systemic changes that create and sustain worker redundancy sharpen and accentuate already existing patterns of inequality and discrimination in labor markets.

BEHIND THE DIFFERING RECORD OF JOB GROWTH

Americans have heard much about the "miracle" of large-scale job growth in the United States in contrast to the virtual cessation of growth in Europe, where unemployment rates in the 1980s rose to well above U.S. levels. This marked a sharp departure from the previous decade, when European unemployment rates consistently remained below 3 percent and, in some important economies, less than 1 percent.

Mainstream economics attributed this change and these differences to "rigidities" in European labor market policies, contrasted unfavorably with "flexibility" in the United States. European governments were urged to reduce the rigidities and move toward greater flexibility if they wished to reverse the inexorable upward movement in unemployment levels.

The reality is that lower rates of overall unemployment in the United States were, as we saw earlier, incomplete and misleading. Disaggregating the numbers revealed sharp differences in levels of unemployment and underemployment by race, gender, and age, to a greater degree than in any of the major European economies.

Solow[23] adds a second caution, observing that while rigidities—reflecting European decisions about the importance of social protection and stability—may explain some of the difference, they do not explain all of it: "Another, additional source of unemployment was superimposed on it some time in the late 1970s," namely, "a nearly universal shift to tight macroeconomic policy, in a natural reaction to the acceleration of inflation after the second oil shock."[24]

Solow observes, correctly, that once unemployment stabilizes at any level, even a high one, theory and policy tend to identify this level as the equilibrium level, below which policy

22. Diane E. Herz and Philip L. Rones, "Institutional Barriers to Employment of Older Workers," *Monthly Labor Review*, pp. 14-20 (Apr. 1989); U.S., Department of Health and Human Services, National Institutes of Health, National Institute on Aging, "Survey Sketches: New Portrait of Aging America," 1993.

23. Robert Solow, "Is All That European Unemployment Necessary?" (Robbins Lecture, Working Paper 94-06, World Economic Laboratory at the Massachusetts Institute of Technology, 1994), pp. 6-9.

24. Ibid., pp. 11-12.

cannot successfully reduce it. Those who make policy, and those who assess it, agree that reducing unemployment no longer merits serious attention, in part because it has become institutionalized in the work of the economists as well as in people's behavior and expectations and in the politics and economics of a society. While Solow argues that macroeconomic expansion would probably reduce unemployment several percentage points without inflationary effects, his analysis explains why this was unlikely to motivate national leaders and parties.

U.S. official unemployment rates are well below those in Europe, but the differences are offset by widespread declines in job quality and security, as measured by earnings, continuity of employment, and provision by employers of nonwage benefits, notably health care insurance and retirement pensions.

Some authors call this the "pauperization" of work.[25] It has shaped a distribution of income that has become steadily more unequal as (1) real earnings stagnated, (2) full-time work became less available and more intermittent and part-time work increased, (3) labor force participation declined for key groups, notably, young black men in central cities, (4) the proportion of well-paid jobs declined, while those with lower pay increased, a reflection of the shift from goods-producing to service work and from predominantly male to mixed sectors, and (5) union density steadily declined, depriving the great majority of workers—estimated at almost nine in ten—of effective advocacy of their economic needs and workplace rights.

Effective and comprehensive labor market policies do not have the power to reverse these forces, but they can blunt their destructive effects and, even more important, change employers' choices that directly affect labor market outcomes.

A recent study of the effects of large-scale computerization of economic activity argues that wise and timely policies, national and international, have the power and the mandate to limit the destructive effects of these new forces on employment levels and opportunities. The authors correctly describe mass unemployment as "an unmitigated social disaster" because of its social, psychological, and political effects, and they characterize its prevention as "a question of the survival of a civilized society."[26] Their comprehensive and practical set of policy prescriptions, and their analysis of the economic changes already well advanced across the spectrum of the developed economies of Europe, Asia, and North America, contrast sharply with apocalyptic scenarios of the end of work offered by other writers.[27]

Among these prescriptions are familiar as well as innovative policies

---

25. Dembo and Morehouse, *Underbelly of the U.S. Economy*, pp. 17-27.

26. Chris Freeman and Luc Soete, *Work for All or Mass Unemployment?* (London: Pinter, 1994), pp. 14, 15.

27. Jeremy Rifkin, *The End of Work: The Decline of the Global Labor Force and the Dawn of the Post-Market Era* (New York: G. P. Putnam's Sons, 1995); Stanley Aronowitz and William DeFazio, *The Jobless Future: Sci-Tech and the Dogma of Work* (Minneapolis: University of Minnesota Press, 1994).

embracing labor market measures, community-based economic development, systematic measures to reduce working time, and measures to curb, control, and compensate for the negative effects on employment of major centers of corporate and financial power that are leading the process of global economic reconstruction in this new Schumpeterian cycle of creative destruction.

POLICIES FOR PROTECTION
AND RENEWAL OF EMPLOYMENT

Our point of departure is the necessity to preserve the ability of people to choose the combination of work and leisure that meets their needs and those of their family, community, and workplace without pressure to impose inappropriate burdens on themselves, their families, their employers, or the community at large. These choices vary over time and place. They involve family, community, and generational relationships that seldom enter the calculations of economists and policymakers.

Policies meeting these tests would not be consistent with an economy that provided secure jobs with good pay—for example, the lifetime employment pattern in major Japanese industries—to a minority of workers while significant numbers were unemployed or underemployed workers as a result of race, gender, age, or geographical location.

Effective labor market policies cannot eliminate but they can counter the effects of these factors. If they are well designed, they will advance economic welfare while protecting those at risk. One of their key effects would be to reallocate the costs and benefits of economic change so that those who have the most to gain—from relocation of operations, adoption of new technology, or redesign of the process of production and distribution—are required to bear some of the social burdens that otherwise fall disproportionately on displaced workers or abandoned communities.

The central concepts are these: retention where possible, retraining when appropriate, reemployment when needed, and opportunities for new entrants to the labor force. A balance is needed between what economists call supply-side measures—dealing with training and retraining and other characteristics and needs of the labor force—and demand-side measures that use incentives, regulation, and other policies to influence and affect the decisions and choices of employers, large and small, private, public, or nonprofit.

Because economic and demographic forces exert their effects over different time periods and geographic areas, labor market policies must include an appropriate range of measures corresponding to these differences.

Hours of work

Among the most important of these measures, requiring progress over a relatively long period of time, is the need steadily to reduce working time, measured not only in hours per day and per year but also over the worker's lifetime. In the century preceding World War II, reducing working time ranked with raising workers' pay at the top of the political agenda of labor and progressive movements.

Between 1900 and 1920, the number of weekly hours of work fell from an average of 60 to just under 50. During the Great Depression, following a period of no change in the 1920s, the level fell to 35 and then stabilized at 40 after the war; they ceased to fall and in recent years have risen.

In the 1990s, the United States shared with Japan the dubious distinction of the longest average number of working hours per year of any advanced economy.[28] Sporadic efforts in other countries—notably, Germany—have won shorter hours for some unionized groups after protracted struggle, but the issue remains dormant in the United States. One important factor has been the stagnation and decline of earnings outlined earlier, a spur to the effort to increase income by working longer.

Even when real wages were increasing in the 1945-75 period, unionized workers welcomed longer hours, paid at overtime rates, which raised incomes and purchasing power in pursuit of higher levels of consumption, the motivation that drove the economy. More recent evidence indicates that as these workers grow older, the burdens imposed by long hours are no longer acceptable; strikes in key auto plants in the mid-1990s sought successfully to limit hours by increasing the numbers of those employed instead of more overtime work. New evidence, theoretical and empirical, supports the view that a renewed effort to reduce working time may now find a favorable reception.

Job retention

The commodification of labor has exposed most workers to an unlimited risk of job loss whenever it suits an employer's wish, prejudice, or whim. The legal doctrine of employment at will embodies and expresses this freedom. Only in limited cases are groups protected from this risk: tenured university faculty, unionized workers, and a few others.

The post-1965 era yielded statutory protection against job loss based on race, sex, age, physical handicap, and other specified factors, but the effectiveness of these shields depends on the resources and political mandate of agencies charged with their enforcement and on the ability of those denied their rights to secure justice individually in courts and administrative agencies, a time-consuming and costly course that has discouraged many. Despite its demonstrated effectiveness in many cases, affirmative action came under relentless attack in the mid-1990s.

Limiting employers' freedom to terminate employment

Curbs and controls on employers' freedom to lay off or discharge unwanted or unneeded employees con-

---

28. Benjamin Kline Hunnicut, *Work without End: Abandoning Shorter Hours for the Right to Work* (Philadelphia: University of Pennsylvania Press, 1988); Juliet Schor, *The Overworked American: The Unexpected Decline of Leisure* (New York: Basic Books, 1991); International Labour Office, "The Hours We Work: New Directions in Policy and Practice," *Conditions of Work Digest*, 9(1) (1990); Fred Best, *Reducing Workweeks to Prevent Layoffs: The Economic and Social Impacts of Unemployment Insurance–Supported Work Sharing* (Philadelphia: Temple University Press, 1990).

stitutes a challenge to labor market policy that will require a mobilization of political will so far absent from U.S. experience, though there are a few modest beginnings on which to build.

One is the first-ever U.S. law requiring some employers to provide advance notice before reducing employment by significant amounts. Experience in other countries—including Canada—supports the view that strong plant-closing and mass-layoff notification requirements can save jobs without placing employers in a straitjacket that prevents them from adapting to changes in markets, technology, or other factors.

In some European countries, reductions in employment are made costly and difficult in the name of both social justice and economic good sense: a stable workforce is an asset that has proved its economic worth to employers in both good and bad times, and the Japanese model of lifetime employment—though it applies to only a minority of the workforce—has been widely praised as a major factor explaining Japan's superior record of productivity and efficiency. Measures to promote stability of employment for the employed in the United States would yield similar benefits, though employers' resistance is likely to be strong.

Community control of economic life

Community-based power to raise and deploy investment capital in order both to conserve existing sources of employment and economic activity and to develop new sources richly deserves attention and support in an era when global capital can and does relocate work not only across the United States but throughout the world.

The Federation for Industrial Retention and Renewal, a coalition of community-based economic redevelopment efforts, has tested a variety of approaches intended to conserve and renew the fruits of urban-based investment of social and private capital, accumulated over many decades. These and other coalitions grew from last-ditch efforts to resist and slow the wave of plant closings that sharply reduced economic activity in New England and other older industrial areas, notably the steel mills in Pennsylvania, in the 1960s and 1970s.[29] Although the record is mixed, it offers some lessons about what works.

The campaign for a "sustainable Milwaukee," the restoration of the economy of the Naugatuck Valley in Connecticut, and the analytic and technical work of the Midwest Center for Labor Research in Chicago are some of the more promising and successful of these efforts. They involve a systematic valuation of the assets—capital and human—that have accumulated over generations of economic development, and a hardnosed, sophisticated, and imaginative analysis that relates these to the local, regional, national, and global possibilities generated by the forces of change. They link sophisticated

29. Barry Bluestone and Bennett Harrison, *The Deindustrialization of America: Plant Closings, Community Abandonment and the Dismantling of Basic Industry* (New York: Basic Books, 1982); idem, *The Great U-Turn: Corporate Restructuring and the Polarizing of America* (New York: Basic Books, 1990).

analysis to effective mobilization of communities, unions, churches, and other forces whose joined voices can command the attention and response of legislative bodies, leaders of industry, and others.

Similar efforts are being developed in Los Angeles, in the work of the Labor/Community Strategy Center, and elsewhere. Their ranks will grow as the lessons of earlier efforts are shared and their accomplishments evoke and support similar activities in other communities. Restoration and renewal of the economic base for viable and stable community life will become more urgent as the effects of economic erosion and dislocation manifest themselves in many ways: more homelessness and poverty, greater instability in family life, and overt hostility to the fabric of governance and toleration that are at the heart of our polity and social structure.

WORK AND INCOME: A NEW SYNTHESIS

Once, men earned their families' living while their wives stayed at home. Then women in increasing numbers went to work and stayed at work as men's wages stagnated, family ties frayed, and women integrated work into their lives and hopes. A volatile economy imposes difficult choices and unexpected contingencies. Our traditional programs and policies dealing with unemployment, retirement, and first-time entry to the labor force assume levels of stability and continuity that no longer exist, nor do our labor force and unemployment databases capture this volatility and rapid rate of change.

The historical dichotomy between work and nonwork no longer reflects reality. When women interrupt their careers to bear and raise children, they are no longer counted in the labor force, though the work they do is central to the stability of the social order and to the life chances of their children. Poor single mothers have been cruelly stigmatized in the welfare-reform debate that has drastically eroded the safety net available to these women and their children, though we know how high the cost can be when large numbers of children grow up in poverty. When people commit their skills and time to housing the homeless, feeding the hungry, or righting the wrongs they see in society's life, they are doing important and useful work that merits recognition and reward.

Social policy creates a semantic dichotomy between earned income and transfer payments; the first ranks higher, the second is vulnerable, especially for those deemed the unworthy poor. This dichotomy needs to be healed. People at all economic levels and at each life stage need and deserve the freedom to choose what combination of work in the labor market and work outside best meets their needs and those of their families and communities.

This freedom to choose acquires special urgency in an era of chronic and continuing inadequacy of paid work for all who want and need it, the erosion of continuity in employment for many, and the marginalization of important groups, notably young black men living in older central cities. The opportunity to get and hold paid work remains the preferred life destiny of most and deserves pride of place in our economic and social policies. The routes into and out of this role need to be multiplied. Alternative ways of meeting one's responsibilities to self, family, and society by appropriate combinations of earnings and income support need to be treated as equally important in our continuing analysis and transformation of our labor market policies and programs.[30]

30. Sheila D. Collins, Helen L. Ginsburg, and Gertrude S. Goldberg, *Jobs for All: A Plan for the Revitalization of America* (New York: Apex Press, 1994), pp. 61-65.

Human Capital Development: America's Greatest Challenge

By THEODORE HERSHBERG

ABSTRACT: Highly developed human capital will be the source of comparative advantage in the twenty-first-century global economy. America's human capital development system—K-12, postsecondary training, higher education, and on-the-job learning—has severe problems that must be corrected if the nation is to compete effectively. Nationally benchmarked standards to measure the educational performance of our students is the best way to proceed.

Theodore Hershberg is professor of public policy and history and director of the Center for Greater Philadelphia at the University of Pennsylvania, where he has taught since 1967.

WHAT follows may sound like doom and gloom, but it is meant to be a wake-up call. The future is not predetermined. Americans can make the necessary changes if they want to. The first step for all of us is to admit that we have a very big problem on our hands that will take a generation to correct. If we fail, we will leave our children and grandchildren a legacy not merely of economic uncompetitiveness and a much lower standard of living, but a seriously diminished quality of life stemming from an enormous gap between a minority of haves and a majority of have-nots that will undermine the basis of civil society and our democracy.

THE SIGNIFICANCE OF HUMAN CAPITAL

It all has to do with a concept called human capital, or the education, skill level, and problem-solving abilities that will enable an individual to be a productive worker in the global economy of the twenty-first century. To understand why this is so, let us examine the arguments made by Massachusetts Institute of Technology economist Lester Thurow in his provocative 1992 study, *Head-to-Head: The Coming Economic Battle among Japan, Europe, and America*.[1]

In the first 25 years after World War II, the global economy was characterized by niche competition. "The United States," according to Thurow, "exported agricultural products our foreign competitors did not grow, raw materials they did not have, and high-tech products they could not build."[2] High-wage products in Germany and Japan were low-wage products in the United States. Imports to America from these countries did not threaten our jobs, and our exports did not threaten theirs.

In these years, America was the undisputed king of the hill. In the late 1940s, America's gross national product (GNP) was half of the world's, and our per capita GNP was 4 times that of West Germany and 15 times that of Japan.

The last 25 years have been very different indeed. By the late 1980s, our share of the world's economy had fallen by half, and in 1990, Japan's per capita gross domestic product (GDP) was slightly larger than ours. In the last 20 years, we have lost our dominance in steel and machine tools, chemicals and autos, and television and consumer electronics. Between 1973 and 1992, while per capita GDP grew 25 percent (adjusted for inflation), real weekly wages for nonsupervisory workers (two-thirds of all workers) fell 1 percent per year. In the last two decades, the top 20 percent of our workers were on a steep "up" escalator, the second 20 percent were standing still, and the bottom 60 percent were going down.

The next 25 years, Thurow argues, will be characterized by head-to-head competition over seven industries that offer high-paying jobs to their workers and bring prosperity and world prestige to their countries. These brain-intensive industries include computers and software, robotics and machine tools, civilian aviation, microelectronics, materials

1. *Head-to-Head: The Coming Economic Battle among Japan, Europe, and America* (New York: Warner Books, 1992).

2. Ibid., p. 29.

sciences, biotechnology, and telecommunications.

Scholarly journals and the popular press have been filled with statistics demonstrating that few new jobs can be filled by unskilled workers and that the largest majority of these jobs demand far higher skill levels than in the past. The days when a poorly educated worker could leave high school and find a well-paying job in a factory are long gone.

But rather than trot out these statistics again, it is more informative to illustrate with three examples why human capital is becoming the comparative advantage of the future.

The first of these concerns product technologies. What is required for companies to invent a product and earn big profits from it? A bit over a dozen years ago, IBM and Apple introduced personal computers on whose sales these companies made a fortune. But in time, other manufacturers discovered how to produce personal computers, and very quickly the prices of these machines dropped precipitously while their speed and power increased many times over. In short, personal computers ceased being unique products and became instead clones or commodities just like so much corn or wheat or potatoes.

Commodities command paper-thin profit margins. The lesson for companies is to invent a product, mass-produce it while profit margins are high, and then, when competitors catch up and thereby force much lower prices, introduce a new product that will put them back on the gravy train.

Product cycles—not how long you can use your widget, but how long before the assembly line that makes it must change—have been shrinking with remarkable speed. In the past decade, the product cycle in the automobile industry has fallen from seven and a half years to six and in several instances to five and four years. The average for all manufactured products has fallen from four years to two, and in the computer industry, it has shrunk to roughly six months.

The second illustration of future trends concerns process technologies. In the nineteenth and twentieth centuries, Britain and America grew rich and powerful creating products. But in the twenty-first century, the advantage based on new products cannot be sustained easily because of reverse engineering, that is, producing more cost-effectively a product someone else has invented. The Japanese have made reverse engineering an art form.

The American electronics industry is a case in point. In the last several decades, four leading new products were introduced into the mass consumer market: the video camera, the videocassette recorder, and the fax machine (all three of which were American inventions), and the compact disc player (invented by the Dutch). But in terms of sales, employment, and profits, all four have become Japanese products.

What used to be primary (inventing new products) has become secondary and what used to be secondary (inventing and perfecting new processes) has become primary. It is instructive to learn that the United States spends 2:1 in research and development on product technologies and Japan spends 2:1 on process technologies.

The third illustration concerns new high-performance work organizations, or how successful companies will be configured in the future. To stay competitive in the global economy, corporate America has been engaged in a dramatic downsizing process. What is unique about this latest round of corporate layoffs is that it affects largely white-collar workers rather than blue-collar workers, as in the past.

When middle managers are eliminated, frontline workers must assume their responsibilities and develop their skills, or the strategy of thinning middle management's ranks cannot succeed. This means that ordinary, shop-floor workers must be able to use computer-aided design and computer-aided manufacturing technologies, manage just-in-time inventories, operate flexible manufacturing systems, and employ statistical quality control. For example, without statistical quality control, Thurow reminds us, "today's high-density semiconductor chips cannot be built—they can be invented, but they cannot be built."[3]

The central argument of *America's Choice: High Skills or Low Wages*, the report of the Commission on the Skills of the American Workforce, was summarized by William Brock, one of the commission cochairs and former U.S. secretary of labor. If every country in the world can now buy "idiot-proof machinery" to compensate for workers with terribly deficient skills, and "if there are people in other parts of the world who will work for $5 per day and they use the same equipment as Americans who want $10 or $15 per hour, either we have to change the way people work here—not only work harder, but smarter, more effectively—or we have to compete on the basis of wages."[4]

Unfortunately, the evidence seems to suggest that America is content to compete on the basis of wages, which means an inexorable trend downward, instead of an effort to build skills up.

What kind of workers must America have in the future? Think about the qualities workers must have if companies are to succeed in product and process technologies. Consider the kind of employees that high-performance work organizations need to succeed absent middle management. They will have to be flexible, adaptable, quick learners and problem solvers. Are these the kind of skills being produced by America's human capital development system?

PROBLEMS WITH
AMERICA'S HUMAN CAPITAL
DEVELOPMENT SYSTEM

I recently came across this ad in a newspaper: "Lost a black shaggy dog. Hair falling from left rear haunch. Under medication for hyperactive thyroid. Blind in right eye. Limps badly after being hit by a car.... Answers to the name *Lucky*." We will be no more lucky than our fictional dog

3. Ibid., p. 52.

4. "Interview: Will Americans Work for $5 a Day?" *Time*, 23 July 1990, p. 12. See also Commission on the Skills of the American Workforce, *America's Choice: High Skills or Low Wages* (Rochester, NY: National Center on Education and the Economy, 1990).

if, as a nation, we fail to come to grips with the statistics cited here.

The global economic competition can be likened to a kite race in which each nation's entry bears its respective flag. Think of it as a two-frame cartoon. In the first frame, the American kite soars into the lead. In the second frame, the kites of other nations pass us by, but we can see why because attached to the tail of our kite is a heavy weight.

The weight represents the results of the National Adult Literacy Survey. In the fall of 1992, the Educational Testing Service, under contract from the federal Department of Education, carried out the most comprehensive survey ever taken of adult literacy. Hour-long interviews were conducted with a national sample of 13,600 individuals above the age of 16. They asked not about old notions of literacy, such as the ability to sign one's name, completion of five years of schooling, and the scores achieved in school-based measures of reading achievements. Their definition of literacy focused on the ability to use printed and written information to function in society, to achieve one's goals, and to develop one's knowledge and potential.

The prose (understanding of information), document (use of information), and quantitative (arithmetic operations) tasks that interviewees were asked to perform were not, in my opinion, particularly demanding. The great majority of high school graduates should be able to perform in the top two of five test levels. Yet fully half of the American workforce—some 90 million adults—fell into the bottom two levels, meaning that they are hopelessly ill-equipped for the jobs of the twenty-first century global economy! Only 15 percent tested at the fourth level, and only 3 to 4 percent, some 6-8 million adults, tested at the highest level.[5]

What explains these results? What is going on in the nation's human capital development system? Let us examine four key components: K-12 education, postsecondary vocational training, higher education, and on-the-job training.

K-12 schools

Suburban parents take considerable comfort in comparisons of their schools with those of the inner cities. On average, the dropout rates of suburban schools are much lower, their performance scores on virtually all measures of academic achievement are much better, and their college enrollment rates are much higher. Yet no comfort should be taken from this comparison. Simply put, it is the wrong comparison. Two others are far more appropriate.

First, we should be comparing our kids to their counterparts in the rest of the developed world because they represent the competition of the future. No matter what test is considered, American fifth, eighth, and twelfth graders on average score at or near the bottom among developed nations in math and science. The good news is that, in some studies, either the top 10 percent or top 30 percent of our 17-year-olds are competitive.

5. Irwin S. Kirsch et al., *Adult Literacy in America: A First Look at the Results of the National Adult Literacy Survey* (Washington, DC: National Center for Education Statistics, 1993), p. 17.

The bad news is that the large majority of our kids score very much below the rest of the developed world.

Second, we should be comparing the human capital of our kids to the skills required by the jobs of the twenty-first century global economy. The mismatch here is stunning. Regarding the skills of all new workers entering the workforce between 1985 and 2000, 78 percent of these workers have the skills for only the bottom 40 percent of the jobs, while only 5 percent of new workers will have the skills for the top 40 percent of the jobs.

Why do our kids fare so badly in these comparisons? Part of the answer is structural. In Western Europe, Canada, and the Pacific Rim, kids go to school 220 days per year; in Japan they go 240 days per year. In many of these nations, children attend school 8 hours a day. In America, our kids go to school 180 days a year and 6 hours a day. When calculated over the full K-12 experience, Japanese students graduate with four more years of classroom time than American students. Little wonder that it takes an American student with a master's of science degree to equal the mastery of statistics possessed by a Japanese high school graduate.

"The great accomplishment of Japanese primary and secondary education lies not in the creation of a brilliant elite . . . but in its generation of such a high average level of capability," writes Thomas Rohlen. "The profoundly impressive fact is that Japan is shaping a whole population, workers as well as managers, to a standard inconceivable in the U.S."[6]

6. *Japan's High Schools* (Berkeley: University of California Press, 1983), p. 322.

Part of the answer is cultural and has a great deal to do with the expectations that parents and teachers have for their children. American parents are far more likely to attribute school success to ability, while Asian parents are far more likely to attribute success to effort. The quality that American teachers treasure most in their students is sensitivity, while Asian teachers treasure clarity.

But the kids should not be let off the hook either. When asked to rate themselves, 75 percent of American primary school students thought they were doing just fine, compared with only 37 percent of Japanese kids. When a national poll compared attitudes about how well students were doing in reading, writing, math, and understanding instructions, students and parents graded students roughly 2-3 times higher than did college administrators and employers.

When American students are compared with students in Korea, China, and other competing countries where academic standards are somewhat more lenient than Japan's, we see that American kids do one-third to one-fifth the amount of homework, watch three times as much television, and, as a result, achieve roughly one-fourth the test score levels realized elsewhere.

Postsecondary vocational training

A little-appreciated fact about the future is that while only 30 percent of new jobs in 2000 will require college degrees, roughly 85 percent of new jobs will require some postsecondary training. Yet for every dollar of taxpayer money we spend on postsecondary training, we spend $55 subsidizing college students. The United States is unique in the world in not having an organized postsecondary training system for the non-college-bound.

Our global competitors do it differently. Other nations spend far more than we do on postsecondary training: Britain, France, and Spain spend twice as much; Germany, three times; and Sweden, six times. When the quantity and quality of postsecondary training programs are ranked, Japan comes out first, Germany second, and America eleventh. Our apprenticeship programs touch only 300,000 workers, less than 0.3 percent of all workers. A German executive put it this way: "America has too many people in college and not enough qualified workers. The U.S. has outstanding universities, but it is missing its middle."[7]

Higher education

While it appears that our K-12 system is in considerable need of fundamental change, our vaunted system of higher education must surely pull our chestnuts from the fire. Here is where we rank highest, here is where we excel. Our universities are the best, a point proven by the fact that students flock here from all over the world.

Unfortunately, what is true about our elite universities is hardly true about all of higher education. America has 3600 colleges and universities: 2100 four-year schools and 1500 two-year schools. By some estimates, however, only 200 to 600 of these schools have selective standards for admission; that is, the balance of these schools rarely reject applicants based on their level of academic achievement.

So why work in high school? Small wonder that the average high school senior does less than one hour of homework per night. "Adolescents are like adults. They do as much as they have to in order to get what they want," writes Albert Shanker, president of the American Federation of Teachers. "The young people who want to go to elite schools must meet high standards, and they work hard. But the rest of high school students know they can get into some college no matter how poorly they do."[8]

Recent research suggests that our colleges and universities add some value. But the results of the National Adult Literacy Survey summarized earlier for all adults reveal some absolutely alarming statistics about the functional abilities of our college graduates. Only 2-5 percent of graduates from two-year colleges and 8-13 percent of graduates from four-year colleges perform at the highest level on the test. Even when we look only at those who have gone on to earn a postgraduate degree or to take some postgraduate courses, fewer than one in five score at the highest level![9]

---

7. Commission on the Skills of the American Workforce, *America's Choice*, p. 65.

8. Albert Shanker, "The End of the Traditional Model of Schooling—and a Proposal for Using Incentives to Restructure Our Public Schools," *Phi Delta Kappan*, 71:353-54 (Jan. 1990).

9. Kirsch et al., *Adult Literacy in America*, p. 26.

On-the-job training

Each year American employers spend about $30 billion on formal training. According to the American Society for Training and Development, $27 billion was paid by 15,000 companies—roughly 0.5 percent of all U.S. employers. Of this group, only 100-200 firms, the largest companies with significant professional and managerial staff, spend more than 2 percent of payroll on formal training. Only about one-third of this $27 billion is spent on our non-college-educated workers, who compose two-thirds of the workforce.

This amount is about 10 percent of total public education expenditures in the United States. Thus almost all our money is focused on the first 15-20 years of life, with precious little aimed at the remaining 40-50 years of working life in an era when technological change requires that education be treated as a lifelong learning process.

Perhaps this is not so surprising. Few chief executive officers of *Fortune* 500 companies come from human resource development backgrounds: 34 percent from marketing and 25 percent from finance. For technical backgrounds, the story is much the same: only 30 percent of American chief executive officers, compared with 70 percent in Japan and Europe, rose to power via technology-based career tracks.

WHAT NEXT?

What does all this mean? It means that if we are to compete successfully in the new world economy and provide jobs that pay wages to keep most Americans in the middle class, we will have to make major changes in the attention we pay to and the money we spend on human capital development.

It is clear, then, that we are in a systemwide crisis. The school system and the human capital development system that helped America and Americans achieve prosperity in a manufacturing era are no longer functional. We no longer need workers who are socialized largely to show up on time, respect authority, and repeat monotonous tasks. We need a different school system for a different economy, a school system that produces graduates who are flexible, adaptable, quick learners, and problem solvers.

Setting national standards—in which we benchmark the performance of our students against the most demanding standards in the developed world—strikes me as absolutely the right strategic direction in which to move. The impact of tough standards can reverberate up and down the human capital development system. Let us set how high the top of the mountain should be for all our kids, and let individual school districts and parents determine how they intend to get their kids to the top.

We must make high school consequential. If our students do not meet these standards, it must be made clear that employers will not hire them, colleges will not admit them, and postsecondary training programs will not enroll them! Significant equity issues exist, particularly in the urban schools attended by so many of the nation's minorities. But the interests of these children are clearly not served by the status quo, and remedies can and must be identified.

One promising intervention, the New Standards Project, is a grassroots partnership of 17 states and large school districts that collectively enrolls about half the nation's schoolchildren. By focusing only on English, math, science, and practical knowledge, the New Standards movement hopes to avoid battles over values engaged in by left- and right-wing ideologues that derailed work on national history standards.

Let us engage in a productive discussion over the key ends to work toward in our schools rather than plunge into a divisive controversy over means such as vouchers and tuition credits. Frankly, if we can agree on appropriate ends, the means become far less important. Finally, let us benchmark our national standards against the most demanding in the developed world because, in a global economy, our children's future standard of living will be determined by the abilities of young people now being educated overseas.

Now is the time to debate these issues. We will need agreements on standards and performance-based assessment protocols for our K-12 students. We will need leaders from business, postsecondary education, and higher education to insist that students meet these standards to continue their training and education or to get a job after high school. With consensus established, we can hold our first graduating class of high school seniors accountable to these standards in seven to ten years.

The human capital development challenge is not one among many—rather, it is the greatest challenge facing America. Creating a future labor force that can compete successfully in the global economy is an intimidating and almost immobilizing task because change must be made in every component of the nation's human capital development system. Yet, if we admit the nature of the crisis, recognize that a generation's effort lies ahead, and get to work now, we can set a course that will take us into the next millennium confident about the future of our economy, assured about our quality of life, and secure in our democracy.

High Technology and Work Tomorrow

By STANLEY ARONOWITZ and WILLIAM DiFAZIO

ABSTRACT: Science and technology developments over the past 25 years have had profound effects on workplace productivity and income. Prevailing wisdom holds that significant levels of investment in plant and equipment and the consequent economic growth lead, in the context of a market economy, to more permanent jobs. The authors contest this claim. They argue that the tendency of technology investment is inherently labor saving, in both goods production and the services. Most new jobs that are being created, primarily in the services, have been contingent, part-time, benefit free, and frequently temporary. Thus there will be a shortage of decent-paying permanent jobs in the future. The authors argue that the premise of economic and social policy must take work as an active presupposition.

Stanley Aronowitz is professor of sociology at the Graduate Center, City University of New York, and director of its Center for Cultural Studies. He is author and editor of 12 books, most recently The Jobless Future: Sci-Tech and the Dogma of Work, *with William DiFazio (1994).*

William DiFazio is professor and chair of the Sociology Department at St. John's University. Among his books are The Jobless Future *(with Stanley Aronowitz) and* Longshoremen *(1986). He is currently working on a book tentatively titled* Ordinary Poverty.

SCIENCE and technological developments have had profound effects on workplace productivity as well as on employment and income. Contrary to the prevailing view that scientifically based technological innovation will lead in the future to a cornucopia of highly skilled, well-paid jobs, we contend that new high-tech regimes, controlled by transnational capital, are labor destroying. Economists and policy experts understand that certain jobs have been made redundant. After all, since the dawn of the Industrial Revolution, when new technologies are introduced they inevitably create new, high-skilled jobs. We argue here that this is no longer the case; we contend that these new computer technologies have already destroyed more jobs than they create and that there is no warrant for believing that this trend will not continue. Moreover, even increased investment will not change this situation, for the progressive diminution of well-paid full-time manual, technical, and professional jobs is a new global condition.

In the past, in industrial-based societies, work and skill were central to economic production. In this new postmodern, postindustrial society, work and skill have been decentered and knowledge has become central. It is to this sea change that we turn.

QUANTUM MEASURES

We do not accept the prevailing wisdom that significant levels of investment in plant and equipment and the consequent economic growth lead, in the current era, to more permanent jobs. To state this proposition more positively, if the tendency of most investment is to save labor in comparison to the part played by machinery in production, then the number of jobs created will be reduced, relatively, in proportion to the unit of invested capital. From the construction of buildings and the production of machinery, the number of workers—intellectual as well as manual— is reduced by quantum measures in computer-mediated labor. Consequently, given the relatively slow rate of global economic growth and especially the long-term tendency to sluggish U.S. growth rates, even when new investment creates short-term employment for machine producers, the number of jobs, in the long-term, is reduced.

We used the term "quantum measures" to distinguish computer-mediated production from that of the mechanical era. There is no question that labor productivity, if measured as a ratio of output to the time required for its production, has dramatically increased. To be sure, the part played by labor in the production of commodities has been reduced, more or less progressively, since the introduction of pulleys and pumps in the sixteenth and seventeenth centuries to power machinery. The rationalization of the labor process into smaller units of repetitive tasks further increased the productivity of labor. Later, at the turn of the twentieth century, we had the application of electromagnetic technologies to engines and motors; we also had the replacement of iron with steel and of other metals with oil-based synthetic materials and the production technologies that accompanied this change. Further, the development of the chemical industry and electrically powered telecommunications accelerated the process of labor displacement.

But, contrary to the optimistic predictions of early advocates of computer technologies, it has not been possible to achieve the utopian (dystopian) dream of the virtually automatic factory in which labor is consigned to the role of maintaining and administering a self-reproducing labor process in most decisive sectors, including professions. In all of this, knowledge, always important, is increasingly central.

New uses of knowledge widen the gap between the present and the future: new knowledges challenge not only our collectively held beliefs but also the common ethical ground of our civilization. The tendency of science to dominate the labor process, which emerged in the last half of the nineteenth century but attained full flower only in the last two decades, now heralds an entirely new regime of work in which almost no production skills are required. Older forms of technical or professional knowledge are transformed, incorporated, superseded, or otherwise eliminated by computer-mediated technologies—applications of physical sciences, intertwined with the production of knowledge, yielding expert systems—leaving new forms of knowledge that are inherently labor saving.

But, unlike the mechanizing era of pulleys and electrically powered machinery, both of which retained the hands-on character of labor, computers have transferred most knowledge associated with crafts, manual labor, and, increasingly, intellectual knowledge to the machine. As a result, while each generation of technological change makes some work more complex and interesting and raises the level of training or qualification required by a (diminishing) fraction of intellectual and manual labor, for the overwhelming majority of workers, this process simplifies tasks or eliminates them and, thus, displaces the worker.

The specific character of computer-aided technologies is that they no longer discriminate between most categories of intellectual and manual labor. With the introduction of computer-aided software programming (CASP), the work of perhaps the most glamorous of the technical professions associated with computer technology—the programmer—is irreversibly threatened. Although the "real" job of programming, which creates new and basic approaches, will go on, the ordinary occupation of computer programmer may disappear just as the drafter, whose tasks were incorporated by computer-aided design and drafting (CADD) by the late 1980s. The invention of CASP is an example of a highly complex program that requires considerable knowledge for its development. But, when CASP's development costs have been paid and the price substantially reduced, much of low-level, routine programming will be relegated to historical memory.

The universalization of computers has increased exponentially the "multiplied productive powers" of labor.[1] In this regime of production, the principal effect of technological

1. Karl Marx, *Grundrisse* (New York: Vintage, 1973), pp. 701-5.

change—labor displacement—is largely unmitigated by economic growth. That is, it is possible for key economic indicators to show, but only for a short time, a net increase in domestic product without significant growth of full-time employment. On the other hand, growth itself is blocked by two effects of the new look to working in America. First, labor redundancy, which is the main object of technological change, is, indirectly, an obstacle to growth. Second, in the wake of the shrinking social wage, joblessness, the growth of part-time employment, and the displacement of good full-time jobs by badly paid part-time mediocre jobs tend to thwart the ability of the economic system to avoid chronic overproduction and underconsumption.

Thus, for many employers the precondition of weathering the new international economic environment of sharpened competition is to ruthlessly cut labor costs in order to reverse the free fall of profits. The drop of profits over the past five years may be ascribed to a number of factors, including declining sales, increased costs of nearly all sorts but especially of borrowing, and the high price of expensive technologies used to displace even more expensive labor. But many corporations experience profit loss in terms of falling prices, a telltale sign of overproduction in relation to consumption. Along with labor-displacing technological change aimed at reducing the size of the labor force, wages must be reduced and benefits cut or eliminated, especially those that accrue on the basis of length of employment. Wherever possible, employers are impelled to export production offshore to areas that offer cheap labor and, like Mexico, free plants and water, and virtually no taxes.

These measures produce chronic overproduction of many commodities that formed the foundation of postwar domestic growth: cars, houses, and appliances. Moreover, consistent cost-cutting leads to a domestic labor force that suffers short-term, that is, security-free jobs. This situation is exacerbated by the accelerated globalization of production and the current international recession, so that raising the level of exports as a means to overcome the structural crisis within the national economy is much more difficult to achieve even as it plays a greater role in foreign policy. In fact, the very notion of exports, just like the notion of a purely national working class in a global economy, is problematic, if not already anomalous.

Here, from the economic perspective, we can observe the effective breakdown of the purely national state and the formation of what might be called the metastate, in which the intersection of the largest transnational corporations and the international political directorates of many nations constitute a new governing class. The institutional forms of rule include multilateral trade organizations such as the General Agreement on Tariffs and Trade and the North American Free Trade Agreement; proliferating international conferences on problems ranging from terrorism and technological change to new forms of international economic arrangements in which business leaders, diplomats, academics, and other experts regularly consult; and increasingly frequent summits of government leaders of the key national states, usually flanked by trade representatives recruited from the international business establishment.

Until recently, from the perspective of these metastates, to the extent that currency regulation remained a national affair, national states were important as the major means for valorization of capital. Labor was regulated within the framework of national law, and police forces and armies were raised in this way. Of course, the nation, with or without the state, remained the context within which culture and ideology are produced, themselves an aspect of control, at least from the perspective of international business. Of course, these functions are still partially served by national states.

However, we may discern, in the various forms of spurious capital formation made possible by informatics, a definite decline in the valorization functions of national treasuries: the emergence of a de facto international currency undermines the power of the dollar, the yen, and the mark as universal media of exchange. Further, international capital has forced many states to relax enforcement of protective labor codes, if not the law itself, leaving employers freer to pay lower wages, export jobs, and import (undocumented) labor. The very idea of a national border in all except its most blatant geographic connotation is becoming more dubious as labor flows become heavier between sovereign states.

Finally, while elements of national culture remain, the past quarter century is definitively the era of media and cultural internationalization, precisely because of available technologies as well as the proliferation of transnational production and distribution companies for (primarily) U.S. cultural products. The international culture industry has destroyed all but a few national film industries: in Europe, France, and Germany but not Britain and Italy; in Asia, India; in Latin America, Argentina's is dead, Mexico's weak, and Brazil's almost nonexistent. American television syndication has reached deeply into the world market, and only Great Britain and, to a lesser degree, France have achieved transnational dissemination in Western countries.

The pressure on profits, and the imperative to subsume labor under the new global arrangements, compose the "rational" bases for the decimation of the industrial heartlands—in both the United States and European countries such as France and Great Britain—as manifested in plant closings, drastic workforce reductions, and the definitive end of the social compact that marked the relationship between a significant portion of industrial labor and corporations since the New Deal and the postwar European compromise between capital and labor.

Ronald Reagan's dramatic and highly symbolic firing of 11,000 air traffic controllers in 1981 may be remembered as the definitive act that closed the book on the old historic compromise between a relatively powerful, if conservative, labor movement and capital. As the American unions whimpered but offered little concrete resistance, employers' groups quickly perceived that it was possible to undertake a major frontal assault on labor's crucial practice, collective bargaining. The ensuing decade witnessed rapid deterioration in union power and therefore a decline in real wages (what income can actually buy) for a majority of workers. Millions of women entered the wage-labor force in part to mitigate the effects of a fairly concerted campaign by employers and conservatives to weaken unions and to reduce wages and salaries beginning in the 1970s.[2]

In the 1980s, the two-paycheck family became a commonplace. Of course, the entrance of large numbers of women into the wage-labor force was also a sign of their growing refusal to accept subordination within the male-dominated family. At the same time, as the computerization of the labor process accelerated, millions of well-paid industrial jobs were eliminated by technological change, and others, within both the United States and other parts of the world, migrated to the global South.

Recall that one of the major terms of the compromise between labor and management forged in the 1930s and 1940s was the exchange of the job control inherent in traditional crafts for high wage levels which, in the era of the U.S. domination of world markets for autos and steel, for example, spread from the crafts to many categories of unqualified labor. When the U.S. labor force was about 60 million, most of the 20 million industrial workers belonged to unions that negotiated steadily increased wages and benefits. At the end of World War II, union strength had grown to nearly a third of the labor force. However, by 1990, when the nonfarm labor force had reached about 105 million, and factory employment was about 22 million, unions represented only 16 percent of the labor force, 12 percent in the private sector.

Although in key industries such as autos, communications, chemicals, oil, electrical, and steel, unionization, as a percentage of the nonsupervisory workforce, had not significantly diminished, collective bargaining no longer determined general wage levels. In fact, union wages were being driven by the low-wage nonunion sector abroad as well as at home. Having surrendered job control, workers were unable, and often unwilling, to control the pace and effects of technological change lest the employer close shop, and their diminished political power made unions virtually incapable of stemming capital flight. The tendency toward union concessions in the form of wage and benefit reductions in the 1980s failed to halt industrial migration. This resulted in lower living standards for many Americans.

As we have argued elsewhere, the surprisingly feeble union response to the concerted employer offensive on the social compact that had driven labor relations for almost forty years may be attributed to one of the tacit provisions of that compact: that labor accept its role as merely another variable factor of the costs of doing business.[3] Fulfilling labor's historical so-

---

2. In the United States, nearly 70 percent of women had entered the labor force by 1990. In recent years, many have been able to obtain only part-time jobs.

3. Stanley Aronowitz, *False Promises: The Shaping of American Working Class Con-*

cial justice agenda became dependent on the health of American business and subordinate to the exigencies of U.S. foreign policy.

Organized labor's ideological subordination in the first decades after World War II seemed to serve American workers' interests well. Real wages rose nearly every year until 1967 and, with short disruptions, continued to improve until the late 1970s. During this period, the American Federation of Labor and Congress of Industrial Organizations was perhaps the most reliable and most powerful nongovernmental organization that provided a social base for U.S. foreign policy, especially its periodic war aims but also its program of intervention in Europe, Africa, and Latin America, where American unions supplied training and financial assistance to "free" (read "anti-Communist") trade unions.[4]

As important as this full-throated patriotic fervor was for disciplining American workers, at least politically, perhaps the most important result of labor regulation since the New Deal has been the emergence of a highly autocratic—in some cases semifeudal—labor bureaucracy to administer the terms of regulation, especially the crucial task of keeping workers in line. The labor baronate is among the most stable of any U.S. institution. In fact, many large unions resemble, in their culture as much as their structure, the large corporations with which they bargain. Far from a social movement, many unions became, in effect, the mirror image of the corporations with which they bargain collectively. Although, since the 1930s, unions have modified the old doctrine of business unionism by adopting a distinct political agenda, their daily operation resembles that of an insurance company, and union leaders take on the aura of chief executive officers.

Even before the debacle of the 1980s, unions in private production and service sectors had ceased to grow, even as they experienced enormous expansion at all levels of public employment after President Kennedy's 1961 executive order sanctioning union recognition and bargaining for federal employees. Yet, in banking and financial services, in the crucial industrial south, and among the rapidly expanding scientific and technical categories, organized labor made almost no inroads, even during the booming 1960s, when ostensibly prolabor Democratic administrations were in power. While the 1947 Taft-Hartley amendments—especially the anti-Communist provisions and restrictions on the use of the strike weapon—certainly halted labor's forward march during the 1950s, labor's vaunted legislative clout was unable to rescind this blight even under the most favorable political circumstances because the Cold War continued to drive labor relations. Perhaps more significantly, with some exceptions—notably, teachers and other public employees organizations, hospital workers and agricultural work-

---

sciousness (Durham, NC: Duke University Press, 1992); idem, *Working Class Hero* (New York: Pilgrim, 1983).

4. Beth Sims, *Workers of the World Undermined American Labor's Role in U.S. Foreign Policy* (Boston: South End Press, 1992). For an earlier study of this question, see Ronald Radosh, *U.S. Labor and American Foreign Policy* (New York: Random House, 1971).

ers—unions had ceased to be a dynamic force in U.S. society.

In those sectors run by computer-mediated work, productivity outstrips growth. Now, "productivity" is a hotly disputed term. The conventional economists' definition focuses on the formula of measuring the ratio of the price of goods and services, adjusted for inflation, to labor costs. In these terms, labor productivity, which had stagnated since the recession, grew in 1992 by nearly 3.5 percent while gross domestic product increased by less than half that percentage.[5] In specific sectors such as industrial production, however, productivity is much higher, perhaps 5 percent, which, in view of the relative stagnation of manufacturing, accounts for the substantial reductions of the labor force in these sectors. Computer-mediated work has spread from offices and the industrial sectors where a high level of corporate concentration prevails, such as autos, machine tools, and steel, to light manufacturing and, more recently, to the professions. Economic growth, which has proceeded in the last decade at a very modest rate (1-3 percent a year), is structurally unable, in the long run, to overcome the job-reducing effects of the technological and organizational changes.

This relatively new development contrasts sharply with the two great periods of U.S. growth in this century: 1900-1925 and 1938-70. Although the average annual growth rate was about 3 percent during these periods, the level of technological displacement was relatively low and offshore capital flight virtually absent, except in shoes and the needle trades. However, internal capital flight began at the turn of the twentieth century, principally in textiles, garments, shoes, lumber, oil refining, and steel. While the distribution of industry changed within the United States from the northeast to the middle west and the southeast, the national workforce grew substantially and so did income.

Of course, much of the prolonged era of general expansion of the economy and the proliferation of jobs corresponded to spurious growth associated with the permanent war economy. That is, much of U.S. economic activity in the last great expansion period is attributable to enormous state investments in military goods that do not circulate but remain within a self-contained defense sector. Real growth, that is, the accretions of capital stock for the civilian sectors of the economy, was severely limited by what might be termed "disaccumulation," defined here as investments in sectors such as public employment, military expenditures, and financial services, the purpose of which is to get rid of surplus capital.[6]

5. *Wall Street Journal*, 9 Mar. 1992.

6. Martin Sklar, "On the Proletarian Revolution and the End of Political-Economic Society," *Radical America* (June 1969). This remarkable article provides a theory, from the perspective of political economy, of the end of real capital accumulation. According to Sklar, the major tendency of contemporary advanced capitalist societies was toward an overaccumulation of capital; thus the task of investment was to get rid of this surfeit, to disaccumulate capital. Hence advertising, the production of waste in the form of planned obsolescence, the proliferation of services, and, of course, in the United States, massive military expenditures.

As we have noted, from the perspective of the individual or institutional investor, putting money in these activities may yield higher returns and is evaluated by neoclassical criteria as a rational choice. However, spurious capital formation, favored since the 1950s over industrial production and transportation, conspired to accumulate debt rather than capital and contributed to the relatively slow growth rate.

SKILL AND KNOWLEDGE

Once craftspersons controlled production. From the point of view of the labor process, the skilled worker of the early, manufacturing phase of capitalism was really no different from the artisan who owned as well as operated the shop. It is our contention that as capitalism developed from its industrial phase to its computer phase, skill was increasingly displaced by knowledge. In this, its latest phase, not only are jobs increasingly destroyed, but skill is destroyed as well.

It is thus that we turn to the debate about skill and knowledge. This debate is framed by the work of Harry Braverman on the labor process.[7] Braverman argued that all workers, including knowledge workers, are degraded in the capitalist labor process. For Braverman, the degradation of work consisted of, first, the directing of technology and labor, under conditions of capital accumulation, against skill. The division of labor is not a neutral process but a force of domination. In the past, a worker's power was based on his skill. He had a historic skill as an artisan. The artisanal worker was a craftworker, whose skill made him autonomous and protected him from the vicissitudes of the labor market. The worker's skill made it difficult for this worker's work to be degraded.

As capitalism developed to its monopoly stage, it launched a continuous assault on the knowledge of the skilled worker by deskilling, that is, by separating the craftsperson from the knowledge of craft that gave him power. For Braverman, this assault was embodied in F. W. Taylor's *Principles of Scientific Management*[8] because it redefined the logic of capital. As in Marx, the development of capital was from the formal subsumption of labor, the control over the product of labor, to the real subsumption of labor, that is, the complete control over labor in the accumulation process. Braverman argued that Taylor's work codified this strategy of capitalist domination. It entailed the degradation of work through the process of deskilling, that is, the separation of conception from execution.

The skilled worker, who performed both the manual and mental aspects of work, was to be systematically separated from his special knowledge of the labor process. He would be transformed into a semiskilled or unskilled worker who no longer was to be involved in the mental work. The workplace would be fractured and a detailed division of labor would become its organizational principle.

7. Harry Braverman, *Labor and Monopoly Capital* (New York: Monthly Review Press, 1974).

8. Frederick Winslow Taylor, *The Principles of Scientific Management* (New York: Norton, 1967).

The new worker would be a nonautonomous, detailed laborer. With the degradation of the skilled worker, new specialized workers were required to do the mental work; professional engineers and scientists, to design the labor process, the machinery, and the new products; and the managers, to command and coordinate the whole process. Under the name of science and productivity the worker was to be dominated.

For Braverman, the second element of the degradation of work was the displacement of labor. Deskilling results in the recomposition of the workforce: less skilled workers will replace more skilled workers, low-wage workers will replace high-wage workers. Workers will lose their jobs. Displacement is a continuous process, and all levels of work—from unskilled workers to even engineers and managers—will be deskilled. Machinery and new forces of organization will replace skilled work, creating permanent tendencies of structural unemployment.

Not everyone agrees with Braverman, and the critiques are quite extensive.[9] But our purpose here is not so much to add another critique as to relate it specifically to the relation of skill to knowledge. In this task, the work of Paul Adler is significant. Adler's work is in direct opposition to Braverman's. Where Braverman theorizes that capitalist technology degrades skill, Adler theorizes that capitalist technology upgrades skill. Thus Adler states, "My own research on basic computerization found very similar changes in the types of skills and in the general upward drift in the amount of skill even for low level employees."[10]

Adler, in disagreement with Braverman's position, views technological change as beneficial to workers. Deskilling only affects a minority of working people. Nor is there a direct relation between deskilling and the creation of low-skilled, low-paid jobs. "There has . . . been some polarization in wages due to the burgeoning of low paid jobs in recent years. But this is the effect not of skill changes, but of a decade of turbulence and of the influx of youth and educated women into the labor force."[11]

As particular old skills are destroyed, new skills are created. In general, the development is uneven and the creation of new skills outweighs deskilling. Overall, this is not true only for the middle-class sectors of professional and technical workers but for the working class as well.[12] With this upgrading of skill, there is an increasing reliance on mental over physical effort, on increased responsibility, education, and experience.[13]

Adler's critique argues that Braverman's definition of skill is inadequate, based on a romantic view of the nineteenth-century craft

9. Three books that deal with Braverman's position but take a different approach are Michael Burawoy, *The Politics of Production* (London: Verso, 1985); Larry Hirschhorn, *Beyond Mechanization: Work and Technology in a Postindustrial Age* (Cambridge: MIT Press, 1984); Paul Thompson, *The Nature of Work: An Introduction to Debates on the Labor Process* (London: Macmillan, 1983).

10. Paul Adler, "Technology and Us," *Socialist Review*, no. 85, p. 82 (Jan.-Feb. 1986).

11. Ibid., p. 83.

12. Idem, "Automation, Skill and the Future of Capitalism," *Berkeley Journal of Sociology: A Critical Review*, 33:3 (1988).

13. Ibid., p. 2.

worker. For Adler, skill must be redefined in the context of modern technological advances:

The dimensions of skill I have identified permit us to understand the manner in which automation is shaping class capabilities in the labor process, by increasing technical culture (complexity), by expanding responsibility (specialization), by broadening intellectual horizons, and by encouraging recognition of labor per se as a historical problem (abstraction), and by forging new forms of group identity that allow the higher form of individuality (collectivization).[14]

Adler understands that the new technologies of high technology and organization have made notions of skill based on craft inadequate. In its place he has put his own notion of skill framed in the context of the requirements of the new labor process. Adler recognizes the need to develop a new paradigm, but he is wed to an analysis that is structured around the key concept of the old paradigm, skill.

We ourselves have criticized Braverman.[15] But here we argue for another notion of deskilling. The history of work in the twentieth century is a history in which machines have increasingly replaced the skills of workers of all collars. In a production process in which science and technology are central, knowledge, and not skill, defines the production process.

The contradictions of Adler's insistence that knowledge is just the current form that skill takes can be seen in the following statement:

In job design the knowledge intensity of new technologies dictates a greater problem-solving component to operator's jobs than traditional Taylorist approaches would suggest. With automation, the number of operators per unit output might fall, but there is typically no net reduction in the average operator skill requirements; on the contrary, higher skills of a new type are usually called for.[16]

There is much to be learned from Braverman and Adler. We agree with Adler that Braverman's analysis is the embodiment of a deep romanticism for a pristine craftsman of an artisanal past. But Adler is equally romantic about the inevitability of technological progress.[17] This can be seen in his arguments against deskilling and the displacement of the workforce. The fact is that there has been significant displacement and deskilling of the workforce. In the United States, 26 million jobs were created from 1973 to 1986. The great majority of these jobs were both low paid and low skilled.[18] Bad jobs

14. Ibid., p. 33.
15. Stanley Aronowitz, "Marx, Braverman and the Logic of Capital," *The Politics of Identity: Class, Culture, Social Movements* (New York: Routledge, 1992); William DiFazio, *Longshoremen: Community and Resistance on the Brooklyn Waterfront* (South Hadley, MA: Bergin & Garvey, 1985).

16. Paul S. Adler, "When Knowledge Is the Critical Resource, Knowledge Management Is the Critical Task," *IEEE Transactions on Engineering Management*, 36(2):92 (May 1989).
17. Adler, "Automation, Skill and the Future of Capitalism," p. 33.
18. "Study of New Jobs since 79 Says Half Pay Poverty Wage," *New York Times*, 27 Sept. 1988. On current income stagnation, Frank Levy states, "By 1975 median family income had fallen by $1,700. It gained most of this back by the end of 1979, but fell sharply in the 1980-82 recession and stood at $26,433 in 1984. This sudden break in trend—twenty-six years of income growth followed by twelve years of income stagnation—is the major economic story of the postwar period." *Dollars and Dreams: The Changing American Income Distribution* (New York: Norton, 1988), p. 17.

with low wages have increased in all sectors of the economy, including college-trained professionals.

The sharp declines in employment are no longer restricted to old line manufacturing firms or old blue collar workers. Plant closings, layoffs, and pay cuts have swept high technology industries as well. In just the first six months of 1985 . . . employment in the computer and semiconductor industries—the core of the new technology—shed more than jobs.

The Bureau of Labor Statistics . . . reported that between 1981 and 1986 more than 780,000 managers lost their jobs as the result of plant closings and layoffs. And the pace has increased, even as the economy entered its fourth year of recovery. In the drive to make the ranks of management "leaner and meaner," nearly all 600,000 middle and upper level executives lost their jobs between 1984 and 1986. Such companies as AT&T, United Technologies, Union Carbide, and Ford are leading the management massacre.[19]

This massacre occurred before the Wall Street crash of 1987. Not only did 50,000 workers, from clerks to investment bankers, lose their jobs because of the crash, but also they were displaced by new computer networks, expert systems.[20]

In our own studies of engineers, architects, and draftsmen who work on computer-aided design (CAD) in New Jersey and New York, however, we found their experiences with the new design technology to be different.[21] In New Jersey, the work of these knowledge workers was degraded; there was clear displacement and deskilling of both engineers and drafters. In New York, however, the architects', engineers', and drafters' work was not degraded, yet new drafters were not going to be hired. New drafters were to be displaced by the technology. An extensive training program was instituted in which the existing drafters were formally trained on CADD. In New York, the goal was to train all the engineers and architects on CADD. This was not the goal of public sector agencies in New Jersey.

Always privileging the creation of new skills as new technologies are developed, Adler would argue here that deskilling and reskilling occur simultaneously. Here is the core of our disagreement with Braverman and Adler. Our contention is that skill itself is no longer central to the labor process. It has been decentered. There has been a vocabulary shift, and knowledge has become the emergent center of production. Knowledge is not just another form of skill, as Adler contends; rather, it redefines the world of work. The past, in which skill was central, is incommensurable with the knowledge-based future. This future embodies a whole new set of alternatives.

Adler's goal is to offer a critique of the view, associated with Braverman, that technological change in the capitalist labor process always entails

19. Bennett Harrison and Barry Bluestone, *The Great U-Turn: Corporate Restructuring and the Polarizing of America* (New York: Basic Books, 1990), pp. 37-38.

20. Manuel Castells, *The Informational City* (Oxford: Basil Blackwell, 1989), p. 342.

21. Stanley Aronowitz and William DiFazio, *The Jobless Future: Sci-Tech and the Dogma of Work* (Minneapolis: University of Minnesota Press, 1994).

deskilling, but he is not willing to question skill. As long as one speaks the language of skill, it is difficult to avoid Braverman's conclusions. Adler's move was to substitute knowledge/skill for Braverman's craft/skill. This move was insufficient. Both forms of skill were based on their relative economic cost and the length of training required.[22] Knowledge/skill required formal training, while craft/skill was based on the experiential knowledge of a trade. Knowledge/skill was an inevitable evolutionary development from craft/skill.

But there is a break between knowledge and skill. CAD, CAM (computer-aided manufacturing), CIM (computer-integrated manufacturing), and other computer-mediated technological innovations have taken over the skill component. In this sense, there has been deskilling. The twentieth century, the industrial capitalist era, is marked by the displacement of skill by knowledge. It is the knowledge component, the conceptual, the theoretical, that is now the basis for the scientific, technological, social relations of production in this latest era of capitalism.

The history of skill is embedded in feudalism and then, in the era of manufacture, in handicraft. Skill was a concrete property that a man could attain only as a result of a long apprenticeship in a trade. The apprentice was trained by his master, and entry to apprenticeship was very selective, often inherited, passed on from father to son, uncle to nephew. Thus skill from its very inception was not open to all. It was a mechanism of exclusion. Even the noblemen were dependent on the skilled craftsman. His learned talent, his special knowledge, gave him a modicum of power and autonomy.

The craftsman thus guarded his skill, the collective property of all those who had learned the knowledge of the trade. They formed organizations of protection, first the guild, then the skilled workers' union, then the profession. Thus it has continued into the modern world, skilled men guarding their territory, which only a few men could enter. Here the case of women is especially significant.

Even as women enter the workforce in great numbers and highly educated (in Adler's sense, more skilled), they are still denied entry into the most skilled sectors of the labor market. Only 3 percent of the top jobs at *Fortune* 500 companies are occupied by women.[23] Further, as John Rule describes:

In fact, the definition of skilled and unskilled work were as much rooted in social and gender distinctions as in technical aptitude. The product of nimble female fingers was often less valued than that produced by men with less dexterity. Josiah Wedgewood in the 1770's paid women flower painters only two thirds of the usual rate for skilled men. . . . Weaving on Dutch looms was taken on by males accordingly defined as skilled and as having a justified restriction over entry.[24]

---

22. Adler, "Automation, Skill and the Future of Capitalism," p. 3.

23. Feminist Majority Foundation, *Empowering Women in Business* (Arlington, VA: Feminist Majority Foundation, 1991).

24. John Rule, "The Property of Skill in the Period of Manufacture," in *The Historical Meanings of Work*, ed. Patrick Joyce (New York: Cambridge University Press, 1987), p. 108. See also Maxine Berg, *The Age of Manufacture, 1700-1820* (London: Fontana, 1985).

The case of the exclusion of women from skilled work points to the problem of the work of both Braverman and Adler. Women are the disruption of the privileged realm of skill. A male property, guarded closely, excluding outsiders, is now called into question. Before this, women trying to compete in the skilled fields of men were always at a disadvantage not because they were inferior, incompetent, weak, or not intelligent enough but because the fields of skill themselves were structured by men. Skill is a male discourse. If women were to succeed, they had to change the field of discourse. In these gendered fields, they could not win. If women forced their way in, the skill was devalued. In Europe and North America, this was true of nonwhites as well. This is not unlike how artisans fought against child labor, not because it was a moral battle but because they were protecting their artisanal territory.[25]

High tech, including CAD, created a knowledge space not burdened with the gendered history of skill. High tech is a male domain, but because it constitutes a technological and social break with the past, it offers a terrain of struggle. A terrain where women's knowledge, theoretical, abstract, aesthetic, and moral, can make an intervention in ways that women have not been able to make in the past, in the realm of skilled work. There is no inevitability, history is on no one's side, but this break with the past offers a space in which transformation is possible. The reconceptualization of work becomes possible. A space has been created in which the discourse of knowledge replaces the discourse of skill.

A JOBLESS FUTURE FOR KNOWLEDGE WORKERS

The economic slowdown that began in the late 1980s witnessed this unique and startling new development in the United States that, for many, constituted nothing short of a profound psychological as well as social trauma. In contrast to all previous postwar recessions, when factory workers and other manual categories bore the brunt of unemployment, now that knowledge work comes to the center, the burden of unemployment falls on different shoulders. Thus, during the recessions of 1982-84 and the longer one of the late 1980s and early 1990s, professionals and managers experienced, for the first time since the 1930s, the dread as well as the reality of redundancy.

In the 1990s, professionals and managers have suffered periods of long-term unemployment, lasting between six months and two years. For those over the age of fifty, losing their job may signal the termination of a career and its replacement by a job outside their field. A large portion of displaced employees are able, for the time being, to find other jobs within their profession, but, because of widespread layoffs in these categories in the recent past, often at a substantial reduction in pay. Many have been forced to take working-class jobs as, for example, parking lot attendants, cab drivers, and salespeople in wholesale or retail trades. Even some lawyers, teachers, and social workers

25. Robert Gray, "The Languages of Factory Reform in Britain, c. 1830-1860," in *Historical Meanings of Work*, ed. Joyce, p. 150.

are experiencing difficulty finding jobs, especially at prevailing salaries. The aerospace industry has been hit very hard, with only "17% finding new jobs in the industry" in California and their "average earnings [dropping] by about one-third."[26]

In the prior half-century, although some professionals and managers, especially in defense-related industries, suffered "frictional"—that is, temporary—unemployment when their employers lost contracts, the competition for their services was too intense in most sectors to permit employers to lay them off. Companies preferred to keep them on the payroll rather than risk being unprepared when business, as it almost inevitably did, picked up. Thus the very idea of unemployment was simply not in the vocabularies of professional, technical, and managerial employees.

However, after 1989, many companies, already awash in debt accumulated during fierce buyout fights or during long-term recessionary conditions, became desperate to cut overhead expenditures. They cut their production and clerical staffs, but in many cases, these reductions were so steep that they were counterproductive. Their only recourse, short of going out of business, was to address their cost problems by turning on those who had themselves been responsible for implementing policies of introducing labor-saving technologies and maintaining the labor process. Technologies such as CAD and CASP are directed at reducing the amount of labor required for design and program writing and, as a recent advertisement by Electronic Data Systems argued, at eliminating these high-priced categories.[27]

Middle managers have been especially hard hit, but so have some engineers and technical categories. The big-three automakers have recently initiated attrition programs for these employees that resemble such programs in the electronics and communication industries. In many computer, electronic equipment, and optical companies, thousands have lost their jobs, albeit with some remuneration. The aircraft industry, partially in response to defense cuts and the depression in airline travel, is hemorrhaging administrative employees as well as factory workers. In the summer of 1992, the postmaster general announced an attrition plan for 40,000 managers in an effort to bring the management practices of this quasi-public agency fully in line with those of the private sector.

Beyond economic conditions, however, it became evident that software is itself a manager of the labor process; no less than the craft machinist or the engineer, the knowledge of the manager has been transferred to the machine. It can issue instructions and provide both information and informed indications for production and administrative decisions. Unlike the mechanical era, when every new technical innovation in the direction of further rationalization signaled the appearance of an army of managers to make sure that the quantity and the quality of the product and the flow of materials were not disrupted in the wake of the increasingly de-

26. Seth Mydans, "Displaced Aerospace Workers Face Grim Future in California Economy," *New York Times*, 3 May 1995.

27. *Wall Street Journal*, 3 Dec. 1992.

tailed character of the labor, much of the work of administration—on the shop and office floor—is now inherent in the computer program.

Just as large amounts of clerical labor were displaced by computerization and by devices such as the answering machine and the personal computer, a significant quantity of managerial labor can now be displaced by the computer's capacity to do the work of coordination. The irony of this development is that the introduction of the computer and other electronic devices to displace manual and clerical labor can be turned on those whose scientific and technical knowledge brought on these displacements. Management and computer consulting firms are widely employed to develop software programs and organizational proposals designed to eliminate knowledge producers. The displacer has been displaced.

In terms of both the decentering of skill and the quantum measures of the new technologies, there are simply not enough jobs for those who are ready and willing to work. There are no signs to justify forecasts that anticipate a reversal in the elements of this judgment: in Europe as well as the United States, unemployment has stabilized for the foreseeable future at more than 10 percent if the real extent of unwork is calculated.

The German labor movement has fought for and won a shorter workweek (despite a relatively unfavorable world economic climate). Short of a new era of militant labor struggle, we anticipate no sharp alteration in labor's policy in the United States and most of the rest of the world. That policy has been to exchange the job security of a minority of the labor force for the solidaristic demand for shorter hours. We anticipate the unchallenged introduction of labor-saving technologies, which will displace both intellectual and manual labor. We anticipate long-term economic stagnation in the post–Cold War era.

Service Workers: Human Resources or Labor Costs?

By BARBARA A. GUTEK

ABSTRACT: In this article, I describe the work performed by service providers, defined broadly, and the changes in this work engendered by an increasing reliance on encounters as a form of service delivery. This delivery mechanism facilitates the view of service providers as labor costs to be managed and reduced rather than human resources to be nurtured and developed. The provision of services by encounters may be a prelude both to the substitution of machine providers for humans and to large-scale unemployment.

Barbara A. Gutek is professor and head of the Department of Management and Policy at the University of Arizona. Among her research interests are women in management, sexual harassment, and service transactions. A fellow in the American Psychological Association and American Psychological Society, her research has been funded by the National Science Foundation and the National Institute of Mental Health. She is the author of The Dynamics of Service *(1995).*

IT is conventional wisdom that the U.S. economy is a service economy and that the proportion of the workforce employed in the service sector, already over 70 percent of workers, is likely to increase. I have my doubts about the increase. I have recently developed a classification of service work that gets below the surface of the conventional wisdom, provides a fresh, more in-depth look at services, and makes me skeptical about any proposed expansion of service jobs.[1] The delivery of service is itself undergoing an important change that parallels the change from handmade to mass-produced manufactured goods and that will have the same broad ramifications for the work of service providers as mass production had for the work of producers of goods. At the heart of this change is a shift from reliance on service delivery, that is, interaction between a service provider and a customer, via relationships to delivery of more services via encounters.

DEFINITIONS: SERVICE RELATIONSHIPS AND SERVICE ENCOUNTERS

People who have a regular dentist, family physician, stockbroker, hairstylist, secretary, or housekeeper, for example, have relationships with their service providers. In a relationship, a customer interacts with the same provider every time the customer wishes a certain kind of service. The customer and provider get to know each other, they expect and anticipate future interaction, and over time, they develop a history of shared interaction that they can draw on whenever they complete some transaction. Over time, relationships become more efficient and effective, especially where a customer and provider interact frequently as, for example, a secretary and manager do. The efficiency in well-developed relationships is one of their strengths as a service-delivery mechanism.

In contrast to relationships, a newer service-delivery mechanism, encounters, consists of a single episode between the customer and provider. Over time, the customer's successive contacts involve different providers, and each provider is expected to be functionally equivalent. Thus a customer should be able to complete a satisfactory service transaction with any of a number of interchangeable providers. Buying a hamburger at McDonald's is a classic encounter, but so is getting a driver's license, ordering airline tickets from an airline reservation center, going to the emergency room or some health maintenance organizations to receive medical care, or going to Supercuts for a haircut.

Encounters constitute a mass-production form for delivering goods and services, and as mass production systems eliminated many of the jobs of skilled craftspersons in manufacturing, so too the mass production of service is likely to eliminate many of the jobs of skilled service providers. Encounters will not be limited to buying a hamburger or obtaining a driver's license, I believe, but many

---

1. The change in service delivery from relationships to encounters is the topic of Barbara Gutek, *The Dynamics of Service: Reflections on the Changing Nature of Customer/Provider Interactions* (San Francisco, CA: Jossey-Bass, 1995).

services traditionally provided in relationships will steadily be organized so that they can be delivered instead in encounters. Finding a way to structure in an encounter format interactions typically provided in relationships is an innovation often considered newsworthy.

For example, a recent report titled "They Rub Customers the Right Way" described the introduction of encounter-style service provided by relationship-style providers, personal masseuses.[2] For $7.95, customers have an 8.5-minute encounter wherein they receive a shoulder and back massage from the next available masseur or masseuse. The provider sticks to a routine, and customers are served on a first-come, first-served basis. A few customers reported having several back rubs in a day, an option made feasible by the small expenditure of time and money involved.

But why stop there? The mass-production delivery of services is starting to encroach on several professions, including medicine and psychotherapy. For example, the managed-care revolution in the United States is starting to document the changes in the quality of worklife for physicians, therapists, and other health care providers, as managers greatly increase the number of patients each primary-care provider is expected to handle and substitute lower-cost, less educated primary-care providers for more expensive and extensively educated ones. Examples of such substitutions include nurse practitioners and physician's assistants for medical doctors; Ph.D. psychologists for psychiatrists, and master's degree recipients for Ph.D. psychologists.[3] For example, Kaiser-Permanente now requires its physicians to be responsible for over 2200 patients, whereas a typical patient load for a physician in private practice is typically 800 to 1200.[4]

SOME CONSEQUENCES OF THE EXPECTED GROWTH IN ENCOUNTERS

As the number and types of encounter systems grow, I can imagine several different scenarios, variations on the growth of the mass production of goods. Growth in encounter systems may come at the expense of relationships; that is, encounters may replace relationships so entirely that receiving medical care in relationships will one day be as archaic as having a personal tailor, a kind of relationship that has all but died out in the United States. Alternatively, growth in encounters may occur independent of the growth in relationships; that is, both may continue to grow, but at different rates, with encounters growing more rapidly. This

2. "They Rub Customers Just the Right Way," *Tucson Citizen*, 18 Nov. 1993.

3. D. K. Clawson and M. Osterweis, eds., *The Roles of Physician Assistants and Nurse Practitioners in Primary Care* (Washington, DC: Association of Academic Health Centers, 1993). See also Melinda Henneberger, "Managed Care Changing the Practice of Psychotherapy," *New York Times*, 6 Oct. 1994.

4. See also J. Erikson, "Newborn Care: Dangers Seen in HMO Pressure for Short Hospital Stays," *Arizona Daily Star*, 19 Sept. 1994; Sherry Jacobson and Bill Deener, "Managed Care Changing Mental Health Treatment: Costs to Firms Are Limited, But So Are Patient Choices," *Dallas Morning News*, 7 Nov. 1994; and S. Woolhandler and D. U. Himmelstein, "Giant H.M.O. 'A' or Giant H.M.O. 'B'?" *Nation*, 10 Sept. 1994, pp. 265-68.

scenario is especially likely if encounters allow more customers to receive services that were formerly available, at a higher cost, via relationships.

Encounters have already made—and increasingly will make—available to a broad segment of the population services that were formerly available to only the elite. Just as standardization of production made more goods available to many more people than did relationship-style production (such as a tailor making a dress), standardization of service often makes services available to people who have not been able to afford them before. Fast-food restaurants, for example, have allowed more people to eat out, and firms such as H&R Block have allowed more people to obtain tax-preparation services. In this view, the growth of encounters will bring new customers to services that they never received before. In the near future, people going home from work may stop in for an 8-minute backrub before picking up their laundry and take-out food for the evening. A rapid expansion in encounter-delivered services could yield a two-tiered system wherein the more affluent receive services in relationships and the less affluent rely on encounters for their services.

While providing service through encounters changes the role of customer,[5] it has more profound effects on the nature of the provider's job. The industrial revolution and the mass production of goods made obsolete many skilled trades, jobs that provided a decent livelihood and interesting, although often physically demanding, work. Will the mass production of service make obsolete many skilled professional and service jobs that now provide a decent (or better) livelihood and interesting, though often mentally demanding, work?

THE JOB OF PROVIDER

I will now describe some of the features of the provider job, features that follow quite naturally from the organization of service delivery. The very nature of encounter systems facilitates the view of workers as labor costs to be cut or replaced by technology where feasible, whereas the very nature of relationships facilitates the view of providers as human resources who differ in talent and effort and whose career development is—or at least has been—closely tied to their reputation for service delivery to customers. I will start by describing the common characteristics of the job of relationship providers and then compare them with their replacement, encounter provider jobs.

Providers in relationships

The whole basis for providing in relationships is quite different from providing in encounters; one depends on some base of knowledge or proficiency while the other depends on the characteristics of the interaction. In relationships, knowledge is embedded in the individual provider; in encounters, it is embedded in organizational procedures and practices.

The role of expertise. Generally, some kind of substantive expertise is required to provide service in relationships. That is, the provider has

5. Gutek, *Dynamics of Service*, chap. 6.

some base of knowledge either lacking in the customer but which the customer needs or which the customer also has but for some reason cannot or does not want to provide to himself or herself. Examples of the former are most of the professions, such as law, medicine, and architecture; examples of the latter include babysitting, housework, and, for some, tax preparation.

The provider's knowledge may be abstract knowledge generally associated with the professions or concrete knowledge such as that required to manicure nails or maintain a yard. The substantive knowledge may require years of education or relatively little training, and experience is generally regarded as an asset, that is, a more experienced physician or manicurist is generally considered superior to someone with less experience. On the other hand, the knowledge base of the field often changes and expands so that any provider must continue his or her education to stay current. Professionals can also stay current by engaging in research or in the development of knowledge in their field. A license, certificate, or the passing of an examination, whether required or merely desirable, shows that the provider has attained the expertise required to provide a given service.

The fact that the expertise is widely recognized through the certification process also means that it is portable. This portability gives the provider options. Providers may opt for an independent practice or take a job in an organization needing their expertise. If the job is not satisfactory, the provider can use the same expertise in another organization or take a block of customers and start an independent practice.

The expertise of the provider draws the customer to a provider in a relationship. In addition, this base of knowledge typically allows the providers a certain amount of flexibility in arranging one's work. Based on their own needs and preferences, providers can choose to meet customers early in the day or late and can order tasks according to their preferences, doing the less desirable chores early or late, bunched, or spread out among other more desirable activities. If providers want, they can also accommodate special needs or interests of customers in meeting early or late or on weekends. For high-status customers, they make special efforts at accommodation, especially if some of the fame or notoriety from the customers extends to the provider.

Becoming a relationship provider. Providers in relationships usually acquire relevant skills on their own, through an apprenticeship to an experienced provider, a formal education program, an internship, experience, and/or a process of certification or licensing. Often people go through more than one of these processes, or all of them, in order to begin their practice as providers.

At the end of the process of obtaining knowledge and demonstrating it, the provider is next expected to find customers on whom she can apply her craft. However, finding new customers may take a while and a provider can lose customers or be fired. The provider is only too aware of this reality and will generally work hard to keep customers satisfied.

Thus relationship providers tend to develop a customer orientation (perhaps without ever using that term!). Being able to attract and retain customers is a key part of becoming a relationship provider.

Career development and identification. Relationship providers tend to develop their careers within their substantive area of expertise, and their reputation is based on their expertise. Providers in relationships tend to identify with their area of expertise, and their loyalty is likely to be to their field or discipline even if they work in an organization. Comparatively few professors or physicians define themselves as employees of universities or health maintenance organizations. Relationship providers tend to be "cosmopolitans" rather than "locals," terms used to distinguish between people who identify with a broad profession and people who identify with the organization in which they work. Some relationship providers are less cosmopolitan than others; a gardener, housekeeper, or nanny may identify with other gardeners, housekeepers, or nannies in only a small geographic area in comparison to the larger geographic area encompassed by professional groups like the American Bar Association or the American Medical Association.

Star providers. In relationships, not all providers are functionally equivalent. There are star providers and other providers. A star provider is defined as one who adds prestige to the organization for whom she works (if she works in an organization) rather than deriving prestige from the organization. Star providers generate more transactions than average or generate transactions based on their own name rather than their company name if they work for an organization. Star providers include Nobel Prize–winning professors, exceptionally prominent lawyers, exceptionally successful stockbrokers and mutual fund managers, well-known management consultants, in-demand speakers or consultants, famous architects, and the like. In most cases, while providers need to please customers, star providers can pick and choose among customers and no longer have to try to please the customer in order to maintain their business. Thus a star provider is in sufficient demand to tip the balance of power between provider and customer in favor of the provider.

Star providers are often suitably arrogant, and stories about them, whether true or not, often emphasize their large egos. The following story about Frank Lloyd Wright is typical. Wright completed a spectacular home late and over budget. Shortly after moving in, the owner, the president of a large corporation, invited a group of very influential guests to dinner. During dinner it started raining and the roof leaked so that water was dripping in on the owner's bald head. Furious, he demanded that someone contact Wright immediately. When he got Wright on the phone and told him that his lovely dinner with his influential guests was ruined by rain falling on his head, he asked Wright what he would do. Wright's response: Move your chair. Whether the story is true is less important than the message it conveys: Frank Lloyd Wright was a star provider who could get away with behavior not tolerated in other architects.

Providers in encounters

The job, indeed the career, of an encounter provider is altogether different. While expertise is the core of the provider role in relationships, delivery process or style is the core of the provider role in encounters. The provider encounters customers, and how that encounter is managed is what is most salient about providing service in encounters. Because all providers are functionally equivalent, they are not differentiated on the basis of substantive expertise; no one person has (or should have) any more expertise than any other. Under these circumstances, other attributes surpass expertise as desired or required aspects of the job. Providers are judged on how well they deliver the service or goods the customer wants, and they are expected to act as if they have a relationship with the customer. Relationships are viewed as the model for encounter providers.

Encounter providers are functionally equivalent, so they are all equally expert—at least in principle—and they all provide the same service. Providing such uniform service necessarily takes some of the challenge and variety out of the job of provider. Thus, in general, relative to providers in relationships, providers in encounters have jobs that are less challenging, more monotonous, more stressful, less autonomous, require less skill, have lower wages, and tend not to provide workers with skills that allow them to advance in the organization. This applies even to highly skilled professionals like the surgeons who work under the Shouldice hospital system, where only hernia operations are performed and they are performed only on patients who are otherwise healthy.[6] Their work is considerably more routine than it is for most surgeons, and it is probably less interesting and challenging.

Providers in encounters are more likely to be nonexempt from various labor laws than providers in relationships, and they are probably more likely to be paid hourly or on a piecerate basis. There may also be differences in fringe-benefit levels and opportunities within the organization, for example, access to tuition-reimbursement programs. Employers seeking encounter providers frequently look to teenagers rather than adults. The proportion of employed 16- and 17-year-olds who hold jobs as encounter providers has increased from 1940 to 1980 from a little over 10 percent to almost 60 percent. Food service work and store clerking—both encounter-provider jobs—have become the prototypical jobs for adolescents.[7]

Let's take a look at six aspects of the job of provider in encounters:

1. Some encounter providers serve simply as decoration.

6. James Heskett, "Shouldice Hospital Limited," in *The Service Management Course: Cases and Readings*, ed. W. E. Sasser, C.W.L. Hart, and J. L. Heskett (New York: Macmillan, 1991).

7. Ellen Greenberger and Laurence Steinberg, *When Teenagers Work* (New York: Basic Books, 1986), fig. 2.3. See also Juliet Schor, *The Overworked American* (New York: Basic Books, 1991), fig. 2.2.

2. Encounter providers have limited decision-making opportunities and autonomy, which creates stress.

3. Selection and training of providers focus on a customer orientation rather than the acquisition of expertise.

4. Job satisfaction and motivation are low among encounter providers.

5. Turnover is high among encounter providers.

6. Encounter providers have little opportunity for advancement.

Decorative work. In some jobs, being attractive is not merely an asset; for flight attendants, sales clerks in certain kinds of stores, some receptionists, and waitpersons, being attractive is a major part of the job. Being attractive always helps, no matter what the job: a variety of social-psychological studies and anecdotes attest to the fact that attractive, tall, and slim people tend to be evaluated favorably and do well relative to less attractive folks. But how is it that serving as decoration should be more common in encounters than in relationships?

Customers engage in relationships in part because of the unique characteristics of the providers. The expertise, care, and concern shown by the relationship provider, whether a stockbroker, nurse, or nanny, are assets found in a variety of people, attractive and not so attractive. In encounters, the contribution of any individual provider is psychologically minimized because every provider is functionally equivalent. If many people could do the provider job and customers might respond more favorably to attractive providers, why not make attractiveness either an explicit or implicit requirement of the job? The problem with decorative work is that customers and others often assume that it requires no other skills. "When only physically attractive people are found in a job, others will assume that (1) physical attractiveness is the most important prerequisite of the job and (2) the job does not require other skills or abilities."[8]

Decision making, autonomy, and stress. A second important way in which provider jobs differ is that in relationships, providers usually get to decide what to do and they also get to do it. In encounters, the decision making has been relinquished and the provider is left with the doing while someone else who never engages in the doing makes the decisions about providing. Thus encounters follow a tradition developed in "scientific management" of divorcing decision making from execution and creating a managerial class to make decisions.[9]

This leads to differences in workload variability. In relationships, providers have uneven and unpredictable workloads; busy periods and slack periods are common. To some extent, some busy periods may be predictable—for example, tax accountants know they will be very busy in March and the first two weeks of April. In any event, the provider is likely to decide herself how to deal with both unanticipated and anticipated time crunches, by, for example, referring some business to others, prioritizing

8. Barbara A. Gutek, *Sex and the Workplace* (San Francisco: Jossey-Bass, 1985), p. 165.

9. Frederick W. Taylor, *The Principles of Scientific Management* (New York: Harper, 1911).

customers, or clearing her calendar of other obligations and forgoing leisure for a while.

In contrast, the provider in encounters has much less control over time demands but typically experiences fewer peaks and valleys in customer demand. Encounter-style jobs are often designed to prevent either busy or slack periods; this is accomplished by, for example, varying the number of providers assigned according to customer demand. During rush periods, more workers are assigned to the provider role, or temporary workers may be hired to help meet the demand. During slack periods, some providers may be assigned to other jobs or laid off. In any case, the work demand is created not only by customer demand but also by management decisions.

Encounter workers rarely have any discretion over when they work or when they work on any particular task. Management and encounter-system designers such as industrial engineers in many cases specify the number of encounters a good provider should complete per hour, day, week, or month. The pace of work in encounters is likely to be especially demanding, creating stress for the provider. Hochschild, for example, discussed the effects of speed-ups mandated by airlines' management on flight attendants.[10] In each of the speed-ups the airlines have experienced in the past 15 years or so since deregulation, fewer flight attendants have been expected to use fewer resources—for instance, no more free drinks or playing cards—to service more customers with the same degree of service.

It is not only in workload and time demands that providers in encounters lack control; they tend to have little latitude in making any kind of decision because their work is often centrally planned, sometimes by a computer; their work is often monitored or their responses scripted.[11] By creating scripts for telephone order takers, encounter-system designers create ways for each provider to complete more orders over a shorter period of time. With each new mandate, workers experience the same kind of pressure that assembly-line workers experience when the line is speeded up. When they are unable to engage in physical slowdowns, providers in encounter-style interactions may engage in psychological slowdowns by failing to smile or engage in other pleasantries that are expected of them.[12]

Selecting and training the provider. Providers in encounters are less likely than relationship provid-

---

10. Arlie R. Hochschild, *The Managed Heart: Commercialization of Human Feeling* (Berkeley: University of California Press, 1983).

11. For example, in discussing the automation of social work, Barbara Garson contended, "The goal of welfare automation is to take every aspect of this overly complex judgement away from the welfare worker and have it made inside the machine—which is to say at a higher level. The aim is to restrict discretion and intervention [usually pro-client] by workers in the local offices." Barbara Garson, *The Electronic Sweatshop* (New York: Simon & Schuster, 1988), p. 102.

12. See, for example, ibid.; George Ritzer, *The McDonaldization of Society: An Investigation into the Changing Character of Contemporary Social Life* (Thousand Oaks, CA: Pine Forge Press, 1993); Robin Leidner, *Fast Food, Fast Talk: Service Work and the Routinization of Every Day Life* (Berkeley: University of California Press, 1993).

ers to learn their jobs on their own or depend almost exclusively on pre-acquired knowledge. Instead, they are likely to receive training that is concrete, not abstract, and that focuses on the details of their job. This training is done through formal programs in their organization by management and support personnel, part of the infrastructure of encounter systems. New recruits hired in cohorts receive their training together. New providers should receive enough training to call them the functional equivalent of a provider who has been doing the same job for years. Besides being told how to behave and what to say, they may also be told what to feel and given advice on creating the proper feeling.

For example, in studying the training program for Delta Airlines flight attendants, Hochschild noted that trainees were encouraged to act "as if the cabin is your home" and "as if this unruly passenger has a traumatic past."[13] Both guidelines were designed to encourage the flight attendant to be pleasant and supportive even in the face of rude behavior from an irate passenger. The worker is thus restricted to implementing standard procedures.

Increasingly for many encounter-style jobs, employers are interested in hiring people who have a service orientation or customer orientation. As providing in encounters has become commonplace, there has been a proliferation of courses teaching providers how to manage their interaction with customers. Some companies specializing in psychological tests for selection have developed or are developing tests to assess customer orientation or service orientation, and some companies are using these tests to help select or train new employees in their new provider roles. Other firms offer training courses to help employees develop a "proper customer orientation." One educational film company, Films for the Humanities and Sciences, lists in its 1994-95 business catalogue six different films on business telephone techniques. Where real expertise that takes years to acquire is required to complete a job, the employer usually cannot demand a customer orientation with the same regularity that employers are demanding it of providers in encounter-style jobs.

Once providers are on the job, they may be constantly reminded to have a customer orientation with posters and signs proclaiming, for example, "The customer is always right." L. L. Bean, Inc., the Maine outdoor clothing and equipment company, prominently displays in its offices a poster called "What Is a Customer?"[14] It includes statements such as "A customer is the most important person ever in this office . . . in person or by mail" and "A customer is not dependent on us . . . we are dependent on him."

Because the encounter structure does not foster close links between customer and provider the way a relationship structure does, employers have opted for trying to select people who have a strong customer orientation and also to socialize employees to continually strive toward satisfy-

13. Hochschild, *Managed Heart*, p. 120.

14. Philip Kotler, *Marketing Management*, 8th ed. (Englewood Cliffs, NJ: Prentice Hall, 1994), p. 22.

ing the customer. Whereas the internal dynamics of relationships foster a customer orientation, managerial coaching and incentives foster a customer orientation in encounters.

Providers, productivity, and job satisfaction. An examination of the popular "job characteristics model" proposed in 1976 leads to an interesting conclusion: the job characteristics of providers who engage in encounters are a perfect prescription for low productivity and low job satisfaction.[15] According to this model, lack of five "core job characteristics" leads to three "critical psychological states," which in turn affect personal and work outcomes.[16] Providers who engage in encounters tend to have low levels of the five core job characteristics: skill variety, task identity, task significance, autonomy, and feedback. Low levels of these core job characteristics lead, in general, to an experienced meaninglessness of work, little responsibility for work outcomes, and little knowledge of the actual results of their work activities. These three "critical psychological states" lead in turn to a variety of negative outcomes: low work motivation, low-quality work performance, low job satisfaction, and high absenteeism and turnover.

A general lack of feedback from customers, low variety, low autonomy, and a narrow task that lacks significance and may be difficult to identify with characterize many jobs held by providers who engage in encounters. It is certainly conceivable that many encounter-style provider jobs lead to negative psychological states in workers and a variety of negative outcomes. If so, creating jobs that lack the core job characteristics is bad job design. Although encounter-system designers have developed jobs that have few intrinsically interesting or challenging features, this is typically not done intentionally. They do not design jobs; they design service delivery systems and the provider job is simply a by-product of the service delivery system. Nevertheless, the resulting job, like the typical assembly-line job, leaves a lot to be desired.

Given the general paucity of positive features of many encounter-style provider jobs, there is little reason for encounter providers to feel any loyalty to their company, and they have no real ties to customers. Why not feel apathetic? But in some cases, employers may be able to attract and hold employees by providing other benefits that are attractive to some workers. For example, airlines offered the opportunity to travel, and they successfully created a glamorous image around the job of flight attendant, an image that new flight attendant recruits and the general public still maintain to a certain extent. Companies may also offer the chance to identify with a well-known and successful organization, which may appeal to some employees. In other cases, it may be difficult to find any clear benefits to the job except that it is a job.

Turnover in encounter jobs. When a job is just a job, and a low-paying one at that, given other opportuni-

---

15. J. Richard Hackman and Greg R. Oldham, "Motivation through the Design of Work: Test of a Theory," *Organizational Behavior and Human Performance*, 16:250-79 (1976).

16. Ibid., pp. 250-79.

ties, employees are likely to leave. Turnover among encounter service workers is very high in comparison to turnover in high-paying high-technology jobs. In the latter jobs, turnover due to employees' leaving to take a job in another company typically runs from about 0.5 to 20 percent per year.[17] In the fast-food business, in contrast, Taco Bell claims to have the lowest rate of turnover among hourly workers, 150 percent; the turnover rate for managers is 20 percent.[18] At McDonald's, overall turnover typically exceeds 100 percent; by some estimates, turnover exceeds 300 percent for counter workers.[19] Turnover is high in other kinds of encounters, too. For example, in the cashier department of a large brokerage firm, turnover exceeded 100 percent.[20] The turnover rate for clerks at some mini-market stores regularly exceeds 140 percent a year. Encounter workers in the hospitality industry also exhibit high turnover.[21]

Scholars and practicing managers disagree on whether or not high turnover in encounter-style jobs is a problem. While some view it as problematic, others regard high turnover as an unavoidable and even a necessary and desirable feature. Those who see it as a problem claim that high turnover affects the quality of products and services, creates significant replacement and recruitment costs, and therefore affects profitability. Those who are more sanguine about high turnover claim that it "ensures recruitment of new blood."[22] One author viewed high turnover at McDonald's in a positive light, as a stepping-stone to a better job: "Because the chain [McDonald's] trains so many high school students for their first jobs, most of its workers quickly advance to higher paying jobs, which explains why McDonald's turnover rate at the store level has historically run better than 100% per year."[23]

In addition, high turnover means that the company will not need a very large pension fund as few employees stay long enough to qualify for a pension. If the high-turnover employees are typically young, as they are in the fast-food industry, then they tend to be healthy and the organization has few health care costs. In general, the indirect labor costs are lower where turnover is high.

Advancement opportunities. The opportunity to advance is one kind of incentive an organization can offer, and it can serve as a mechanism for reducing turnover.[24] Since encounter-style jobs are by nature routine, if the employee becomes bored with the job,

---

17. Figures taken from a presentation by Richard Bowman, AT&T, 25 Mar. 1993; personal communication with Geza Bottlik, 1993.

18. M. Nalywayko, "The Link between Quality Operations and Quality Service" (Paper delivered at the conference "Activating Your Firm's Service Culture," First Interstate Center for Services Marketing, Arizona State University, Phoenix, AZ, 28-30 Oct. 1992).

19. John F. Love, *McDonald's: Behind the Arches* (New York: Bantam Books, 1986), p. 5; Ritzer, *McDonaldization of Society.*

20. James Heskett, *Managing in the Service Economy* (Cambridge, MA: Harvard Business School Press, 1986), p. 100.

21. Roy C. Wood, *Working in Hotels and Catering* (London: Routledge, 1992), pp. 95-96.

22. Ibid., p. 96.

23. Love, *McDonald's*, p. 5.

24. Rosabeth M. Kanter, *Men and Women of the Corporation* (New York: Basic Books, 1977).

advancement is likely to be attractive. One problem, however, is that a good frontline provider delivering encounters does not have the chance to exhibit the qualities needed in a supervisor or manager. Following the rules and regulations to the letter and delivering the goods or service with a smile are not the prime qualities needed in professional, middle-management, or executive positions.[25] In order to demonstrate their ability, providers will probably have to quit their job and go elsewhere. Unfortunately, the longer a person has been working in encounter-style jobs, the more difficult it will be to convince any employer that she is capable of doing anything other than routine work.

One way to advance that is available to some encounter providers is to become an exception provider. An exception provider handles special problems, cases that require discretion beyond that given to the frontline provider. Garson noted that "at airline reservation offices special 'Flagship' or 'Gold Card' phone lines are manned by exception workers who deal with frequent flyers or travel agents. They're freer to deviate from the script."[26]

SUMMARY AND CONCLUSION

Encounters occur in encounter systems. These systems are designed and managed to be efficient, that is, to provide service to the greatest number of customers for the least amount of time, provider time, or money. In an encounter system, managers are always looking for ways to cut costs. In relationship-based service, providers are often the largest—and sometimes the only—cost. From the perspective of the relationship provider—the physician, professor, manicurist, gardener, or babysitter—that is as it should be. If a high proportion of the customer's dollar is not going directly to the service provider, the customer is not being well served.

These providers are accustomed to thinking that they embody the services customers are seeking, that they are the reason why customers are there. But such providers constitute labor costs in managed organizations, such as managed health care (for example, Kaiser Permanente), managed food delivery (for example, McDonald's), managed haircuts (for example, Supercuts), or managed back rubs. When physicians, nurses, and therapists are viewed as the labor costs of health care establishments, or hairstylists are viewed as the labor costs of a salon, or social workers are viewed as labor costs in an agency, replacing relationship-style service with less expensive encounter-style service—with its less expensive, more specialized workers—is one strategy for cutting costs.

Once jobs have been created so that in principle all providers are interchangeable and functionally equivalent, it makes sense to consider automating the provider job. That is, of course, already happening as automated messaging systems have replaced live operators, automatic teller machines (ATMs) are replacing bank tellers, and automated check-in services are starting to re-

25. Heskett, *Managing in the Service Economy*, p. 61.
26. Garson, *Electronic Sweatshop*, p. 105.

place hotel clerks.[27] Thus the replacement of relationship interactions with encounter interactions has direct implications for the quality of the working life, pay, and career opportunities of service providers, fewer of whom will have the luxury of a relationship provider career. In addition, the replacement of relationships with encounters has implications for the number of jobs available as machine providers replace human providers.

The standard comeback, and one that has served reasonably well in the past, is twofold: first, production could not expand rapidly enough with the existing workforce (thus, the often cited example that there are not enough people in the country to handle all the switchboards necessary to control communications in the United States today), and, second, new and often better jobs are created to replace those that have been deskilled or automated. The economy has managed just fine without blacksmiths, for example.

Commodities continue to be created, and some think that information, rather than being part of service, will emerge as the new commodity that will create jobs for workers whose jobs have been eliminated as agriculture, manufacturing, and now service are being produced less expensively. That may be the case, but I am not among those who are optimistic about the ability of information or any other new commodity—whatever it might be—to create enough well-paying jobs to provide a reasonable standard of living for a rapidly expanding world population.[28]

Marvin Harris expressed the point quite eloquently over a decade ago:

As productivity in manufacturing and mining rose, surplus labor was drawn off into the production of information and services. What next? With microchip computerization of information-and-service jobs the fastest growth industry in the United States, who can doubt that the same process is about to be repeated in the service-and-information fields? But with one difference: There is no conceivable realm of profitable employment whose expansion can make up for even modest productivity gains among the nation's sixty million service-and-information workers.[29]

I have painted a picture of an inexorable transition in the delivery of services, but do we really need to accept, in some form, the scenario I have portrayed? I will be spending the next year at the Udall Center for Public Policy at the University of Arizona exploring this issue, but I am sure that public policy interventions can alter the scenario I have described.

First, we do not have to accept the profit motive that characterizes encounter systems as a substitute for an older ethic of caring, however imperfectly implemented in many relationship provider jobs today. But without some intervention, that is what we will have, and it will be hard to change once in place. As an academic, I am personally concerned about changes in higher education; I

---

27. Customers can check in and out of some Hyatt Hotels by using an ATM-like machine called the Touch and Go Instant Check-In. "Bypassing the Front Desk," *Business Week*, 3 Oct. 1994, special advertising sec.

28. Marvin Harris, *America Now: The Anthropology of a Changing Culture* (New York: Simon & Schuster, 1981).

29. Ibid., p. 179.

am not ready to accept "managed" higher education.

Unfortunately, I do not now have any brilliant ideas to prevent the loss of relationship-style jobs or, for that matter, encounter-style jobs, but I would encourage a number of activities that might generate such ideas. Thus for a second suggestion, I would like to encourage both public awareness and public debate about the changes that are taking place. Are these changes what the public wants? In *The Wealth of Nations*, Adam Smith contended that it takes 18 easily trained and easily replaced people, each doing a very specialized repetitive task, to make a high-quality pin. But do we believe that 18 narrow-content specialists each teaching a single lecture can provide a better course than a single professor teaching the full semester? Or that a single skilled surgeon can be replaced by 18 different narrowly trained medical technicians?

Third, we need data from companies and agencies as well as more traditional academic research. Do services delivered in relationships have a higher quality than services delivered in encounters? Further, we need to compare the cost of relationship-style service delivery with encounter-style service delivery. I believe that encounters are not necessarily a more cost-effective delivery system.[30] It would be a real shame if the substitute of encounters for relationships yielded merely fewer good jobs and more profit for owners but not more effective service.

Finally, we need to consider not only the quality of service but the quality of service jobs. What kind of jobs does the public want available, for now and for future generations? Parents encourage their children to go into the various professions because they often provide interesting, flexible, and remunerative work. The replacement of relationship-style professional jobs with encounter-style provider jobs will destroy these positive aspects of professional jobs. We need to find out if and under what circumstances the public is willing to expend more resources to provide relationship service jobs that they can recommend to their children.

30. Gutek, *Dynamics of Service*, chaps. 3 and 7.

The German Apprenticeship System: Lessons for Austin, Texas

By ROBERT W. GLOVER

ABSTRACT: With a strong economy bringing skill shortages in technical jobs, Austin, Texas, has sought to learn the essentials of the German apprenticeship system for the development of its local youths and to help resolve labor supply problems encountered by local employers. Going beyond the conventional research and study tours, Austin has invited direct participation from European training experts and has established an apprentice exchange for Austin youths with the Chamber of Small and Medium-Sized Firms and Crafts in Koblenz, Austin's sister city in Germany. The Capital Area Training Foundation, an industry-led, nonprofit corporation, was formed to guide the development of the school-to-work system through its affiliated industry steering committees established in each of the region's major industry sectors. These steering committees decide on the industry's approach to working with schools, confirm industry skill standards and curriculum frameworks, provide career information, and organize opportunities for active career exploration and work-based learning.

Robert W. Glover is presently a research scientist at the Center for the Study of Human Resources at the Lyndon B. Johnson School of Public Affairs of the University of Texas at Austin. From 1978 to 1982, he served as chair of the Federal Committee on Apprenticeship. In 1990, after participating in several national and international studies regarding school and work, he focused his efforts on school-to-work issues in Austin.

NOTE: The National Center for the Workplace, the Charles Stewart Mott Foundation, the German Marshall Fund, and the Center for Learning and Competitiveness provided financial assistance for this research.

THE German apprenticeship system has drawn the interest of Americans seeking better ways to prepare youths for employment. What practical steps can be taken to learn from the German apprenticeship system? Is there any utility in sending American youngsters to Germany? How can the American business community be organized to increase its efforts in the professional development of youths? What roles can local elected officials play in fostering this process? This article examines the experience of Austin, Texas, in seeking to learn from the German experience.

The German apprenticeship system has attracted the attention of American policymakers because it has demonstrated the ability to produce high skills in a majority of German youths while conferring recognition and status to a wide array of occupations not requiring university training. Fully two-thirds of all young people completing secondary education in Germany enter apprenticeships. About 90 percent of them will complete training, pass their comprehensive examinations, and obtain credentials. High proportions of German firms offer apprenticeships, and the ratio of youth to adult unemployment in Germany is among the lowest of any nation in the world. Apprentices must find their own training slots, with information and counseling assistance provided through occupational information centers (*Berufsinformationszentrum*) operated by the public employment service (*Arbeitsamt*). Training is offered in about 375 apprenticeable occupations under standards agreed to nationally by industry. These standards outline the scope and duration of training, the duties and tasks of the occupation, and provide a curriculum outline and a common framework for the assessment of skills in examinations.

Officially entitled the Dual System, German apprenticeship derives its name from the fact that training is provided in two locations: in firms that provide practical instruction and in vocational schools (*Berufsschulen*) that offer related theoretical instruction. Apprentices usually spend one or two days in the vocational school and the remainder of the week with their firms. A portion of the time with the firm may be spent in interfirm workshops. These special industry facilities, most of which were built with federal subsidies, are operated by the German Chambers. Instruction at the interfirm training centers is especially helpful for smaller firms that are unable to offer the full range of the required training in a given occupation at the work site.

Many Americans have made study trips to examine European approaches to occupational training for youths. Several of these trips have produced thoughtful reports, and a growing body of competent publications is available in English regarding the German Dual System.[1]

1. See, for example, Glenda Partee, *European Lessons from School and the Workplace* (Washington, DC: Council of Chief State School Officers, 1991); Emily Gantz McKay, *The Forgotten Two-Thirds: An Hispanic Perspective on Apprenticeship, European Style* (Washington, DC: National Council of La Raza, 1993); Stephen F. Hamilton, *Apprenticeship for Adulthood: Preparing Youth for the Future*

In its community partnership to implement a school-to-work system, Austin, Texas, is moving beyond the study trips and reports to incorporate lessons from Europe by developing more continuous and meaningful contact with our European partners through establishing training exchanges and making direct use of the training expertise and advice of experienced European training officials. We also have invited European professionals to advise us and to work with us in developing the system. In February 1995, a Swiss training consultant with extensive experience in Zurich banks moved to Austin to help establish apprenticeship programs.

SPECIAL FEATURES OF THE AUSTIN LABOR MARKET

By almost any measure, Austin currently has a robust economy. Unemployment in May 1995 stood at 3.2 percent, the lowest rate in Texas and one of the lowest of any metropolitan area in the nation. In 1994, employment in the Austin metropolitan area grew at 6 percent, or about double the population growth rate of 3 percent. The Austin area, which contained only one-eighteenth of the population of Texas, accounted for nearly one-quarter of all gains in manufacturing that occurred statewide in 1993.[2] From 1984 through 1994, manufacturing employment in Austin grew by 55.7 percent compared to the state's 0.3 percent.[3]

The most dynamic component of Austin's economy has been the high-technology electronic industry. Hiring activity at major and small corporations has continued unabated at firms such as Motorola, Advanced Micro Devices, National Instruments, Applied Materials, Crystal Semiconductors, Apple Computer, Origin Systems, and others. Today Austin boasts nearly 825 high-tech companies employing approximately 85,000 persons. Employment growth in this sector has expanded at 6.9 percent per year over the last decade.[4]

Austin's high-tech job market continues to expand. New semiconductor wafer fabrication plants are currently under construction by Motorola and Advanced Micro Devices at $1 billion apiece—in East Austin near some of the poorest neighborhoods in the county. These two firms alone are anticipated to add 3000 new employees over the next five years. In addition, as many as 400 jobs become available annually through turnover in the industry.

The entry-level qualifications for these jobs currently range from 10th-grade tested skills for certain operator jobs to an associate's degree for technicians' positions. However, skill requirements are rising fast in this industry so that all jobs will soon require proficiencies at the technician or two-year college level or its equivalent in scientific or technical courses.

(New York: Free Press, 1990); Joachim Munch, *Vocational Training in the Federal Republic of Germany*, 4th ed. (Berlin: European Center for the Development of Vocational Training, 1994).

2. Angeles G. Angelou and Melissa Stokes, "Economic Review and Forecast: 1994-95" (Report, Greater Austin Chamber of Commerce, 1994), p. 2.

3. Angeles G. Angelou and Melissa Stokes, "Economic Review and Forecast: 1995-96" (Report, Greater Austin Chamber of Commerce, 1995), p. 4.

4. Ibid.

Nine universities and colleges are located in the area's three central counties. Together they have a student enrollment of 100,000 and produce approximately 15,000 college diplomas annually compared with 5000 high school graduates produced in the same area. Of the college and university students, about 11,000 graduate from the University of Texas at Austin. Most college students graduate in nontechnical areas. Because Austin is an attractive area, many try to stay here, even at the price of being underemployed in jobs usually occupied by individuals with less education.

However, the area's schools and training providers have not kept pace with the demand for workers trained in technical fields at the subbaccalaureate level. Of 26,000 students enrolled in Austin Community College for college credit courses each year, less than 1000 receive an associate's degree or certificate. Approximately 100 students per year graduate as electronics technicians, of which 90 had already worked for high-tech firms. Thus only 10 new technicians are graduated to the labor market whereas labor market projections show that at least 400 are needed by the industry over the next 5 years. Part of this problem is capacity because Austin Community College encounters difficulties in keeping pace with the changing laboratory equipment needed for training in high-technology occupations.

Another facet of the Austin labor market is the common use of temporary service firms. Temporary service firms are used for a variety of purposes. A frequent aim is to avoid the expense and commitment of hiring permanent workers, thus providing a company with greater flexibility in downturns. Some local manufacturers try to have as many as 40 percent of their workers as temporary workers. A second prevalent use for temporary service is as a screening device. Rather than hiring permanent workers and placing them on probation, one local computer manufacturer hires all its initial production workers as temporary workers, retaining the best as permanent employees once they have proven themselves. Some firms use temporary service agencies to supplement their recruiting and training of new workers, especially in tight labor market conditions. For example, one newly established electronics assembly firm paid a temporary agency to recruit and train its production workforce in soldering techniques.

The use of temporary agencies varies significantly by firm and changes through time. This complicates the task faced by job applicants trying to develop a permanent attachment in the Austin labor market. They need to understand which temporary jobs lead to permanent status and which do not.

In the present labor market climate, emphasis is on knowledge and skill development rather than on the attainment of credentials. Some teachers of block training classes offered by Austin Community College have found their classrooms emptied before the end of the course because all their students had been recruited into jobs. In fact, to reduce this problem, the college has banned temporary job agencies from recruiting in classes.

In short, even though the Austin labor market is strong, it poses serious challenges to youths who lack specialized skills or credentials and special connections to employers. While low-wage jobs in industries, such as fast food and retail, are commonly available, the fresh high school graduate confronts serious competition from college students and college graduates for jobs that have greater potential for producing income and benefits.

In this environment, the development of work-based learning as found in German-style apprenticeships offers Austin several advantages. By developing their own technical workers, Austin employers can alleviate their supply problems in technical fields and produce more loyal workers who are less likely to jump to competing firms. Many of Austin's high-technology firms already provide tuition reimbursement to help their incumbent workers through school; what is needed at this point is to develop work-based learning that is structured and connected with school. Trainees can become familiar with current production equipment at their job sites, which will reduce the financial pressures on Austin Community College to continually acquire the latest expensive equipment for use in school laboratory settings. By conducting training at work sites as well as in classrooms, training capacity can be expanded rapidly in high-demand occupations. Most of all, Austin youths will benefit. Apprenticeships offer teenagers clear, structured pathways to career positions, personal connections with employers, and training and credentials in specialized skills in short supply. All of these factors help youths to compete more effectively with more generally educated college graduates.

GLEANING LESSONS FROM ABROAD

At the outset, I should point out that Austin does not aim to replicate the German education and training system. Clearly, the United States cannot adopt the German approach wholesale, nor should it want to. Germany's education and training system is embedded in a set of cultural practices that will not transfer well to American soil. In perhaps the most widely cited example, Germany uses a three-track system in lower secondary schools that most Americans find unacceptable because it forces youths to make a choice about their future even before they become teenagers. Rather than trying to replicate the German system, a better approach is to identify essentials that underlie the German approach and to find appropriate ways to adapt them to practices in the United States.

Austin has taken several initiatives to glean the essentials in lessons from abroad. Background research gathered during 1991-92 by a student-faculty team at the Lyndon B. Johnson School of Public Affairs at the University of Texas identified six key common elements between youth professional development practices in Germany and those in Japan, where apprenticeship is not used. First, under both systems, youths know that effort and achievement in school are clearly and unmistakably needed to qualify for high-quality training and jobs after high school. Second, society has high expectations for the standards that all youths need to meet in school. Third, employers make early connection with youths, hiring them in their teenage years. Fourth, the process of preparing adolescents for the workplace is viewed as a joint responsibility of schools and firms. Fifth, experiential learning systems for youths on the job are well developed. Sixth, industry takes major responsibility for assessing and certifying the skills of youths.[5]

In the fall of 1993, with funding from the German Marshall Fund of the United States through the Center for Learning and Competitiveness, the Greater Austin Chamber of Commerce sponsored a Comparative Learning Team sent to Switzerland, Germany, and Denmark to examine governance and financing of apprenticeships. The team found most impressive the large scale of European apprenticeship, its systemic approach, and the responsibility that industry widely assumed jointly with schools for the professional development of youths. European planners start by calculating need and assemble resources to meet that need; in contrast, Americans typically begin by examining available resources and calculate how many can be served with these limited resources.[6]

5. Robert W. Glover et al., *Bridging the Gap: Implementing School-to-Work Transition in Austin, Texas* (Austin: University of Texas at Austin, Lyndon B. Johnson School of Public Affairs, 1993), pp. 8-9.

6. Center for Learning and Competitiveness, *School-to-Work Transition in the U.S.: The Case of the Missing Social Partners* (College Park: University of Maryland, School of Public Affairs, 1994), p. 19.

Whereas Europeans develop systems to serve all people, Americans design limited programs to serve special populations whose needs were used to justify the expenditure of public funds in the first place. Americans attempt to conserve public funds by reserving eligibility for services only to "deserving" individuals who can demonstrate the need for them. As a result, American programs often are stigmatized and balkanized into numerous, inflexible, overlapping, duplicative, narrow efforts for separate populations; the programs have uneven coverage and inadequate overall resources available, and they serve the needs of neither trainees nor employers very well.

The Mayor's Task Force on Apprenticeships and Career Pathway Programs for Austin Youths strongly recommended making good use of Austin's sister-city relationship with Koblenz, Germany. Biannually since 1989, Austin has sent a delegation of elected officials, educators, and representatives from industry and the community to Koblenz. These one-week visits have often included a stop at the facilities of the Chamber of Small and Medium-sized Firms and Crafts (Handwerkskammer Koblenz). The 1994 delegation of 33 persons—the largest sent to date—focused on the Dual System, visiting schools, training facilities, and firms.

A primary focus of our sister-city relationship has been on creating youth exchanges. Several educational exchanges have blossomed between schools in the two cities, ranging from a double-degree program between the Graduate School of Business at the University of Texas at

Austin and the School of Corporate Management in Koblenz, to visits between primary school students and educators at the Schenkendorf Primary School in Koblenz and the Summitt Elementary School in Austin, as well as increasing electronic connections through the Internet. Currently we are building on this sister-city relationship to offer German apprenticeships for Austin teenagers in collaboration with the Chamber of Small and Medium-sized Firms and Crafts.

In another approach to understand essentials, we have asked our German colleagues to identify the key components of their system for us. The advice we have received has been thoughtful and challenging. Mr. Karl-Jürgen Wilbert, executive director of the Koblenz Chamber of Small and Medium-sized Firms and Crafts, emphasized that the provision of knowledge and skills is linked to required job experience; the vocational training is proximate to the work site; the on-the-job training uses state-of-the-art equipment and takes place under real-life conditions; access to the Dual System of Vocational Training is open to all; upon completion of the vocational training, the young person is a certified skilled worker and can enter the workforce immediately; and the contents and requirements of the training are geared to subsequent vocational mobility and a willingness to undergo further training.[7] Dr. Wilfried Prewo, executive director of the Hanover Chamber of Industry and Commerce, emphasized three themes in his response:

First, you must have a private-public partnership with clear-cut responsibilities: the training companies must be in the driver's seat and be willing to lead. The government should have its hands off the steering wheel; it should pave the way by setting national standards and grease the wheels with tax credits and, on the state and local level, provide vocational schools. Chambers of Commerce or other forms of private industry councils should act as catalysts, organizing the joint effort of companies and mediating between the private and public sector. Second, the system must be work-based: in the mix of school-based and work-based learning, two-thirds of the apprentices' time should be spent in the workplace. Lacking workplaces, you must simulate them perfectly. Trainees must be treated as employees, not students. Third, you must build a system: aim for a system and not for just another program. And bring it up to scale fast with a highly generous tax credit for companies that start training.[8]

ORIGIN AND PURPOSE OF AUSTIN'S SCHOOL-TO-WORK SYSTEM

Austin's efforts to improve school-to-work opportunities trace back to 1991 with various waves of activities, beginning with pilot programs undertaken by the Greater Austin Chamber of Commerce through its School-to-Work Transition Committee. In May 1992, the Austin Project, initiated by Walt and Elspeth Rostow,

---

7. Karl-Jürgen Wilbert, Presentation to the Mayor's Task Force on Apprenticeships and Career Pathways for Austin Youth, Austin, TX, 17 May 1993.

8. Wilfried Prewo, "School-to-Work Transition and High Performance: The German Approach" (Paper delivered at the workshop "Education That Works and Work That Educates," Austin, TX, 6-7 June 1994), p. 18.

was launched to mobilize the community to eliminate poverty through strategies of investing in families and youths. Developing paths into work and professional life is an essential component of the Austin Project's ambitious effort to invest in youths on a continuous basis from the prenatal period through the entrance into work at a scale that meets the needs. The project emphasizes prevention and secures the participation of the neighborhoods involved.

Greater impetus for learning from our German partners came in a third wave of initiatives stemming from the efforts of Austin mayor Bruce Todd in March 1993. Mayor Todd had just returned from an exchange visit to Koblenz, where he reviewed the workforce development system, especially its initial training system for youths found in the Dual System. What he observed impressed him deeply, and he resolved to use his influence to establish an Austin equivalent of the German apprenticeship system. Mayor Todd made improving school-to-work transition one of his three priority goals for the new City Council beginning in June 1993, and he called on the Greater Austin Chamber of Commerce to work with the city to implement a system of school-to-work opportunities in Austin. In collaboration with chamber officials, Mayor Todd convened the Mayor's Task Force on Apprenticeships and Career Pathways for Austin Youth, chaired by Sharon Knotts Green of Motorola.

Over the following year, the task force interviewed students and business leaders and investigated practices in other localities across America and in other nations in order to gain a better understanding of the issues. Both the executive director and the deputy director of Handwerkskammer Koblenz made visits to Austin to observe representative programs and companies, to review existing school-to-work pilot activities, and to offer advice. By the time the new city council was in place, the task force had produced an interim report that outlined agreement on a dozen principles and raised several questions for subsequent study. The mayor and the city council responded by allocating $200,000 in seed monies under its Opportunities for Youth Program in the 1993-94 city budget.

By the spring of 1994, the task force, working closely with the Greater Austin Chamber of Commerce, had agreed to form a new industry-led, self-governing, nonprofit corporation entitled the Capital Area Training Foundation.[9] The mission of the foundation is to promote regional workforce development and to guide and support the establishment of a system of school-to-work opportunities across the Capital Area. To foster industry-level collaboration, the foundation has established steering committees in major industry sectors of the Austin-area economy. In the fall of 1994, the Capital Area Training Foundation won local school-to-

9. The original name of the organization was the Austin Training Foundation, but Austin's school-to-work system subsequently expanded into a regional effort, focusing on the 10-county Capital Area, and the name of the organization was changed accordingly. The term "industry" as used in this article is meant to designate both employer and worker representatives.

work implementation grants from the federal government to test its approach. Through these grants and city seed monies, modest funding has been made available to the steering committees to help them put their ideas into action. In all cases, such funding has been augmented by contributions from industry and schools.

The city of Austin has important roles in this endeavor. The Austin City Council provided the initial seed money to begin the Capital Area Training Foundation as an independent entity. Second, the city has a voting representative on the foundation's board of directors to help ensure that public interests are served. Third, as an entity with 10,000 employees of its own, the city of Austin is an important participating employer itself. Finally, the mayor has convened several of the industry groups. We have been pragmatic and opportunistic about organizing the steering committees, recognizing that there is no one best way. Generally, industry steering committees have been organized through the chief executive officers or local managers, whose support is vital to success. Steering committees are composed of small executive-level groups concerned primarily with strategic issues. Depending on the needs and preferences of the industry, various subcommittees and temporary special-purpose task forces are formed to accomplish specific tasks. A major focus of the industry efforts concerns the implementation of industry skill standards and qualifications. Opportunities for active career exploration and work-based learning are also issues addressed.

The design of the Capital Area Training Foundation gives industry influence and ownership in the region's school-to-work system. By establishing a self-governing, industry-led institution concerned with the preparation of entry-level workers, the foundation aims to mobilize industry to become an active partner with schools in the development of future employees. After all, those who know most about an industry's needs—representatives of the firms and workers themselves—are in the best position to make decisions regarding initial preparation of the industry's workforce. The training foundation and its steering committees offer considerable advantages over traditional approaches to involving industry in vocational education, especially school-based advisory committees.

Most of all, this initiative eventually aims to improve the preparation of a majority of Austin's youths by engaging them in learning, connecting learning in school with applications in the real world, and providing incentives to motivate students who are weary of conventional approaches to instruction—through communicating more clearly what is required for success in the modern workplace, building hope for youths who see no attractive futures for themselves, and making these hopes real by creating clear, direct, and immediate paths to work and further learning.

GLOBAL LEARNING THROUGH INTERNATIONAL TRAINING EXCHANGES

As an integral part of its school-to-work initiative, Austin is developing international training exchanges for its youths. The idea for Austin's initiative in this arena began with a generous and ingenious offer made in June 1994 by Mr. Karl-Jürgen Wilbert, executive director of Handwerkskammer Koblenz, to place Austin youths in German apprenticeships preparing them to work in occupations of their choice. The Austin youths will serve in accelerated apprenticeships lasting from two to two and a half years.[10] They will be employed by German employers as regular apprentices and will take related instruction in schools and interfirm workshops with German apprentices. They will take the regular final comprehensive examinations, and those who pass will receive full German credentials.

In August 1994, the Mayor's Task Force on Apprenticeships and Career Pathways for Austin Youth began recruiting interested high school graduates who were no older than 20 years of age. Applicants and their parents were interviewed by a screening panel of representatives from the Austin business community, the school district, and the Austin-Koblenz sister-cities program. The initial group of Austin youths selected began their apprenticeships in January 1995 in a variety of occupations, including machine builder, steel fabricator, electrical installer, automobile mechanic, automobile electrical technician, baker, cabinetmaker, and carpenter. Special arrangements for language training and any other needed tutoring are being made by the Handwerkskammer Koblenz. A monthly fee of DM100 per apprentice for administering and monitoring training contracts, normally paid by German employers sponsoring apprentices, is funded by the Capital Area Training Foundation.

Arranging for living accommodations has presented a more significant challenge than placing the youths as apprentices with German employers. If the costs of room and board are fully monetized (that is, paid in cash rather than contributed), the expenses may run as high as $7000 per year per apprentice. The cost of housing and food exceeds most apprentice training stipends. Indeed, this is why most German apprentices live with their parents or relatives.

What potential benefits does such an apprentice exchange offer Austin? First, it provides Austin teenagers access to serious occupational training as well as all the benefits of studying internationally. Second, it offers rich opportunities for comparative learning. The program provides Austin with a direct window to view the day-to-day operations of the German Dual System through the eyes of our youths. When the apprentices return to Austin, they will make presentations about their experiences in Koblenz and the training they are receiving. Third, this unusual high-profile initiative provides opportunities to educate Austin employers, parents, students, teachers, the me-

10. German youths who have successfully completed schooling in the college preparatory (*Gymnasium*) track and passed their college entrance examination (*Abitur*) are eligible to serve in accelerated apprenticeships. The Austin-Koblenz exchange takes advantage of this provision to shorten the term of apprenticeships for recent American high school graduates who are assumed to have the equivalent of an *Abitur*.

dia, and the general public about the approach that the Germans take to the professional formation of their youths. We are organizing teams of Austin employers in each of the chosen trades to review and monitor the training to help ensure its relevance to the Austin labor market so that the youths will have job opportunities in their fields on their return to Austin. This arrangement offers important side benefits in getting Austin employers acquainted with the German approach to the professional formation of youths. Fourth, it strengthens motivation for language learning. Youths who never performed well in school in English courses are now excelling in foreign language training, and we have found new allies for our school-to-work endeavors among Austin's foreign language teachers. Finally, our global learning initiatives aim to raise the status of our new vocational-technical training and help distinguish it from traditional efforts.

CONCLUSION

American employers tend to complain about schools and to demand that schools perform much better before they will hire youths. This approach contrasts markedly with employer attitudes in other nations where the professional development of youths is viewed as a joint responsibility. As much as schools do need to improve, American firms likewise need to adopt high-performance practices to keep up with the demands of international competition. The move to high performance necessarily involves an increased focus on learning and training generally. In short, American learning systems at school and at work need to be improved simultaneously and need to be meaningfully linked.

Building an effective school-to-work system is a long-term endeavor, for it implies significant changes both in school instructional practices and in hiring and training practices regarding youths. It is also an incremental process. We should not tackle more than we can accomplish well; maintaining quality and making continuous improvements are key considerations. We need to work at it, being alert to new opportunities and points of leverage for extending and improving structured work-based learning. In this process, no single model can be imposed on all industries and all youths. A better strategy is to offer industry a menu of options for providing structured work-based learning to students and educators in various forms. There are a variety of ways to begin. Options include short-term projects devised collaboratively by industry professionals, teachers, and students that emphasize group learning processes, interdisciplinary learning, and the application of academic knowledge acquired in school. Work-based learning options can include learning-rich summer jobs and internships, community service learning opportunities, apprenticeships, as well as designs and devices to integrate school and work that have not yet even been invented. Career academies, school-based enterprises, and technical preparatory programs can provide platforms to connect schools with industry and to develop pathways to careers. Ultimately, as the Germans have shown us, we need to develop training options for youths that bring them to full qualification to work in an industry.

Austin wants to install the essentials of the German apprenticeship system. We are emphasizing the acceptance by industry and schools of joint responsibility for the professional development of youths; the development of work-based learning and its integration with school-based learning; and providing teenagers with access to serious occupational training that leads to careers. Still dependent on seed monies for this endeavor, we aim to develop continuous funding for the system from local sources based on the key principle underlying the financing of German Chambers, namely, using the authority of government to raise the funds but keeping decision making in private hands.

Given the strong orientation of American firms toward short-term profits and the stress on restructuring and cost cutting, making long-term investments in youths is currently not an easy proposition to sell, even in tight labor markets. At this writing, implementation began only several months ago and we are measuring progress in terms of hundreds of work-based learning positions created, including 100 new positions for youths in electronics. Yet to reach any meaningful scale of participation in the program, firms will need to recognize that working with schools to hire and train youths is more than a community service activity; it is in the firms' own longer-term economic interests. With leadership from its mayor and generous assistance from European partners, Austin is trying to make this case to its business community and to organize industry-led institutions to establish an effective school-to-work system. Only through sustained efforts by numerous champions across the Austin community can the full vision be realized.

ANNALS, *AAPSS*, 544, March 1996

The End of Hawaii's Plantations: Back to the Future?

By LAWRENCE W. BOYD, JR.

ABSTRACT: This article explores the response taken by Hawaii's people and society to workers displaced by the closing of sugar and pineapple plantations. Rooted in culture, history, and a labor market that is institutionally different from that of much of the United States, the response to structural unemployment is both unconscious and systematic. Also explored is the potential impact these closures can have on Hawaii's economy and society. Will Hawaii go back to the future and return to a society dominated by a business oligarchy such as existed throughout much of the plantation era? Or will it go back to the future as happened with the Democratic Revolution of 1954 and the birth of the modern Hawaiian economy? Can we distinguish between the two approaches today? These questions will be resolved based on whether Hawaii's people decide on a renewal of traditional ideas and beliefs or on an overthrow of these ideas.

Prior to earning his doctorate in economics, Lawrence W. Boyd, Jr., was a coal miner who was an activist in the United Mine Workers and then became a displaced worker. He is currently employed as a labor economist at the Center for Labor Education and Research at the University of Hawaii at Manoa. He has also been a union organizer for District 1199 in Pennsylvania, a health care union.

NOTE: The author thanks Ah Quon McElrath, Guy Fujimura, Leonard Hoshijo, Joanne Kealoha, and others who read and commented on earlier drafts. In addition, Gregory Pai, director of state planning, and Xijun Tian of the Research and Economic Analysis Division, Department of Business Economic Development and Tourism, were generous with their time and advice. I also thank participants in the International Longshoremen's and Warehousemen's Union's Tourism Institute who patiently educated me about the meaning of "aloha" and Hawaiian sovereignty.

IN Hawaiian, "aloha" has many meanings: love, generosity, affection, compassion, mercy, welcome, as well as hello and good-bye. The definition is complex because the word encompasses a philosophy and a culture. To speak of Hawaiian aloha is to mean right action based on generosity, often without reciprocity between givers and takers; it is something that cannot be commercialized.[1] It is part of the tangled web of culture in Hawaii that has mixed many different ethnic cultures into a larger whole. For workers displaced from their jobs, it means that they are viewed as members of a community who are deserving of generous support. Thus Hawaii's cultural heritage has helped create a social consensus of support for displaced workers.

This view can be contrasted with one often adopted toward displaced workers, one that holds them as objects to be managed. More often than not, they are seen as a problem to be solved, or ignored, depending on one's view of politics and economics. Sometimes they are even viewed as having created their own problems. In Hawaii, the approach taken toward them is both unconscious and systematic. It is a product of culture and history rather than a single neat idea or political program (although these, too, play a role). It is also the product of a labor market whose institutional framework is different from that found on the mainland. Yet if displaced workers are treated differently in Hawaii, there are also similarities that exist worldwide.

Sugar and pineapple production has played the same role in Hawaii's economy as steel production has played in Pittsburgh, coal mining in West Virginia, and automobile manufacturing in Michigan. Jobs on Hawaii's plantations, like many manufacturing jobs on the U.S. mainland, have been lost through a combination of international competition and mechanization. Thus there are important similarities in the forces that are displacing workers on the mainland and those in Hawaii. Like manufacturing and mining workers, plantation workers in Hawaii have also been relatively well-paid union members. Therefore structural unemployment will also have similar effects on the Hawaiian economy.

In 1992, Hawaii's sugar and pineapple industries began to shut down completely. Dole's pineapple production was shifted to Thailand while plantations on Lanai and their processing plant in Honolulu were shut down. Of 11 sugar plantations, 6 have ceased operations or will have done so by 1996. Should the farm bill before Congress in 1995 eliminate the protection that sugar enjoys, all of Hawaii's remaining plantations will close. Closures on this scale are unique in Hawaii's economic history and portend the end of more than 100 years of plantation agriculture.

Previously, employment in the sugar and pineapple industries had

---

1. An example of aloha is the hanai pattern of child adoption practiced in rural areas as late as the 1930s. A hanai child was given by its true parents to its foster parents as a mark of love and respect. The hanai child in turn often received greater attention by its foster parents than did their own children. This practice continued somewhat differently and was also taken up by other cultures when parents would offer a child they could not care for to friends. "Hanai" means "to feed" in Hawaiian.

declined gradually as plantations became more mechanized and their operations consolidated. As a result, other sectors of the economy, especially tourism, were able to absorb these workers as they were displaced. Recent closures, however, have been more than the Hawaiian economy can absorb. Up to this point, unemployment in Hawaii has always been a result of national recessions. Today's unemployment, on the other hand, is created by the structural change going on within the state economy. In general, policymakers in state government, private economists, business interests, and labor have not fully understood the difference between the unemployment created by a national recession and the structural unemployment created by the virtual closure of a major industry. The effect of this closure on the economy has been the longest period of economic stagnation in the state's history as well as a financial crisis for its government. Furthermore, the lack of understanding about the roots of the state's economic problems has prevented a fully developed response to it.

Culture, Hawaii's high union density, the ad hoc responses of state government, the role of the plantation workers' union, and the growth of other sectors of the economy have led to displaced workers being treated fundamentally differently in Hawaii from the way they are treated on the mainland. The institutional framework of the labor market in Hawaii is different and reflects the evolution of politics and the state economy. It also constitutes a system of responses to these problems rather than a thought-out plan or political program.

On the mainland, displaced workers enter a labor market that has undergone what *Business Week* has described as a revolutionary transformation of labor. This labor market has high risks and high rewards as well as winners and losers. The fundamental difference between the old labor market and the new labor market is that workers had greater security in the old one.[2]

The comparison between *Business Week*'s vision of this new labor market and other markets is striking. In financial markets, individuals can hedge their bets; that is, they can balance a risky investment with a less risky one. In this way, individuals who are risk averse can minimize their risk. By contrast, workers entering this new labor market cannot minimize their risks. Obviously, any financial market that operated like a casino would soon collapse. Today's new labor market, on the other hand, is a crapshoot, with each roll of the dice producing some winners and many losers. In the old labor market, workers could hedge their bets because unions provided job security, job stability and lifetime jobs existed, and there was a social safety net.[3]

2. The substance of the argument was taken from "The New World of Work: Beyond the Buzzwords Is a Radical Redefinition of Labor," *Business Week*, 17 Oct. 1994; "Business Rolls the Dice," ibid.

3. It has been suggested that education and skill training are means of reducing risk. The problem is forecasting what skills and education one would need. Unlike financial markets where risk-minimizing strategies are well known, choosing this type of training is also all or nothing. See "New World of Work"; "Business Rolls the Dice."

In this new labor market, the problem associated with dislocated workers is not that they cannot find other jobs but that they cannot find equivalent jobs. As Jacobsen, Lalonde, and Sullivan point out,

> The costs of worker displacement go beyond income losses due to unemployment and do not end with reemployment. On the contrary, displaced employees incur large losses, amounting to as much as $80,000. While there have been efforts from policy makers to establish programs to assist the thousands of workers who have been displaced, the existing system prevents them from implementing these effectively. In addition, these programs merely help workers adapt to lower incomes.[4]

The system in Hawaii lessens these costs and can thus help focus attention on the broader issues involved with worker displacement.

The main difference between Hawaii and the mainland is that the labor market is much closer to the one that existed on the mainland during the 1950s and 1960s. Unions play a major role, with about 30 percent of the workforce covered by union contracts. Importantly, two-thirds of the workers in the tourism industry are covered by union contracts. One of the two unions that has organized the visitor industry is the same one that organized the plantations, the International Longshoremen's and Warehousemen's Union (ILWU). Furthermore, all full-time jobs provide health care through Hawaii's prepaid health care law, and a strong social safety net exists.

4. Louis S. Jacobson, Robert J. Lalonde, and Daniel G. Sullivan, "The Costs of Worker Dislocation," *Challenge*, 37(1):56 (Jan.-Feb. 1994).

Thus many former plantation workers have gone directly into tourism, with a collective bargaining contract negotiated by the same union as on the plantations. Their wages and benefits are equivalent to or better than what they earned before. Furthermore, the ILWU historically has been involved in social issues such as housing. Hawaii does not necessarily have better individual retraining or other programs than those found on the mainland. Nevertheless, the response to displaced workers in Hawaii is a systemic one.

Consequently, in this article I first assess the economic impact of plantation closures. I then provide an overview of the evolution of the political economy of the state. Third, I describe how various plantation closings have been handled, especially the joint problems of housing and jobs. Fourth, I examine how these closings, and the economic and political questions they raise, appear to be undermining the social consensus that exists. I conclude by raising the question of whether labor markets and, by extension, the question of displaced workers should be placed in the wider context of national policy decisions.

THE PROBLEM

One way of measuring the impact of displaced workers on the economy is to use the state input/output tables. As Table 1 indicates, between 1983 and 1993, approximately 7000 jobs were lost directly in the sugar and pineapple industries. The impact of this direct job loss led to a total loss of 16,000 jobs throughout the state

TABLE 1
DIRECT AND INDIRECT JOB LOSSES ON HAWAII'S PLANTATIONS, 1983-93

Industry Sector	Direct Jobs	Total Jobs	Income Loss
Pineapple/field-workers	1,117	1,755	$53,010,130
Pineapple/cannery	1,863	5,082	$220,292,140
Sugar/field-workers	1,829	5,666	$178,906,690
Sugar/processing	2,179	3,466	$105,397,240
Total	6,988	15,969	$557,606,200

SOURCE: Hawaii Department of Economic Development, Business and Tourism, *Hawaii State Input Output Model*, 1988.
NOTE: Income loss is in 1993 dollars.

economy. The net loss in personal income was nearly $558 million. It is quite possible that if direct job losses were counted from 1992 through projected job losses into 1996, the numbers would equal those from the 1983-93 period.

Since 1983, the total loss in jobs and personal income has represented 5 percent of all jobs and 4 percent of all income in Hawaii. The economy, however, boomed between 1983 and 1991, creating approximately 100,000 jobs. The convergence of a strong union, the unionization of the service sector, state commitment to aid these workers, and a vibrant economy lessened the problems that displaced workers faced and the effect that these job losses had on the economy. Beginning in 1991, however, these job losses were combined with the effects of the national recession. Since the end of the recession, job losses of the same magnitude, actual and projected, have been occurring over a much shorter time period, two to three years. The shock of job losses within agriculture cannot be made up by other sectors in such a short time. Slow economic growth has in turn created potentially serious problems for recently laid-off workers. How these problems are resolved in Hawaii has much to do with the evolution of Hawaii's economic and political system.

LABOR, LAND, AND
POLITICS IN HAWAII

Hawaii's labor market resembles the labor market that has existed on the mainland, but in some important respects it has evolved independently from the mainland. There are two seminal events that have determined much of Hawaii's modern history. The first was the organization of Hawaii's plantations by the ILWU in 1944 and the 1946 strike in the sugar industry that demonstrated its success. The second was the Democratic Revolution of 1954 that overturned Hawaii's old political system. These events have largely shaped Hawaii's political economy and labor market.

Before these events, Hawaii's economy and political system were dominated by an oligarchy whose financial power rested on control of the islands' economy through the Big Five. The Big Five were corporations that evolved out of Honolulu merchandising stores, or plantations, which acted as agents for sugar planters. These agents, or factors, secured loans, transportation, and supplies and marketed the sugar produced by the islands' plantations. Eventually they came to control much of the land, 90 percent of all sugar production, all of the pineapple production, transportation, banking, and much of Hawaii's economy. To maintain this sort of financial dominance, the Big Five also had to dominate the territory of Hawaii's political system.[5]

The ILWU as an organization functioned as both a union and an economic and political opposition to the Big Five. For example, the ILWU responded politically to the recession of 1949 and the mechanization of the plantations. In a letter to the chairman of the Hawaiian Senate's Ways and Means Committee, the regional director of the ILWU in Hawaii, Jack Hall, pointed out that the workforce was becoming "progressively smaller" in the sugar and pineapple industries. As he noted, employment had been 54,000 in 1932, 31,000 in 1941, and less than 20,000 in 1949. He pointed out, "The reduction in the work force is continuing because of further mechanization and improved production methods." Moreover, outside of these industries, there were only two other major sources of jobs: "military employment and the tourist trade." Military employment was "being decimated." He suggested, "The tourist trade is likely to fail us when we need it most—in the period of a national recession."[6]

Hall went on to say that it was the "*responsibility* of government . . . to provide employment for all who are able to work if private industry is unable." It was also the "responsibility of government to provide adequate subsistence to residents of our community who are unable to work." Hall also explained how these "responsibilities" should be paid for.[7]

Hall argued that the tax structure was "highly" unfair. "Few of our taxes," he said, "take into consideration the principle of 'ability to pay.' Over 94 percent of our income is derived from flat rate, or regressive taxes." Therefore part of the solution was "a better balance between regressive and progressive taxes." Hall and others displayed a sophisticated knowledge of state public finance, one that is sadly lacking today. As Hall put it, "Additional new taxes . . . are not desirable in a period of economic recession."[8]

Rather, it was desirable for the legislature to float a bond issue of "not less than 20 million dollars for public improvements." These projects should "require a minimum of expenditure for materials and supplies and a maximum for personal services." While this might appear as nothing very new to those who are somewhat familiar with Keynesian economics, it was new for Hawaii

5. For a detailed history, see Lawrence Fuchs, *Hawaii Pono: A Social History* (New York: Harcourt Brace Jovanovich, 1961). It should be noted that Hawaii did not become a state until 1959. The Big Five were American Factors Ltd., Castle & Cooke Ltd., Alexander Baldwin Ltd., C. Brewer & Co., Ltd., and Theo. H. Davies & Co., Ltd.

6. Jack Hall, "The Political and Economic Situation in the Territory of Hawai'i" (Report to joint meeting of the executive boards of Locals 136, 142, and 150, ILWU Library).
7. Ibid.
8. Ibid.

during this period. In fact, nationally, it is doubtful that many officials in labor, government, business, or the union movement displayed the understanding of the relationship between fiscal policy and the economy that Hall did. It is also doubtful that many unions understood their state's tax structure as well as the ILWU did. As Hall's letter suggests, the ILWU at this point in time had a clearly thought-out political and economic program.[9]

In 1950, the ILWU developed a plan to cope with the introduction of new technology on the plantations and the effects of the declining workforce. The plan called for the union to work toward a meaningful share of the benefits of technology for the workers who remained on the plantations and to negotiate early-retirement plans for those forced out of the industry. The union also would work politically to pass legislation that dealt with unemployment, housing, and social services. Furthermore, the union would begin organizing efforts in service industries such as tourism and retail stores, which were also dominated by the Big Five. Surprisingly, the ILWU was able to successfully carry out almost every element of this plan.[10]

The ability of the union to work successfully toward these goals was a result of a convergence of the union's own successes in organizing and the political upheaval known as the Democratic Revolution of 1954. Until 1954, the Republican Party, which was directly tied to the Big Five, had controlled the major political institutions in Hawaii: the state legislature, the nonvoting delegate to Congress, and the territorial governor. Union organization barred discrimination based on political preference and loosened plantation managements' control over plantation voters. In 1954, the Democratic Party won two-thirds of the seats in the House and a 9-to-6 majority in the Senate. A simple change in which party was in the majority does not deserve to be called a revolution, however. The term implies some form of social upheaval.

That social upheaval rested on the Democratic Party's having become the party of Japanese, Filipino, and Chinese immigrants. Although the growth of the labor movement obviously added votes to the Democrats, the ethnic component of the Democratic Party was largely led by young, upwardly mobile, middle-class professionals. Not only labor but also small business joined what amounted to a political coalition that led to this overturn.[11]

During this period, the ILWU had been under attack repeatedly as a Communist union. At one point, between 1948 and 1952, the ILWU was seen as trying to take over the Democratic Party and was opposed by the new forces that had come into the party. As Hall later wrote, "We made a grievous error in 1948 when we tied ourselves to the Democratic Party.... Some of our worst enemies have been Democrats, masking as liberals and friends of the workers."[12] The victory in 1954 could not really be described as a win for labor;

9. Ibid.
10. Ibid.

11. See Fuchs, *Hawaii Pono*, chap. 13.
12. Cited in ibid., p. 312.

rather, it combined a labor upheaval with an upheaval among Hawaii's various ethnic communities who had been discriminated against.

The 1956 election gave the Democratic Party a second decisive victory. One historian stated, "For Hawaii, 1956 was what 1936 had been in the states—endorsement of the New Deal and repudiation of the Old Guard policies."[13] At this point in time, the political program outlined by Hall in 1949 was enacted with several additional points. The legislature increased spending on education, lowered tuitions at the University of Hawaii, and increased teachers' salaries. It doubled welfare assistance and expanded public housing. It also raised the minimum wage, increased unemployment benefits, and extended workers' compensation coverage. Tax laws were rewritten to make the system more progressive. Finally, a bill was passed that encouraged investment from the mainland.

As a political and economic opposition to the Big Five, an issue that evolved naturally for the ILWU was housing. When the 1946 strike occurred, a central demand of the union concerned perquisites. These were the value that plantations added to wages for "free" housing and medical care to comply with minimum wage standards. Plantations not only hired labor; they also traditionally provided housing and medical care to their workers. Once the Fair Labor Standards Act was passed in 1937, plantations began to unilaterally add the costs of housing and medical care on to wages in order to bring wages up to the minimum wage level. In other words, the equivalent of rent and insurance premiums was tacked on to the wages and deducted as though money had actually changed hands.[14]

By 1946, most workers were very dissatisfied with their housing and medical care. The union demanded the creation of a labor-management housing improvement fund and a classification of housing by type and quality of building. Furthermore, the union demanded that perquisites be eliminated in favor of rents, with wages adjusted to cover those rents, and that plantation housing be operated on a not-for-profit basis. From the beginning of the negotiations, management was ready to eliminate perquisites because of the complexity of the calculations and the potential tax payments. Other union demands included a 16.5-cent wage increase, a union shop, a 40-hour workweek, a job classification system, and an end to discrimination based on race, creed, color, or political activity. Negotiations quickly stalled on the issues of perquisites, wages, and the union shop, and a 79-day strike ensued.[15]

Although the ILWU did not win all its demands, the strike was seen as an overwhelming union victory. Perquisites were eliminated, rents were listed as part of the union contract, and wages were raised to cover these rents. Thus, virtually from its inception, the ILWU became concerned with a key issue, housing, important to displaced workers.[16]

13. Ibid., p. 327.

14. Edward D. Beechert, *Working in Hawaii: A Labor History* (Honolulu: University of Hawaii Press, 1985), chap. 15.

15. Ibid.

16. Onomea Sugar Company and International Longshoremen's and Warehousemen's Union, *Contract*, 30 Jan. 1947, sec. 7, "Conver-

The ILWU expanded its role in housing over the years, becoming one of the major community nonprofit organizations providing low-income housing. In 1994, the union reported, "The lack of secure housing for working people remains one of our primary social problems. Hawaii's loss of industrial jobs and the growth of yet unorganized, lower wage businesses make home ownership an even more distant goal for 60 percent of the population."[17]

The ILWU currently operates six low- or moderate-income rental projects, aids workers in keeping housing during plantation shutdowns, and actively participates in homeless-shelter issues and self-help projects for homeowner-built housing. In addition, thousands of housing units have been purchased. Collective bargaining contracts state that companies may not evict residents from housing or close housing without providing alternatives.

The social and political changes outlined have operated in a specific economic context as well. A long boom began in 1959 and lasted into the late 1970s. Federal government expenditures on defense in Hawaii grew to be a major sector of the economy. Statehood opened the door to economic expansion by companies other than the Big Five. Beginning in 1960, with the advent of jet airline service to the islands, tourism began to rapidly overtake agriculture as the leading sector of the economy. After the recession of the early 1980s, the economy boomed again until 1991. Indeed, by 1987, the unemployment rate on Oahu was only 2.5 percent and business interests were concerned about a labor shortage.

Thus several things have combined in Hawaii to lessen the problems that displaced workers face:

— the development of a service sector within the economy that could provide jobs for them;
— a strong union, which has understood the evolution of the industry it organized from a very early period;
— a strong union presence in the service sector, a presence that has caused wages and benefits to rise substantially;
— the transformation of the economic and political lives of people in the plantation villages as a result of union organization; and
— the uniting of people from different ethnic cultures in the plantation villages as a result of union organization.

In addition, the state government has basically maintained a commit-

---

sion of Perquisites and Minimum Guarantee" (Center for Labor Education and Research, University of Hawaii, Labor History Archive, ILWU Contract File). "Summary of Transcripts of Negotiations 1948," sec. 23, contains a history of what was agreed on in 1946 and records of negotiations on this issue covering the 1948 agreement. Management did not want housing to be covered under the collective bargaining agreement, but the union did. Eventually a joint management-labor committee was agreed on. See "Summary of Transcripts of Negotiations 1948" (Center for Labor Education and Research, University of Hawaii, Labor History Archive, ILWU Contract File).

17. "Housing Report" (Report delivered at the twentieth convention of ILWU Local 142, Honolulu, HI 19-23 Sept. 1994, Center for Labor Education and Research, University of Hawaii, Labor History Archive, ILWU Contract File), p. 1.

ment to aiding displaced workers. Furthermore, the state government has also appeared to follow an implicit policy of expanding employment as gross state product rose and expanding bond-financed public works projects during recessions (unfortunately, during booms as well).

The New Deal came late to Hawaii and has operated in a much different historical and cultural context from that on the mainland: one of prosperity rather than depression, one of aloha rather than narrow self-interest.

RECENT PLANTATION CLOSURES

Beginning in 1992, declining employment in agriculture was accompanied by a series of plantation closures. This presented a different set of problems to all concerned with the problem of dislocated workers. Closures had to be negotiated between the union and the company. The state often had to intervene as a partner in retraining and, in one instance, as a loan guarantor. Ultimately, workers on these plantations had to decide whether or not to accept wage concessions in order to continue working. Workers also had to seriously assess their future and decide what type of career and retraining they wanted to have. What has begun to emerge from these closures is the realization that a way of life is ending, with no clear alternative available. The result has been anxiety and stress for the workers involved and soul searching for many policymakers and residents.

Prior to 1992, the last major plantation shut down was Puna Sugar 10 years earlier. The company and the ILWU negotiated an agreement that led to 3300 acres of land being turned over to former employees. The land was to be transferred in five-acre lots; however, ultimately, the land was turned over in one-acre lots to former Puna employees who wanted it along with some major earth-moving equipment from the plantation and $2 million for infrastructure development. Consequently, these workers could develop small farms that grew coffee, papaya, truck-garden crops, and flowers. Those who did not want the land received the value of the land in cash. Many employees had previous experience outside of the plantation in agriculture. When these employees were polled by state government officials about the type of training they wanted, "strong interest was indicated for training in marketing, production, fertilization, disease, weed control, and financing."[18] The state appropriated supplemental funds to the state Extension Service, the University of Hawaii's local community college, and the Hawaii Employment Service to carry out supplemental training. Although no follow-up study was done, anecdotal evidence suggests that many former Puna employees successfully entered diversified agriculture and the tourist industry or moved on to other plantations.

In contrast to this relatively benign ending, the most recent plantation shutdowns on the Big Island of Hawaii have been far more difficult.

18. State of Hawaii, Department of Labor and Industrial Relations, "A Study of Displaced Sugar Workers Focuses on Puna Sugar Co., Ltd.," Dec. 1982, p. 10.

These shutdowns occurred in some of the most isolated parts of Hawaii, with little alternative employment available. These plantations, as federal judge Lloyd King described one, functioned as a "quasi-government" that supplied housing, utilities, and medical service.[19] This in turn meant that these services also had to be transferred from a plantation to other agencies.

Perhaps the most difficult closure was that of Hamakua Sugar, the second-largest plantation in the state, which in 1992 announced it would shut down after a final harvest in 1993. Hamakua went through a long and agonizing bankruptcy proceeding. As the union described it,

The situation at Hamakua Sugar is entirely different. It is a disorderly liquidation forced by bankruptcy. Hamakua Sugar will be shut down in March [1993] and the sugar crop will be left in the fields. The company has no money to pay severance benefits owed to the workers under the union contract. Medical coverage with Hamakua Infirmary will end and there will be no company to run the housing.[20]

The short-term remedy was to allow the plantation to complete its final harvest.

In a complicated arrangement, the bankruptcy court allowed the harvest to go forward after the state agreed to guarantee the loan for operating expenses. Workers voted on a concession contract that essentially gave them a 5 percent production pay raise and a 20 percent share in the profits if a profit did occur. The clinic has been transformed into the Hamakua Health Center and is run as a not-for-profit corporation. Fortunately, the last harvest was profitable.

Unfortunately, the problem of housing for the 430 families who lived in six main camps at the plantation has not been resolved. With no other private or government entities willing to take over the camps, the ILWU formed the nonprofit Hamakua Housing Corporation. It has secured the initial funds necessary to keep the infrastructure operating. The substandard condition of these camps also presents enormous obstacles. Proposals concerning the turnover of the camps to Hamakua Housing Corporation will be decided in court. As the union has reported, "The non-profit corporation could fail under the weight of physical, legal, political, or internal problems."[21] Currently the situation appears to have stabilized, and residents are working on long-term plans.

The closure of Hilo Coast Processing Company during this same period presented different problems. The company's owner, C. Brewer, wanted to renegotiate contract provisions concerning severance pay and medical coverage. These negotiations did lead ultimately to severance pay being awarded, continued medical coverage, and retiree benefits. In addition, the company has offered one- to five-acre plots rent free for five years; former employees could engage in diversified agriculture on the plots. Most of these workers had bought

19. "Judge Rules on Hamakua Case," *Honolulu Advertiser*, 16 Dec. 1994.
20. "What's Ahead for the ILWU in 1993," *Voice of the ILWU*, p. 3 (Dec. 1992).
21. "Housing Report," p. 3.

their own homes through a union program. As their unemployment benefits end, it is unknown whether these workers can meet their payments without further assistance.

These closings can be compared with what happened on the island of Lanai. In 1993, Castle & Cooke, which own Dole Pineapple, phased out all pineapple operations on Lanai. These operations were the major center of Hawaii's pineapple production. At the same time, the company was developing major resort hotels on the island. It appeared natural that the workers on the former plantations would get jobs in the tourism industry. It appeared natural, at least to everyone except the agricultural workers involved. For most of these workers, English was a second language, and culturally they were not prepared for the type of work that the service industry demanded. For example, many workers came from cultures where it was impolite for someone to look directly at another person when they were speaking. The ILWU funded a pilot class on getting hired in the tourist industry before the shutdown announcement.

Subsequently, a state grant made a full-scale training program possible. An important part of the training was an orientation to the tourist industry that encouraged pineapple workers to consider hotel employment. As Honorata Nefalar, a twenty-year employee, explained, "I gained confidence in myself. . . . I'm not afraid to face people now. In fact, I think a lot of people learned a lot of social skills from the classes. It's cute to walk up to old Filipino workers who say, 'Hello, how are you?' "[22] As Nefalar indicates, many of these workers simply had cultural problems with the face-to-face encounters found in service jobs. For example, almost all plantation workers grew up speaking pidgin, a dialect of English that is difficult for outsiders to understand. In addition, they grew up in tightly knit plantation villages where strangers were rare, especially wealthy white strangers. Thus the curriculum integrated literacy training, English as a second language, and the vocabulary of the hotel industry along with skill modules on various aspects of the hotel industry.

The Lanai workers also maintained their traditional housing contract. The ILWU, the Lanai Company, and Lanai Resort Partners signed an agreement that covered 280 rental units in five housing projects. The agreement determined rents based on size and condition of the rental units. (Rents range from $13 to $650 a month.) It also placed the rental housing program under the administration of a joint union-company housing committee. The housing committee, composed of four union members, four management members, and an unaffiliated community representative, administers the written agreement, makes housing assignments based on seniority, and establishes conditions for eviction. The agreement also fixed rents for retirees within a range of $13.50 to $98.35 a month.

22. Cited in "Lanai Pineapple Workers 'Graduate' to Hotel Work," *Voice of the ILWU*, p. 3 (Mar. 1991).

The shutdown of O'ahu Sugar was also orderly, and the union was able to negotiate a severance allowance, a moving allowance, and continuation of the medical plan for six months. Worker education, retraining, and housing relocation were financed from a state grant. The problem of housing has largely been left unresolved both here and for the planned Wailua shutdown in 1996 (also on Oahu). The difficulties in negotiating housing for these workers arises because real estate development is planned for these lands, with homes selling at $500,000 and up in nearby communities. At O'ahu Sugar, the housing was turned over to the city of Honolulu largely so that the company could avoid any liability for housing.

The ILWU has formed the Ewa Housing Foundation to raise funds and operate 84 rental units for the elderly. Many of these units are occupied by retirees from O'ahu Sugar. The ILWU has also participated in a project by the city of Honolulu to rehabilitate and sell to ILWU members and pensioners houses in three plantation villages. This project was planned for residents who had had jobs and incomes, all of whom were displaced by the shutdown. The ILWU is now advocating relief programs for those unable to find adequate employment.

At Ka'u, also on the Big Island, sugar production is scheduled to shut down in 1996. Housing will continue to be provided for five years at standard rents ($39.20 to $58.80 per month). After that time, housing will be sold to tenants at 20 percent below market value. Most have already bought their housing. In addition, there is an Agricultural Land Program for Displaced Workers. Under this program, workers will pay no rent for five years on leases that run year to year. Up to 15 acres is provided for raising livestock and five acres for nonlivestock farms. Many details remain to be worked out at Ka'u, which is in the least populated part of the state. One problem is that plantation workers do not generally have experience with small-scale agriculture.

Although each shutdown has been different and those involved with them have had to confront many different challenges, there has been a common general approach. First, the closures were negotiated, thereby bringing together the union, the company, and state and local government. Beginning in 1994, all parties in these negotiations have addressed the twin problems of jobs and housing for displaced workers. Second, reasonable retraining has been established which meets displaced workers' desires and the demand for their services in the area. Third, the union is strongly committed to work through the problem of housing even though it has not always been completely successful. The main problem with these closures has been the slow growth of the economy, whose condition is partly a result of the scale of these closures.

ALOHA?

"Aloha" means both hello and good-bye. In an ironic sense, bidding aloha to the plantations and the workers who built them can mean good-bye to an old system and hello to a new system at the same time. The reason for this is that these closures have the potential to destroy the communities and culture that sustain the current social consensus about what should be done about them. If plantation closures in Hawaii have not followed the pattern that factory, mill, and mine closures have followed on the mainland, they may yet do so. As one observer noted, almost gleefully,

> With the decline of Hamakua Sugar, we are seeing the end of more than an industry. We are bidding aloha to a political power base spawned by the labor movement and rooted in a way of life. Hawai'i will never be the same, and neither will the power structure within the state legislature.[23]

The ILWU in Hawaii has been effective politically because of the geographical breadth of its membership and the very culture of which it is part. It has been able to exert political influence in rural areas where union strength is normally absent.

The decline of sugar and the rise of tourism have effectively split the county comprising the Big Island of Hawaii into a prosperous west side and an economically troubled east side. This has led to calls to split the county into two separate county governments. It has also led to the election of two Republican county commissioners from the west side of the island. One of them, Jim Rath, has called the Big Island "the most antibusiness . . . county in the world." Referring to east-side political leaders, he has said, "If they can't overtax it, unionize it, and regulate it, they don't want it." Furthermore, he claims that the west side is "supporting an east-side welfare system."[24]

The most recent state elections, in 1994, reflected the same sort of polarization. Business interests backed Republican Patricia Saike while—with one exception—the labor unions backed Democrat Ben Cayetano. A third candidate, Frank Fasi, mayor of Honolulu, formed the Best Party and ran also. Saike essentially called for the end of "mandates," a code word for the islands' prepaid health care system and temporary disability insurance. At the same time, she attempted to win over labor votes with her advertising. Cayetano won with 37 percent of the vote, with Fasi finishing second.

Ironically, nearly forty years after the reform legislature of 1956, the 1995 legislature began to move in precisely the opposite direction. The state's financial problems appear to have been resolved on the basis of interest-group power rather than overall social and economic policy. The budget was balanced through a combination of regressive taxes and spending cuts with no thought given to the economic consequences of these actions. The tourism subsidy was maintained at the same level while higher education was cut. The legislature took the first steps toward reforming workers' compensation at the expense of injured workers. The new budget, although it avoided the worst extremes, has the potential to delay Hawaii's recovery and thereby

23. Chuck Freedman, "Key Institutions: Can You Name the Big Five?" *The Price of Paradise*, ed. Randall W. Roth (Honolulu: Mutual, 1993), 2:82.

24. Quoted in Jeff Barrus, "East Side—West Side," *Hawaii Business*, p. 20 (Nov. 1994).

increase the polarization that already exists. The polarization occurring on the Big Island, however, could be an isolated circumstance.

Other closures are occurring in counties such as Honolulu where alternative jobs exist and it is possible the transition will be a smooth one. On Lanai, the transition to tourism left behind only a small percentage of the displaced workers. Furthermore, despite an estimated budget shortfall of $350 million, the state legislature approved bills for state aid to displaced sugar workers.

If the present course of events appears to be moving in contradictory directions, what of the future?

BACK TO THE FUTURE?

The significance of the plantation closures and the social issues raised by displaced workers lies in what sort of society Hawaii will be in the future. The organization of plantation workers into the ILWU, that union's political agenda, and the power exercised by plantation workers helped pull Hawaii out of colonialism. The closings raise deep questions about land use, water, the political structure, the environment, economic development, housing, and social policy. They also come at a time when no obvious solutions are being presented that are acceptable to all segments of society.

Essentially, the business community has taken up the questions of taxes, regulatory burdens, labor costs, governmental efficiency, and mandatory health care and has decided the burden is too great. It calls for reductions in governmental employment, reform of workers' compensation, an increased subsidy for the tourism industry, reductions in the permitting process, and an end to prepaid health care. Presumably, a healthy business climate will allow small business to be "an engine of growth" for the economy, although such an outcome is dubious at best.

On the other hand, the economic history of Hawaii could be described as a 35-year boom punctuated with occasional returns to normalcy. Most portions of society have benefited from the Hawaiian economy. The poverty rate is about half of what it is on the mainland, and real wealth from development has been spread among both developers and home owners. Unfortunately, the boom that ended in 1991 left many union members with virtually flat real wages. During 1989, inflation on the islands was as high as 9 percent. For example, real wages for workers in the tourism industry began to rise only after the bust because all parties anticipated a boom. Thus, on the one hand, there is a large segment of workers whose living standards have been stagnant or eroded by inflation. On the other hand, there is a large body of employers who appear to want to reduce labor costs. Conflict would appear to be inevitable. Will it be back to the future that existed before 1954?

Or will it be back to a future that is a renewal of 1954? What is needed now is the sort of political program enunciated clearly by the ILWU in 1949, when Hawaii faced a similar situation. Regressive tax increases, public sector layoffs, and budget decisions that affect the economy adversely should be avoided. Bond-financed projects, such as school construction, that do aid the economy should be approved. Where cuts are absolutely necessary, the savings should be weighed against the economic impact as well as the services that government provides. A return to this sort of program has long-term benefits for all and could bring together a social consensus that aids displaced workers and smooths the transition out of plantation agriculture.

Can Hawaii's experience contribute anything that will benefit others who struggle with the problems of structural unemployment? One point, which would please many conservatives, is that individual states can successfully cope with many of the problems with displaced workers by employing traditional values. That success, however, rests on a New Deal social structure that includes strong unions that can raise the standard of living of workers in the service sector; a big government that aids in retraining and housing and also uses fiscal policy to affect the economy; a traditional culture of social solidarity that leads to a consensus in which people believe that these measures should be enacted; and, of course, a sector or sectors that are creating jobs that displaced workers can move into. All of these require conscious action, yet some of them are diametrically opposed to a large body of conventional wisdom. Hopefully, Hawaii's successes will be noticed and incorporated into other states' activities while other states' failures will not be imported into Hawaii. Perhaps all that Hawaii can ultimately offer is wisdom: Hawaii aloha.

Dislocation Policies in the USA: What Should We Be Doing?

By ROSS KOPPEL and ALICE HOFFMAN

ABSTRACT: This article examines whether retraining helps dislocated or displaced workers find new jobs or receive comparable pay. Dislocated or displaced workers are experienced workers who are dismissed due to work-site closings or significant downsizings. The authors compare dislocated workers who received retraining to dislocated workers who did not receive retraining. They find that retraining fails to improve the probability that workers will get new jobs, get full-time jobs, get higher pay, receive decent benefits, experience acceptable working conditions, have reasonable commute times, or get new jobs with a future, that is, with reasonable security in continued employment.

Ross Koppel (Ph.D., sociology) is president of Social Research Corporation, Wyncote, Pennsylvania. He conducts research and consults on work, research methodology, training, and new technology. He also teaches sociology at the University of Pennsylvania.

Alice Hoffman is a research affiliate at Bryn Mawr College. From 1966 to 1986, she was on the faculty at the Pennsylvania State University; from 1987 to 1992, she was director of the Dislocated Worker Unit in the Pennsylvania Department of Labor and Industry.

> I am a former steelworker. I worked at U.S. Steel ... for 21 years. After the mill shut down ... many of us made a mistake: we chose job retraining. ... After job retraining there were no jobs to fit the training.
> —Dislocated Fairless Hills steelworker

> When we first came [to the job center], we were told that we had better be prepared to take $5 an hour if we wanted jobs in this area.
> —Civilian employee at Williams Air Force Base

Each year about 2 million American workers are dismissed from their jobs because their work sites are closed or greatly downsized. While there are many reasons for these mass layoffs, the primary solution proposed for these unneeded workers is that they should seek training to improve their skills.

This article examines the value of current training efforts for experienced workers who are dismissed due to work-site closings or significant downsizings—worker dislocation or displacement. The law defines dislocated and displaced workers as individuals with three or more years of experience at a workplace who have been laid off and are unlikely to return to their previous industry or occupation.[1] Training is an attractive solution to worker dislocations because both liberals and conservatives believe in training as a form of self-improvement, because most current training is cheap, and perhaps because training is a seemingly positive action that does not raise questions about employment policy. Training is seen as the route to a flexible workforce, enabling dislocated workers to shift with market changes and technological developments.

Training dislocated workers thus responds to a variety of needs: offering hope to workers, an active response by government, a sense of relief for former employers but without their incurring obligations or expenses, and the promise of a more competitive workforce for communities and for the nation. In addition, training for dislocated workers is one of the few social programs that survived recent federal cuts.

We, however, do not join the training bandwagon. Our data and those of others do not support the value of training as presently provided, and we are skeptical of the current political proposals that promote voucher systems, where workers are supposedly free to select the training provider of their choice. While seemingly a good, market-oriented idea, vouchers are likely to reduce much of the already minimal guidance workers now receive. Workers unfamiliar with training institutions, labor market needs, and training requirements will enter a market of slick advertisements and cutthroat proprietary schools. Regulation is often nonexistent, and placement data are deeply flawed or simply not available. Worse, as we demonstrate, current training efforts do not help the vast majority of dislocated workers. Current training proposals make no improvements but perpetuate the failures of the existing system. This system is especially disappointing in light of growing worker dislocation

---

1. In this article, we use the term "dislocated" to reflect both dislocated and displaced workers. There is a distinction in the technical literature that we need not worry about here.

and thus of training as its putative solution.

OUR QUESTIONS

While training appears to be among the most enlightened policies for dislocated workers, training as currently provided does not appear to be the most effective solution. It may not even be a solution at all.[2] Despite the broad faith in training for dislocated workers, both researchers and dislocated workers find that existing programs do not lead to jobs with replacement wages.[3] Our data and many similar studies reveal that job training programs often do not lead to any jobs.

In our research, we compare dislocated workers who received training to dislocated workers who did not receive training. If training works, we would expect that, when compared to those without training, those with training would be more likely to get new jobs, get full-time jobs, get new jobs with a future (that is, with reasonable security in continued employment), secure higher pay, receive decent benefits, experience acceptable working conditions, and not be forced to commute dramatically longer than they were required to by the old jobs.

Using these and other criteria, we find that, surprisingly, post-layoff training or education as currently provided does not work any better than does no post-layoff training or education. Training for the dislocated workers we studied did not make a difference in finding a job, in wages, in job security, or even in working conditions or commute time.

OUR STUDY

We conducted almost 500 interviews with workers from two sites of dislocation: the USX Corporation's Fairless Hills steel mill in Pennsylvania and the Williams Air Force Base in Chandler, Arizona. Our research differs from most studies of dislocated workers in a fundamental way: it draws its information from the affected workers themselves rather than from the agencies that attempt to provide assistance. It is subject to the workers' misrepresentations and misunderstandings of the helping agencies' efforts. On the other hand, this study avoids the inherent biases of attempting to demonstrate the efficacy of the helping agencies.

While the subjects of our research were dislocated workers and not welfare recipients, the conclusions have some application to both populations because the helping agencies and schools typically serve both populations. In fact, the programs were designed with the disadvantaged populations as the main target of planned interventions.

SALIENCE OF DISLOCATION AND TRAINING

Worker dislocations are increasing; downsizing continues to trend up. Since World War II, each reces-

2. Walter Corson et al., *International Trade and Worker Dislocation: Evaluation of the Trade Adjustment Assistance Program* (Princeton, NJ: Mathematica Policy Research, 1993).

3. U.S., Department of Labor, Office of the Chief Economist, *What's Working and What's Not: A Summary of Research on the Economic Impacts of Employment and Training Programs* (Washington, DC: Department of Labor, 1995).

sion has left higher rates of long-term unemployment. Of those who had held their jobs for three years or more and were laid off in the recession of 1973-75, 51 percent lost their jobs permanently. Of those laid off in the downturn of 1981-82, 64 percent lost their jobs permanently. Of those laid off in the recession of 1990-92, 85 percent lost their jobs permanently.[4]

The dislocation rate, moreover, is not confined to marginal firms. In the last 15 years, the *Fortune* 500 companies, by themselves, have dismissed more than 340,000 workers a year. These companies now employ about 10 percent of the workforce, half of their 20 percent share of workers two decades ago.

As is evident in the business pages of any newspaper and in the statements of corporate leaders, large-scale layoffs are a basic corporate strategy. Companies compete to demonstrate their mastery of what Labor Secretary Robert Reich calls the butcher metaphors: cutting to the bone, cutting out the fat, getting lean. Of course, not all workers are slashed; those remaining in the euphemism-generation industry are working overtime. Mass layoffs are called downsizing, restructuring, right-sizing, or reengineering.[5]

In addition to general and often counterproductive corporate trends involving mass layoffs,[6] several factors encourage or facilitate worker dislocation:

1. Even when the jobs remain in a firm or locale, they are often shifted to workers with lower pay and fewer benefits. Manpower, Inc., a temporary employment firm, is now the nation's largest employer, hiring 1.5 million workers each day. The number of temporary workers has tripled in just one decade, to 2.1 million. Also, many tasks are routinely "outsourced" (another euphemism), sometimes to former employees—at 40-70 percent of their former wages and with fewer if any benefits.

2. Unemployment figures are softened by the armies of former employees who have set up shop for themselves or who are obliged to work in jobs that do not use their skills (underemployment). Part-time work—especially part-time work that is involuntary—has increased dramatically in the past several years; of 22 million part-time workers, 4.5 million sought but did not secure full-time work.

3. Technology, not surprisingly, is a major contributor to dislocation and a major impetus for training as the solution to unemployment. Technology has long been the promised killer of jobs, but this impact has been mixed with the millions of jobs it has created. Many observers came to believe that technology was just a one-edged and friendly sword that created far more jobs than it cut. The other edge, however, is becoming sharper—exactly as logic and productivity gains would predict.[7]

---

4. U.S., Department of Commerce, July 1992. The specific dates of the recessions were November 1973–March 1975, July 1981–November 1982, and July 1990–June 1992.

5. The U.S. Department of Labor is currently sponsoring sessions titled "Responsible Restructuring."

6. See the work of economist Eileen Appelbaum, Economic Policy Institute, 1995.

7. Consider the historical example of the sector that most benefited from technology-

4. Automation, a form of technology, has long held such high promise and such low realization that it came to be viewed as a hollow threat. Reports on the paperless office lined the shelves. But no longer. Now automation—in the form of, for example, automated teller machines, voice mail, automatic data transfer, digital everything—is seriously affecting service jobs. Automation is finally realizing its potential, especially in the occupational sector—service—that holds most of the jobs and almost all of the job growth.

5. Global competition and multinational corporations oblige American workers to compete with every other country's labor force. India, just one example, illustrates how high-tech and service jobs have found succor abroad. Hundreds of American firms, such as IBM, Texas Instruments, and Hewlett-Packard, are the new virtual viceroys, with assembly plants in the Bangalore area and other parts of the subcontinent. These hardware companies are following the digital raj of American banks, which have long used Indian software writers. In fact, during just one recent fiscal year, 1993-94, software revenues in India jumped 55 percent.[8]

6. The residual of the English empire also helps in other ways. The well-educated workers of Ireland have been servicing American insurance companies' clients for decades. Each day, planes leave New York City's JFK airport with insurance files and claim forms. Irish workers write letters and process forms. The planes return to American shores each evening with completed paperwork.

7. Employers are aware of their increasing leverage. Recruiters offer lower wages but demand more experience and education.[9] Offices are peppered with empty desks, and Rolodexes spin more freely, relieved of entries for former colleagues and friends. Job insecurity and the problems of survivors occupy water cooler conversations and employee assistance plan counseling sessions.

8. The reduced power and scope of unions—now only 11 percent of the private sector workforce is unionized—facilitate worker dismissals and the use of contingent labor. The labor market is also influenced by the reduced emphasis on the military-industrial sector associated with the Cold War. Consolidation of military-industrial firms and elimination of their jobs have placed many high-tech, high-pay workers on the market.

9. New office designs save space and avoid embarrassing questions. Emerging offices will offer hotel-like arrangements, where offices and desks are scheduled by the hour. Employees are provided file cabinets and drawers at a central location for their papers and personal effects. Dismissed employees will leave no trace.

---

induced improved productivity, direct agricultural production. It used to employ 80 percent of the workforce; now it uses 2.5 percent.

8. The more complete explanation for this extraordinary rise is that new laws prohibited American firms from temporary import of Indian software engineers. Thus even more work than usual was obtained from Indian software writers in India.

9. Peter T. Kilborn, "In New Work World, Employers Call All the Shots," *New York Times*, 3 July 1995.

For these and other reasons, worker dislocation is growing. Moreover, the focus of dislocation is shifting. Mass layoffs used to be a phenomenon of the manufacturing sector and of blue-collar workers. But in the 1980s and 1990s, dislocations have increasingly affected middle- and upper-middle-class workers.[10] In addition, older workers are now as affected as younger workers. Equally significant, as real wages decline for so many American workers, families have diminished abilities to absorb economic shocks and to spend time in training or job searches.[11]

BACKGROUND TO OUR STUDY

From their inception, federal programs to aid the unemployed were predicated on the idea that long-term unemployment is caused by some deficiency in the worker.[12] Therefore the remedy was and is to correct that deficiency. Perhaps the worker lacks the appropriate technological skill; if so, skill training should be provided. Perhaps the worker is unable to speak English well; English-as-a-second-language programs were developed. If the worker was not able to read directions, literacy programs were created. The focus was on the individual, and the solutions were individual. The fact that the causes of dislocation are corporate and societal was and is not addressed in the three major programs for dislocated workers.

Three programs

By the 1990s, in addition to unemployment compensation, there were three basic programs to assist the jobless created by three pieces of legislation: the Trade Readjustment Act/Trade Adjustment Assistance (TRA/TAA), the Job Training Partnership Act (JTPA), and the Workers Adjustment Retraining Act (WARN).

TRA/TAA, passed in 1974, compensates workers who lose employment as a result of free trade policy. These programs were amended in 1988 to emphasize workers' participation in training. They were further augmented by laws related to the North American Free Trade Agreement. In cases where it can be demonstrated that employment loss was due to foreign competition, workers are entitled to an additional 52 weeks of unemployment benefits.

In reality, however, researchers (e.g., Corson et al.) have found few differences in employment and earnings between those who took training and those who did not, suggesting that there was no "strong evidence that the training had a substantial positive effect."[13] That is not surprising; the law, as implemented, often defeats its intentions. One prime example is that dislocated workers are almost always required to take training

10. Bruce Nussbaum, "Downward Mobility: Corporate Castoffs Are Struggling Just to Stay in the Middle Class," *Business Week*, 23 Mar. 1992, p. 57.

11. Aaron Bernstein and Wendy Zellner, "The Wage Squeeze: Productivity and Profits Are up a Lot; Paychecks Aren't; Is the Economy Changing?" *Business Week*, 17 July 1995, pp. 54-61.

12. The Manpower Development and Training Act of 1962 and the Trade Adjustment Assistance Act of 1974. The latter was to compensate workers for income lost due to import competition.

13. Corson et al., *International Trade and Worker Dislocation*, p. xxi.

in fields different from their former employment. This rule, intended to block redundant or superfluous training, effectively prevents workers from building on existing skills. As a result, workers do not improve subsequent earnings or build on career ladders.

Perhaps more destructive to the intent of the law, previous administrations defined foreign competition in the most restrictive ways possible. At the steel mill we studied, securing TRA benefits required a lengthy appeal and re-appeal process. While eventually successful, the certification came nearly two years after the layoffs. By that time, most of the dislocated workers had already suffered two years of unemployment and had exhausted their unemployment benefits. Many were difficult to reach with information about the new benefits; many could not afford to commence a training program.

JTPA replaced the Comprehensive Employment and Training Act (CETA), which had provided training for the unemployed and had created jobs in the public sector. During the Carter administration, rising unemployment created pressure to increase the available jobs under CETA. The number of slots was doubled, resulting in some ineligible enrollments that provided grist for investigative journalism and created a climate in which the Reagan administration decided to abolish the program. However, bipartisan congressional advocates changed the program and substituted a new title: the Job Training Partnership Act of 1982. JTPA represented a major policy shift from a program to create jobs to a program designed to meet the labor market needs of employers. Its value for dislocated workers has also been questioned because it emphasizes service to the poor and disadvantaged.[14]

In reality, JTPA programs, often dominated by local businesspersons or for-profit training schools, sometimes do not represent the best interests of the unemployed. Many training institutions teach skills that are not needed for jobs that do not exist. Some businesses offer months of on-the-job training with subsidized wages for skills that can be learned in little time.

WARN legislation mandates that advance notice be given to employees when a company is closing or is going to lay off a large number of its workers. Its purpose is to give workers 60 days' notice before termination of employment. In reality, however, WARN's promises are less generous than they seem.

WARN legislation was altered significantly from its original form. More bluntly, WARN was crippled at birth. The 60 days' notice as set forth by the legislation does not allow sufficient time for the social and employment agencies to organize the needed services for dislocated workers. Also, many far-reaching exemptions were added to WARN that allow employers to lay off workers without notice. Recent studies suggest that many employers simply ignore WARN rules.[15]

14. Sar A. Levitan, Peter E. Carlson, and Isaac Shapiro, *Protecting American Workers: An Assessment of Government Programs* (Washington, DC: Bureau of National Affairs, 1986), p. 47.

15. Work by John Addison and McKinley Blackburn, cited in Sylvia Nasar, "Layoff Law Is Having Slim Effect: Plant Closing Rule Full of Exceptions," *New York Times*, 3 Aug. 1993.

In sum, the three programs that provide assistance to dislocated workers offer a patchwork of legislative initiatives administered by a variety of agencies with differing goals and interests. While programs may not directly conflict with each other, requirements are confusing and funding is often capricious. Workers and even service providers are frequently uncertain of the laws and regulations. Information appears scarce and is often misleading; a significant proportion of workers rely on informal, sometimes ill-informed networks for training and funding information.

Schools and training institutions often recruit dislocated workers with well-honed advertisements that do not reflect job market realities. Workers seldom receive appropriate guidance about local labor markets or about job experience requirements. While there are undoubtedly thousands of honest schools and training institutions that serve dislocated workers, many exist primarily to collect government training funds or private fees.

DISLOCATION FROM TWO SITES

We studied steelworkers laid off from USX's steel mill in Fairless Hills and civilian employees laid off from Williams Air Force Base. Both locations had warned of their closings for more than a year, and both had already dismissed most of the workers at the time of our interviews in 1993 and 1994. Both locations were venerable institutions that had offered good benefits and average or better wages.

At Fairless and at Williams, we conducted 25- to 40-minute telephone interviews with former workers. At Fairless, the final sample of 174 was randomly drawn from the 2500 steelworkers who had worked at the plant. At Chandler, the sample of 128 was randomly drawn from 700 civilian workers who had worked at the base.[16] In both cases, we had previously established relationships with union officials, job assistance personnel, local and state JTPA officials, unemployment insurance office staff, the labor-management committee (at Williams), the union-operated job center (at USX), social workers, and others.

FINDINGS: DOES
TRAINING WORK FOR
DISLOCATED WORKERS?

Our two research sites are extraordinary in the degree of assistance provided to the workers who were laid off. The steel mill received special help and grants from the state and federal governments. It had an on-site job center run by the union that offered job search workshops, help with complicated forms, counseling, and a friendly face. The job center coordinated efforts with the local JTPA offices, which referred workers to training, provided assessment tests, and supplied individual funding support. The air force base had a specially funded office, the Job Employment Training Service, on the

16. Seven hundred workers attended the initial base closure meeting. We obtained a list of those attendees. In fact, about 1200 worked at the base. We could not secure the full list of 1200.

base that similarly coordinated services and provided assistance. This office also offered workshops and had trained peer counselors.

At both locations, the workers received special funding and exceptional programs, such as support for training, support for workers while in training, and extra counseling. Also, at both locations, the staffs of the on-site assistance centers were caring, knowledgeable, and familiar with the difficulties faced by the workers. Yet, as our data demonstrate, even under these circumstances, the training provided to the workers seldom made the workers whole again.

We asked seven questions about the worth of training. The first was, Does post-layoff training or education help dislocated workers find jobs? The answer was no. Training or education did not help dislocated workers get new jobs. In both locations, those who took training were no more likely to find reemployment than were those who did not.[17] Also, the effect of training did not differ when controlling for previous wages or for original education level, which has a separate and important effect on job search success.

To examine another measure of training efficacy for getting a job, we asked the workers who took training whether their training helped them find jobs. This is a question about the respondents' perceptions and therefore differs from the preceding analysis, which is a statistical correlation. The answers are equally sobering, especially for the former steelworkers. Only 30 percent of the former USX workers said training was helpful in securing other jobs. Among Williams workers, 57 percent said the training was helpful. In neither case did training receive a rousing endorsement. Moreover, the expected bias would have been in favor of training's efficacy. That is, the workers' desire to feel that they had not wasted their time would probably have biased their answers in favor of showing training to be useful. This finding, thus, is especially strong.

We again emphasize that our two sites represent some of the best opportunities for dislocated workers to receive training and support under the current system of regulations. It is therefore especially noteworthy that training did not result in higher probabilities of finding new work.

The second question we asked about training was whether it helped dislocated workers find full-time as opposed to part-time work. Millions of workers are obliged to accept part-time work when they are seeking full-time work. Presumably, training or education should enable workers to secure full-time work if so desired. However, we found that training did not alter the proportions of dislocated

---

17. At the steel mill, 32 percent of workers enrolled in training or education courses after they were laid off. At the air force base, 41 percent of workers enrolled in training or education courses after they were laid off. In both locations, those who took training were no more likely to find reemployment than those who did not. At the steel mill, 65.5 percent of those who took training found jobs. However, almost the same percentage, 61.7 percent, of those who did not take training also found jobs. At the air force base, 68.0 percent of those who took training found jobs; a slightly higher percentage, 77.8 percent, of those who did not take training also found jobs.

workers who accepted part-time versus full-time work.[18]

The issue of part-time work is seldom examined in studies of worker dislocation. This oversight is serious. At Fairless, for example, 63 percent of the dislocated workers found jobs. But 20 percent of those with jobs were employed part-time. A little arithmetic reveals that only half of the dislocated workers are employed full-time.

The third question we examined was whether the dislocated workers who enroll in post-layoff training or education get jobs that pay adequately both in percentage terms compared to the previous wages and in dollars. The answer is that there was no relationship at either site between taking training and subsequent wages.

Without taking training into consideration, the pre-layoff wages at Williams were $14.08 an hour and the post-layoff wages were $10.17. At Fairless Hills, the pre-layoff wages were $13.78 an hour and the post-layoff wages were $9.63. When taking training into account, the differentials were not altered meaningfully. The mean post-layoff wages for Fairless Hills workers with later training were $9.27 an hour. That is $0.53 less than the mean post-layoff wages for Fairless Hills workers without later training. Similarly, the mean post-layoff wages for Williams workers with later training were $9.91 an hour, $0.42 less than the mean post-layoff wages for Williams workers without later training.

Part of the explanation is that dislocation is a great leveler; those with higher original wages will be brought down more than will those with lower original wages.

Moreover, these losses underestimate the actual losses of the dislocated workers because

— only those with jobs have wages (these data do not reflect the "zero" wages of those without jobs);
— the take-home pay of part-time workers and those without overtime will be significantly less than it was before the dislocation;
— these data do not reflect the loss of benefits or other perks; and
— many work sites start reducing wages three years before they actually close,[19] and thus pre-post wage comparisons underestimate the real loss.

The fourth question we investigated was whether post-layoff training or education helped dislocated workers get new jobs with decent benefits. Again the answer was no. There was no positive relationship between post-layoff training and subsequent job benefits. In general, most workers saw their benefits deteriorate or evaporate with new jobs. At Williams, only 9 percent of all workers said they had better benefits in

18. At Fairless, 19 percent of those with training worked part-time compared to 21 percent of those without training who worked part-time—a meaningless difference. At Williams, the difference was equally trivial: 9 percent of those with training and 14 percent of those without training accepted part-time work.

19. Louis Jacobson, Robert LaLonde, and Daniel Sullivan, *The Costs of Worker Dislocation* (Kalamazoo, MI: W. E. Upjohn Institute for Employment Research, 1993).

their subsequent jobs. Almost half—45 percent—said that their new jobs offered no benefits, and 16.5 percent said they now received fewer benefits.

Among Fairless workers, only 5 percent said that their benefits improved. Almost two-thirds of those with new jobs said the benefits were worse. A third reported that they received no benefits, and 12 percent—including some workers with working spouses—had no health insurance.

Our fifth question was, Does post-layoff training or education help dislocated workers get new jobs with acceptable working conditions? Again there was no training advantage. Among both USX and Williams employees, there was no difference in relation to whether or not dislocated workers took training.

On a different note, although training did not influence later working conditions, we did find that former USX employees generally enjoyed better working conditions in their new jobs: fully 77 percent reported that they do not miss the heat (steel is poured at 2700 degrees Fahrenheit), the dust, the asbestos, the confrontational labor relations, or the hours.

Our sixth question was, Does post-layoff training or education help dislocated workers get new jobs that do not require dramatically longer commutes than were required by the old jobs? We found that post-layoff training made no significant difference in travel time.

In our seventh question, we asked the respondents to evaluate the outlook for the jobs they had found after the layoffs. Whether respondents had post-layoff training or education did not affect job security.[20]

DISCUSSION AND CONCLUSION

Our research on two very different sites of worker dislocation indicates that post-layoff training or education as currently provided is not efficacious. Workers who enrolled in training or education programs after dismissal did not do any better than those without additional training or education. Training for the dislocated workers we studied did not make a difference in finding jobs, in wages, in job security, in outlook, in working conditions, or even in commute time. Moreover, our two research sites were extraordinary in their levels of help, support, guidance, and coordination with other agencies. Most dislocated workers receive far less assistance than do the workers at Fairless or Williams. The failure of training to make a difference in our two sites suggests that training at most other plant closings will have even more dismal results.

20. At Williams, 70 percent of the former workers saw an acceptable future for their new jobs, and 30 percent were quite positive. Only 30 percent were pessimistic about their new jobs. Note that 5 percent had already been laid off of their subsequent jobs (these we count in the pessimistic column). At Fairless, 44 percent of the former steelworkers with new jobs said that the outlook for their new jobs was good. This is lower than the 70 percent of former air force base workers who were optimistic and may reflect the lower unemployment rate in Arizona, where the base is located, at the time of the layoffs. Correspondingly, 56 percent of the former steelworkers were pessimistic and saw little hope for their new jobs. As with the air force base workers, 5 percent had already been laid off from new jobs.

What does the research literature say?

As we indicated earlier, most studies of training for dislocated workers are based on interviews with providers of services and training. These studies are inclined toward cheerful and perhaps self-serving results. Also, most researchers are supportive of education and training. Hence even serious and responsible studies of training outcomes typically conclude with caveats such as "the available quantitative evidence . . . [brings] the cost effectiveness of retraining [into] question. Nevertheless, the authors of the evaluation reports reviewed are unanimous in cautioning that the impact of training programs may be understated in their empirical analyses."[21]

However, a recent and comprehensive review of controlled studies and evaluations of short-term training for dislocated workers corroborates our findings. The 1995 U.S. Department of Labor analysis states,

Current evaluations indicate that short-term skills training has not been particularly successful in producing earnings gains for dislocated workers, but the evidence is not entirely conclusive. In three studies, which were effectively random assignments, workers offered relatively short-term training plus job search assistance showed no significant increase in earnings or employment when compared to workers receiving job search assistance alone.[22]

Even more corroboration is found in studies of economic loss from dislocation. A 1993 study by Jacobson et al. found a total lifetime earnings loss of $80,000, 72 percent of which was due to permanently lower wages.[23] Their figure very closely parallels our estimate of wage loss. Similarly, Levitan and Mangum's 1994 report finds that wage losses are often in the range of 24 percent and are higher for those who do not find work in the same industry.[24]

Why do current forms of training fail?

Our basic task, of course, is not to seek parallel findings but to understand why current forms of training for dislocated workers are so ineffective. We offer some reasons.

Short-term training. Current training is almost always short-term. But short-term training is seldom sufficient to help dislocated workers. Dislocated workers, by definition, are experienced. They are also often skilled. It is unlikely that a program lasting only a few months will improve their ability to secure new jobs in difficult labor markets.

On the other hand, longer-term educational efforts that provide more broadly based skills and knowledge appear to be effective for dislocated workers. The skill most needed in high-tech environments is not high

---

21. Duane E. Leigh, *Assisting Displaced Workers* (Kalamazoo, MI: W. E. Upjohn Institute for Employment Research, 1989), p. 142.

22. Department of Labor, *What's Working and What's Not*, p. 53.

23. Jacobson, LaLonde, and Sullivan, *The Costs of Worker Dislocation.*

24. Sar A. Levitan and Stephen L. Mangum, *The Displaced vs. the Disadvantaged: A Necessary Dichotomy?* (Washington, DC: George Washington University, Center for Social Policy Studies, 1994), pp. 6, 7.

tech; it is the ability to learn and make sense of the information provided by the technology. Programs that focus on the technology instead of learning, concepts, and reasoning miss the point. The Department of Labor review states, "A study of dislocated workers, and several which examine older college students, ha[s] found significant positive impacts to long-term training. More general evidence on returns to higher education also suggests that long-term training pays off for some dislocated workers."[25] Longer-term education allows workers to build on their existing skills and to put their experience in broader contexts. Honest educational efforts—for example, at least a year or two at community college—also provide credentials, which can be especially helpful in tight labor markets.

Ignoring labor markets. Many training programs teach skills that are not in demand or that are not marketable without additional experience. No matter how good the training, if the skill is not needed, most graduates will be disappointed. Also, schools and training programs advertise to the most vulnerable. Few dislocated workers are aware of future labor market demand, and it is not reasonable to expect them to be.

Predatory preparatory schools. Many training institutions offer excellent programs with a serious concern for labor demand and placement. Others exist primarily to fleece the federal coffers and personal savings and to dash personal hopes. Regulation is spotty. Some private industry councils are not up to the job of oversight.

Disadvantaged versus dislocated. Most programs for dislocated workers are stepchildren of programs for the disadvantaged. Often the agencies are ill prepared to help those with résumés, skills, and experience.

In 1993, for example, almost 9 million people were unemployed in the nation. The programs discussed here assisted only 164,826 of them, or under 2 percent. Of those 164,826, almost 90 percent (147,000) either were high school graduates or had some post–high school training. Only 17,000 had less than a high school education. Yet most programs are focused on the small fraction with less than a high school education.

No longer just a blue-collar affair. Plant closings and mass layoffs used to be the curse of the working class. No more. A nasty equality has struck the middle and upper middle classes. Because most jobs are now in the white-collar and service sectors, and because technology is aiming at those sectors, traditionally safe jobs will increasingly become vulnerable. Older workers and educated workers are at risk. Whither middle management?

Despite the recent vulnerability of middle-class workers, most training programs for dislocated workers still maintain a blue-collar model of guidance and training. That model is often vestigial. Will former managers or engineers want to be retrained as air conditioning repairmen or truck drivers? Will they be pleased with 30 percent pay cuts or even less job stability than before?

25. Department of Labor, *What's Working and What's Not*, p. 53.

Neglect of the community. Few programs incorporate community-level issues in their plans or solutions. When a plant goes down or when a large number of workers are laid off, the entire community is affected. Small and large businesses fail, businesses that were dependent on the now laid-off workers are themselves endangered. Ironically, it is in these local businesses that the former workers naively expected to find new jobs.

Equally important and seldom studied are effects on and of real estate values. Communities with large layoffs suffer depressed real estate values, which prevent dislocated workers from moving away for employment elsewhere. The workers cannot sell their houses, and so they cannot relocate.

In simple language, a community where there has been a mass layoff is a lousy place to look for work. But that is where the former workers are, and they cannot easily leave.

Poor counseling and guidance. Our two research sites offered some of the best help available. Even at these locations, counseling about options and programs was inconsistent and often poor. At Fairless, only 24 percent of the dislocated workers received any job counseling. At Williams, more than 71 percent received job counseling, but some Williams workers told us that the counseling focused on the need to accept lower wages. Few workers received adequate information on available schools, programs, and job requirements.

Personal costs. When asked to compare their current situations with their expectations at the time of the layoffs, almost all of the workers expressed disappointment, anger, or worse. Few appeared to have been able to predict the impact of the layoffs. At USX, for example, 11 percent of the former workers reported that their children had to drop out of school because the families could not afford tuition or because the families needed the income; 27 percent reported deterioration in health since the layoffs (9 percent felt better).

Comparatively few researchers or evaluators have examined the costs of dislocation in terms of losses to families, downward mobility, loss of credit, loss of property, political alienation, or a worker's worsened self-definition.

In sum, our examination of the help given to dislocated workers shows that the gap between good intentions and failed programs seems particularly wide. Some of the gap is undoubtedly due to the embattled genesis of the enabling legislation. Some is probably due to the American belief that we are each responsible for our destiny, even if that destiny is affected by foreign trade or by others' foolish investment decisions. Whatever the cause, dislocated workers are not being well served by their government.

Only a portion of the dislocated workers who are eligible for services were actually reached with services. When training for new jobs was successfully completed, however, it was often in fields with few or no job opportunities. Few programs demonstrated concern for the financial and psychological strain of job loss and subsequent retraining.

WHAT WOULD WORK BETTER?

We do not conclude that training programs for dislocated workers are useless. Training is valuable if it is focused on skills that are in demand. Longer-term education is needed if dislocated workers are to be prepared for new careers and for the expertise required in advanced economies. Genuine education, moreover, has been shown to be effective with dislocated workers, a claim that cannot be made for short-term training.

Our recommendations to improve training include the following:

1. Training should be targeted to fields where there are proven job opportunities with adequate incomes. It is both wasteful and callous to offer job training for nonexistent jobs or jobs that do not pay living wages.

2. Training should be long enough and comprehensive enough to provide realistic new career paths. Training should be accompanied by income support that makes that training economically feasible.

3. It must be recognized that many dislocated workers are increasingly white-collar. Guidance and educational programs must reflect their needs and abilities.

4. Dislocated workers require programs that build on previous work experience and education. These are different foci from those that are appropriate for the disadvantaged.

5. Help with child care and transportation seems simplistic, but real-life problems of child care and the like can vitiate the most elaborate reemployment strategy.

6. Better oversight of training referrals and of training institutions is desperately needed. Evaluations should measure job outcomes after more than 13 weeks. Evaluations should follow program graduates for 18 months. Evaluations should include information on both trainees and their employers.

7. No amount of training or assistance will help if there are no jobs. Economic development and job development policies must be considered. Job creation and community-level issues need to be included in efforts to deal with worker dislocation. Not all problems can be solved at the individual level. New résumés or better phone techniques do not generate jobs in a community. The problems are economic and social; economic and social solutions must be addressed. In this context, a standby public service employment program is one effective tool for addressing the problems of the dislocated while providing useful services that would otherwise be neglected.

8. The dissemination of information to dislocated workers should occur at a much earlier stage than it currently does so that programs may begin while income support is still available. To facilitate this goal, WARN must be both extended and enforced.

9. The current minimum wage encourages employment of low-skill and low-tech workers. These workers are most vulnerable to dislocation and dependency. The minimum wage should be raised to a level that will sustain a family—an increase of at least 35 percent.

10. Outreach efforts, including radio and television public service announcements, should be used more

extensively to increase participation rates in effective programs.

11. Vocational and career counseling must be improved because workers and service providers are often ill informed.

12. Funding levels and allocation formulas are inadequate to meet demand. Amendments to JTPA (the Economic Dislocation and Economic Adjustment Act), for example, reach only about a tenth of dislocated workers.

The apparent failure of training for dislocated workers is not addressed in the proposed plans of either political party. The patchwork of programs and policies, the lack of coordination, the short-term focus, and the capricious nature of funding waste resources and people's lives. Continued structural change and demilitarization of the economy will increase the number of dislocated workers. The problem of ineffective training is growing.

Dislocated workers are traditionally people with good work histories and skills. Their job losses are due to factors out of their control. Even in a frugal era, we can recognize that a failure to address their needs will incur long-term costs to society, costs that may be avoided by effective and timely policy.

Dislocation Policies in Western Europe: Past, Present, and Future

By THOMAS SAMUEL EBERLE

ABSTRACT: Within the past two decades, the "brutal American management methods," which caused a national upheaval against Firestone in the 1970s, have become common practice in Swiss and other European corporations. These practices include global sourcing, dislocation of work to Third World countries, and workforce reductions by rationalization. In the middle of this general trend, Volkswagen in Germany set a countermodel: by introducing the four-day workweek, it redistributed work in the existing workforce, increased the sense of solidarity, and avoided layoffs. Volkswagen's actions added new fire to the heated European debate on how to deal with unemployment: by further deregulation or by work-time reduction and redistribution of work? In Europe, quite in contrast to the United States, an ongoing tension exists between modernization and the traditional culture, a tension manifest in a deep schism within the population.

Thomas Samuel Eberle teaches sociology at the University of St. Gallen, Switzerland. He is the former vice president of the Swiss Sociological Association and served as an editor of the association's newsletter and of its publishing company, SEISMO. His sociological practice activities include the training of managers, social workers, project managers, and others. He has written on the topics of the sociology of work, culture, communication, and methodology.

IN 1978, when Firestone Tire and Rubber Company shut down its factory in Pratteln BL, Switzerland, laying off hundreds of workers, there was a national outcry blaming the ruthless American style of management. Thirteen years later, when the prestigious Swiss company Swissair dislocated work to a Third World country to cut costs, there was little protest. The Swiss had quickly learned to accept ferocious measures of rationalization as a means of survival in an ever more competitive world economy and to live with a formerly unknown rate of unemployment.

Can cultural brands of capitalism survive in an increasingly globalized world economy?

FIRESTONE SHUTS DOWN
ITS SWISS PLANT IN 1978:
THE STORY OF A SHOWDOWN

Switzerland is a placid country with a long democratic tradition and an industrious, highly qualified workforce. The Swiss are fairly pragmatic; they try to reach consensus rather than engage in ideological conflicts that might result in political confrontation and stalemate. This mind-set can be found in nearly all areas of their lives. On the political level, it is manifested in the federalistic structure of the nation, with 26 fairly autonomous states. It is also seen in the way all major political parties take part in the government, leaving no significant political opposition. Also, it is manifest in political referendums, where the people vote, several times per year, to accept or refuse a modification of the constitution or a specific new law proposed by the parliament. On the cultural level, the Swiss managed to weld together four different cultures with four different languages (German, French, Italian, and Rhaeto-Romansh).

On the economic level, the pragmatic mentality is best expressed by the special industrial relations between the labor unions and the employers' association, which stand in sharp contrast to those in other European countries. There was only one general strike in the country, for five days in 1918, after World War I—an outstanding event that is prominently marked in Swiss history books. In 1937, however, the mighty employers' association of the machine and metal industry and all major labor unions signed a peace treaty in which they agreed to handle disagreements in good faith, to accept a formal multistage procedure of conflict resolution, and to firmly exclude strikes. This peace treaty, made in a time of economic and political crisis—Fascist Italy to the south and Nazi Germany to the north and soon to the east, in Austria, and west, in France, as well—has been renewed ever since. If a company, a branch, or an industry was in trouble, the labor unions and the employers' association searched to reach a mutual agreement on how to share the burden.

In this spirit, there were many Swiss entrepreneurs who, during the economic depression following the oil crisis in 1973, suffered tremendous losses in trying to save the lives of their companies and to avoid layoffs. When Firestone announced its shutdown of its Swiss production plant in 1978, putting 600 workers out of their jobs, this was perceived as a profit-obsessed American management decision lacking all social responsibility. Many headlines in the Swiss press were exceptionally harsh: "Firestone: Brutal End," "Brutal Stroke of the Pen," "Brutal Decision of Firestone," "More than 600 Workers out of Job," "The Firestone Shock," "Now the Workers Feel Cheated," "Fierce Fight for the Firestone Jobs," "A Village Fights a US-Giant!," "From Rage to Consternation."[1] The labor unions called for a two-day strike; a demonstration in front of the plant was held by some 3000 people. The government intervened in favor of the workers, and solidarity was expressed throughout the country, even by political parties who represented employers' interests.

What had happened? Firestone's tire factory in Pratteln was founded in 1935 and celebrated as the most modern tire factory of the world. Three-quarters of the shares were owned by the Swiss family Dätwyler and one quarter by Firestone. In the late 1960s and early 1970s, the competitiveness of the company declined, partly because Firestone prohibited the licensed Swiss plant from exporting its tires to Holland and Belgium. As a consequence, in 1973 the family members sold their shares to Firestone. Firestone, at the time known for its conservative management policies, committed several managerial mistakes, however; it was late to recognize the market shift to radial-ply tires, kept a nonrational multiplicity of products, and even had to call back a vast number of sold tires. Facing a loss of market share, the company urged the workers and employees of the Pratteln plant to accept short-time work several times plus a general reduction of work time and wages and also reduced the workforce from 1600 to 837 within five years—firmly promising to keep the factory alive by these measures. But in 1978, the board in Akron, Ohio, decided to shut down the Pratteln plant, together with another one in Calgary and even one in Akron. The Swiss labor force, after all the sacrifices, felt betrayed.[2]

A brief economic analysis revealed the structural problems Firestone was facing.

The radial-ply tires reduced the demand for bias-ply tires. Radials lasted twice as long and thus generated worldwide decline of demand, leaving large overcapacities in the tire industry. In addition, the production costs in Switzerland had soared significantly; when the U.S. dollar began to float, the Swiss franc reached a hitherto unseen high, making imports cheap and exports expensive. Locally, however, things looked different: sales were good; stocks were low; and within the Firestone group, the Swiss plant still was leading in quality. A general consensus emerged that the factory could be saved, be it by help of the government as the political left requested or by structural reorganization as the political right claimed. Solidarity was

1. All headlines were translated from German and French to English by the author. Corresponding to the sequence of titles, the sources are *Blick*, 23 Mar. 1978; *Solothurner Arbeiterzeitung*, 24 Mar. 1978; *Journal du Valais*, 23 Mar. 1978; *Der Bund*, 23 Mar. 1978; *Pratteler Anzeiger*, 28 Mar. 1978; *Bündner Zeitung*, 23 Mar. 1978; *TagesAnzeiger*, 30 Mar. 1978; *Blick*, 30 Mar. 1978; *Journal du Valais*, 24 Mar. 1978.

2. *Neue Zürcher Zeitung*, 12 Apr. 1978.

expressed by all the political parties, by the members of the parliament and the government of the state Basel-Land, and even by the federal secretary for economic affairs.

Then an event unique in Swiss economic history happened. A delegation of high-ranking political representatives—two members of the state government, a federal expert in economic affairs, and the Swiss ambassador to Washington—traveled to Akron to present their views on the economic situation and a proposal of measures by which Firestone could save the Swiss plant. American business executives are said to dislike government representatives. Accordingly, Firestone received the Swiss delegation only by members of the second and third rank. The Swiss felt insulted. The Americans, on the other hand, were reportedly quite puzzled about the vehement reaction in Switzerland; in America layoffs happened all the time.[3]

Firestone stayed with its original conclusion and shut down the Pratteln plant. And criticism stayed with Firestone. Two well-known German newsmagazines, *Die Zeit* and *Der Spiegel*, reported the case under the headlines "Exploited and Betrayed" and "Falsehood and Deceit."[4] "The human being is of no value to these Americans. To them, we are only numbers," *Die Zeit* quoted one worker as saying. "Hire and fire, in the United States the order of the day, is considered by the Swiss like the raging of a bull in a china shop." Indeed, the Swiss consensus concerned above all the culturally inadequate, non-Swiss, American management style, which just ignored the social partnership the Swiss had practiced for the past forty years. The Swiss resented the fact that all the important Firestone decisions were made in Akron, far away from the place where they were to be implemented; they were neither based on local knowledge nor discussed with the local management and workforce. The shutdown was announced as a fait accompli; even the American top manager of Firestone Switzerland insisted he was surprised by the decision in Akron.

But the same top manager refused to reveal the crucial financial figures. This stirred up considerable suspicion, as wages and salaries had been higher and profits substantial during the Dätwyler era.[5] One member of parliament concluded, "Foreign corporations acquire companies in order to shut them down. The production is dislocated to those places with the fewest social obligations. American bosses, too, shall not treat their employees like this, for we are no banana republic."[6] Only five days later, Firestone announced a multi-million-dollar project in Thailand to increase the production capacity of its Thai subsidiary.[7]

SWISSAIR DISLOCATES
WORK TO BOMBAY:
THE SITUATION 15 YEARS LATER

Thirteen years after the Firestone layoffs, Swissair announced it was moving its revenue accounting de-

3. Ibid.; ibid., 14 Apr. 1978.
4. *Die Zeit*, 7 Apr. 1978; *Der Spiegel*, 5 June 1978.
5. *TagesAnzeiger*, 30 Mar. 1978.
6. *Basler Zeitung*, 13 Apr. 1978.
7. *Neue Zürcher Zeitung*, 19 Apr. 1978.

partment to Bombay, India, costing 150 jobs and saving Fr8 million. This measure, part of the general revenue improvement program called Move, was implemented within three years. Although the company attempted to accomplish it with "natural leaves" and internal transfers of the persons concerned, dismissals were inevitable. For those affected, a "social plan" was worked out together with the employees' union. Financially, the transfer paid off well for Swissair: in Bombay, it is easy to find qualified people, and they cost only 10 percent—including 35 percent social costs—of what personnel cost in Switzerland.[8]

At the beginning of the 1990s, airline companies found themselves in their most severe crisis ever; they lost within two years what they had earned in two decades. In 1991, they were struck by the gulf war; in 1992, the price war began due to worldwide overcapacities. As this price war continues, Swissair has been attempting to remain a global carrier by a thorough organizational restructuring. In 1992, 40 percent of the total costs were personnel costs; therefore the reduction of personnel was a major source of cutting costs. And it still is; in the summer of 1995, Swissair announced that it would reduce its workforce by another 1600 jobs by 1997.[9]

Compared to the Firestone shutdown, the reaction was extremely moderate. The dislocation of work to Bombay and the job reduction between 1991 and 1993 was met with a comment by the employees' union, VPOD, that "the future of the company is endangered by making the personnel bleed to death."[10] Following the announcement of 1995, the mayor of the city of Kloten, where Swissair is the biggest employer, said he was "stunned" by the extent of the reduction, while the spokesman of the Aeropers, the association of cockpit personnel, stated that they had expected this development but think that "the board is saving the company to death." VPOD called the reduction "unacceptable" and "irresponsible" and protested the procedure; like Firestone, Swissair did not invite the unions to participate in the preparation of this decision, which was, according to a union spokesman, "against the rules."[11]

Certainly, a sudden shutdown of a production plant causes higher shock waves than does a transfer of work or a reduction of jobs that takes place over a two-year period. The dismissals at Swissair have been embedded in a broader strategy that relied on natural leaves, fostered early retirement, and allowed for internal displacements. And, in contrast to Firestone, Swissair has offered from the outset to work out a so-called social plan together with the unions to reduce the hardships of dismissal. In addition, it created a so-called transfer organization (outplacement service), which offers counseling, training, and further education to the persons concerned. But Swissair's traditional role as a "model employer" in the country seems to belong to the past.[12]

---

8. Ibid., 11 July 1991; ibid., 10 Aug. 1993.
9. Ibid., 19 Aug. 1992; ibid., 20 Aug. 1992; ibid., 14 Sept. 1995.
10. Ibid., 20 Oct. 1992.
11. Ibid., 14 Sept. 1995.
12. Ibid.

AN AMERICANIZATION OF SWITZERLAND?

In my view, the differences between the Firestone and the Swissair cases cannot account sufficiently for the difference in the reactions of the Swiss public. The two cases were not selected at random. Rather, they symbolize a major change in Switzerland: people are getting used to the fact that their national economy, too, is affected quickly and unpredictably by the whirlwinds of the world economy; that their country, too, is hit by layoffs and unemployment; and that Swiss corporations, too, dislocate work to Third World countries in order to survive. What in the case of Firestone was considered as a brutal and ruthless American style of management is becoming common Swiss practice. Swissair is by no means the only Swiss company that could be cited, but, as the national flag carrier and a traditional model employer, it certainly is the most symbolic of the trend.

Besides the turbulent changes in the world economy and the global political system, notably the disintegration of the Communist bloc in Eastern Europe, it is above all the emergence of visible unemployement that has formed a new vista on economic matters. Between World War II and the mid-1970s, unemployment in Switzerland was plainly nonexistent, at least in the public mind; the official figure fluctuated around 0.3 percent. In 1990, it soared to 0.65 percent, and then, within four years, it hit a record high of 4.5 percent.

Of course, these figures do not represent the actual unemployment but only the number of reported unemployed. Besides the increased pressure of the world economy on local corporations, they also represent a particular change in mentality: unemployment now is considered to be a fact, and to be unemployed has become a legitimate status. Until the mid-1970s, to be unemployed was considered to be a shame, expressing a lack of motivation to work. "Everybody who wants to work can find work" was the general saying. Thus many Swiss were too proud or ashamed to report themselves as unemployed to public authorities. There was a tendency of employers to first dismiss women and save the jobs for men—based on the traditional family model that men have to support a family while (married) women earn only pocket money. Moreover, many women just returned to their households when they lost their jobs and never showed up in the statistics. This was one factor that held the official figures low. The second was that, other than women, it was foreigners who lost their jobs, and they then either were expelled or returned voluntarily to their home countries. This way, Swiss unemployment was partly exported and showed up in the statistics of other countries, above all those of southern Europe.

In the face of the recession following the oil crisis, Switzerland introduced mandatory unemployment insurance in 1977. Before, the voluntary insurance had covered less than 50 percent of the unemployed; in earlier recessions, it had covered only about 20 percent. The general insurance evoked new behaviors and attitudes. To get unemployment benefits, many more unemployed persons now reported to public authorities, and many more foreigners stayed in the country. This made the unemployment rate soar, and the higher it became, the more it felt legitimate to report as unemployed. Undoubtedly, these new behaviors helped make the official statistics more representative of the actual unemployment rate. Thus it can be argued that unemployment in Switzerland has not really increased but has only become more visible.[13]

The general public, however, is hardly inclined to view the soaring unemployment rate as a statistical artifact but rather perceives it as a pure fact. Also alarming are the front-page news stories about new layoffs, new restructurings implying a reduction of the workforce, and new dismissals. The Swiss economy is obviously under increasing pressure and seems to be losing ground in international competition. Being pragmatic, the Swiss view this development as a challenge, one that may be frightening but that clearly makes further rationalization, structural adaptation, and new technological and social innovations inevitable. Like others, Swiss corporations have clearly adopted the strategy of global sourcing and moving their production plants away from Switzerland to markets abroad. And they openly admit it[14] without stirring up social unrest as Firestone did. In this sense, an Americanization is taking place: social responsibility and solidarity are being challenged more and more and often are being replaced by a pervasive economic rationality. The progressing globalization of the world economy will continually increase this trend, making the competition even harder and the pressure to rationalize even stronger.

NEW FORMS OF SOLIDARITY:
THE VW SOLUTION

In the middle of this general trend that is taking place in all Western European countries, Volkswagen Corporation (VW) in Germany has put forward an alternative: instead of firing people, it introduced the four-day workweek in 1993. Naturally, this move gained a lot of publicity. Never before had a big corporation reduced work time to such an extent in order to redistribute work and avoid mass dismissals. In the press, the so-called VW solution was praised as an act of solidarity between management and the workforce, as a sign of social responsibility by a big corporation, and as proof that economic difficulties can be

---

13. For a detailed economic discussion of this explanation, see Niklaus Blatter, "Arbeitslosigkeit: Tatbestände, Erklärungen, Lösungsansätze," *Forum Helveticum*, 6:8-27 (1995); Hans Schmid and Eckehard F. Rosenbaum, *Arbeitslosigkeit und Arbeitslosenversicherung aus ökonomischer Sicht* (Bern: Paul Haupt, 1995). For a comparison with other European states, see Hans Schmid, Peter Füglistaller, and Marcela Hohl, *Vollbeschäftigungspolitik: Der Wille zum Erfolg* (Bern: Paul Haupt, 1993). For an analysis of unemployment in Switzerland and economic and social remedies, see Hans Schmid, "Arbeitslosigkeit in der Schweiz: Diagnose und Ausblick," *Forum Helveticum*, 6:43-63 (1995).

14. For example, the personnel manager of the Swiss-Swedish corporation ABB. See René A. Lichtsteiner, "Neue Arbeitsplätze schaffen und Arbeitslosigkeit vermeiden: Lösungsansätze aus der Sicht einer grossen Arbeitgeberin," *Forum Helveticum*, 6:75-81 (1995).

mastered without causing mass unemployment.[15]

The reasons for the economic problems were clearly visible. The car industry, like the tire industry in the 1970s (as shown by the Firestone case) or the airline business in the 1990s (as shown by the Swissair case), was struck by large overcapacities. In the mid-1990s, the worldwide production potential amounts to about 40 million cars annually, while less than 30 million are sold per year. VW already reduced its workforce from 130,000 in the 1980s to 100,000 in 1993, promoting voluntary leaves via early retirement at the age of 55. But in 1993 a further reduction of another 30,000 people seemed necessary. A cost reduction of 25 percent was considered to be inevitable, as VW had fallen far behind foreign—above all, Japanese—competitors.

The car industry, the heart of industry in the twentieth century, still is a paradigmatic example for rationalization. In the 1920s, Henry Ford realized a technical version of what Frederick Taylor had proposed in his "scientific management." It was copied by all of Ford's competitors. In the 1980s, the new managerial revolution took place, again in the auto industry. It occurred first in Japan, with buzzwords such as "just-in-time production," "lean management," and "simultaneous engineering," and then in the United States with "total quality management," "business reengineering," and so on.[16] VW is still in the process of discussing and implementing these—as well as its own—new management concepts. To pair them with adequate behavior, the personnel division set the strategic goal of developing "multifunctional, mobile, entrepreneurial and human workers and employees."[17] These attributes are set to become the selection criteria for the future workforce.

Meanwhile, the VW solution builds on solidarity with three pillars. The first, the four-day workweek—that is, the reduction of the weekly work time from 36 to 28.8 hours and a corresponding reduction of wages and salaries—was introduced for everybody, including the top management and the board members. That means that even those in positions with much responsibility, working 50 or 70 hours a week, had to accept substantial pay reductions. The second pillar is the introduction of block times. Under this arrangement, each worker or employee may interrupt work for three or more months per year while staying in a regular contract. Block times suit primarily singles and younger people and should be used for study and

15. For the specifics of the VW solution, see Peter Hartz, *Jeder Arbeitsplatz hat ein Gesicht: Die Volkswagen-Lösung* (Frankfurt: Campus, 1994); Peter Haase and Thomas Kuhn, "Neue Arbeitszeitmodelle bei der Volkswagen AG—innovative Ansätze für mehr Wettbewerbsfähigkeit und wider die Massenarbeitslosigkeit," in *Innovatives Personal Management*, ed. R. Wunderer and T. Kuhn (Neuwied: Luchterhand, 1995). For the diverse reactions in the press, see Volkswagen Corporation, "Das VW-Modell der Vier-Tage-Woche im Spiegel der öffentlichen Meinung" (Manuscript, [1994]).

16. James P. Womack, Daniel T. Jones, and Daniel Roos, *The Machine That Changed the World* (New York: Macmillan, 1990).

17. In German, all these words begin with an "M": "multifunktional, mobil, mitgestaltend, menschlich." Therefore the concept is called the "M4 employee."

training. To support this, VW has founded a coaching (consulting) company.

The third pillar may be the most peculiar: the relay race (*Stafette*). The relay race is a plan to distribute work among different age groups. Young people after apprenticeship may work 20 hours a week; after 24 months, they may work 24 hours; and after 42 months, they may work the full 28.8 hours of the four-day workweek. Similarly, people at the age of 56 who are not retiring are obliged to reduce their weekly work time by 4 hours and to receive less pay accordingly. At 60 years of age, they must drop another 4 hours a week, or 2 months a year. The idea behind this is a contract between the generations: younger and older people step back in favor of those who need work and money most, middle-aged people with families. As there are many families whose grandparents, parents, and children work at VW, this generation contract can often be transposed directly into family terms, as solidarity between family members.

Can this new approach serve as a model for the future? There is a personal, an organizational, and an economic level to consider. So far, only the four-day workweek has been implemented. Two years later, the majority of the workforce still praises it as an act of solidarity that is "typically VW" (in the good sense). No surprise: every third or fourth person would have been personally hit by a mass dismissal without it. And as the average wage per month of a VW worker was DM4500 ($3250) compared to the DM3500 ($2500) that is the average in the metal industry, they were still better off after the 20 percent work and wage reduction than were most of their colleagues. Many of those in key positions who work a lot of overtime, however, feel rather exploited by the new regulations.

On the organizational level, the four-day workweek for everybody causes a lot of problems. One top manager puts it this way: as a rule of thumb, the four-day workweek is suitable for production—to produce less, people work less—and maybe as a means to reduce the fat in the administrative overhead, but in many areas (development, sales, marketing, financial services) work reduction is fatal. Furthermore, the four-day workweek requires a huge amount of coordinating work, as the company is run for five days a week with people who are there for only four days. Even in small units, more than 150 different work-time models have been developed. On the economic level, experts note that the four-day workweek increases the costs of each work unit instead of reducing them, prevents conventional economic structures from necessary adaptations, and endangers Germany's overall competitiveness.[18]

Indeed, the VW solution is probably only a provisional solution. Maybe the company's board simply had to agree to it. In the big corporations in Germany, half of the members of the supervisory committee are by law representatives of the workers and employees, while the other half represent the shareholders. At VW, the *Betriebsrat* (works council) and the unions have for historical reasons always been stronger than they have

18. Personal interviews by the author.

at other corporations. The biggest shareholder, the state of Lower Saxony, which owns 20 percent of the shares, is represented by the Social Democratic governor. Other corporations have clearly signaled that they are not willing to copy the VW model. But even within VW, the fundamental conflict may be just postponed. The radical cost cutting and rationalization measures within the company will drastically increase work productivity. The next model of the popular car Golf, due out in 1997, will be produced in only 24 hours of work per car, compared with 38 hours now. Unless the market will allow for many more sales, the workforce or its work time has to be reduced significantly again by 1998. The union leaders of IG-Metall predict they will go on fighting for job security for all, while VW's chief executive officer, Ferdinand Piëch, threatens to join the great German corporate flight abroad.[19] Whether the company will be able to avoid layoffs and dislocations and proceed with its solidarity pact as it moves into the next century remains to be seen.

THE ONGOING TENSION BETWEEN MODERNIZATION AND NATIONAL CULTURES

Let us now broaden the scope. What are the prospects of work in the future? What will the twenty-first century look like? Will there be work for everybody who is willing to work? Or will work become a scarce good, reserved for privileged people? For nearly two decades, there has been a heated international debate in Europe on this issue.[20] One group of scholars argues that technological rationalization and new management techniques increasingly wipe away jobs, continually diminishing the number of jobs in relation to the potential labor force. The new jobs will not balance the number of jobs that are lost, and more and more people will be pushed out of the economic system. Moreover, this will happen forever, without a return ticket. The future society will be a "two-thirds society"; there will be work left for only two-thirds of the population. The protagonists of this theory call for a new distribution of work by shortening the work time of each person. This would be a just solution and put everyone, they contend, back in a job. Many representatives of labor unions and of leftist political parties adhere to this view.

Another group of scholars reject this analysis firmly. They repudiate the underlying assumption that a general saturation is being reached, and they assure us that the economy will create enough jobs for everyone if the general frame conditions are modeled adequately. They explain the steady rate of unemployment of 10 percent and more in many industrialized states in two ways: (1) as a mismatch of demand and supply of labor concerning qualifications and regions and (2) as a result of the welfare state, which reduces the mobility

19. See Bill Powell, "Germany's Angry Autoworkers," *Newsweek International*, 11 Sept. 1995, p. 37.

20. For a recent renewal of the debate, see Christian Lutz, "Unsere Zukunft—eine Zweidrittelsgesellschaft?" *Neue Zürcher Zeitung*, 14-15 May 1994, p. 23; Thomas A. Becker, "Zukunft der Arbeit—nur für Akrobaten? Argumentationsdefizite des Szenariums Zweidrittelsgesellschaft," ibid., 2-3 Sept. 1995, p. 17.

of people. In such a context, the shortening of work time would not distribute work more justly among the population but, worse, would reduce general wealth. Many managers of big corporations and other proponents of the upper-middle class support this view.

This discussion is likely to go on far into the twenty-first century. In the social market economies of Western Europe, the long-term unemployment rate makes the first group call for a redistribution of work, while the second blames the existing political and legal restrictions as causal factors and demands deregulation. Will this debate result in a political stalemate, or will global competition advance economic rationality at the expense of social responsibility and solidarity, as I proposed in the case of Switzerland?

A new modernization theory provides a suitable framework to discuss this in more depth. According to Peter Gross,[21] modernity is advanced by three core processes: (1) "optioning," or the creation of more and more options; (2) detraditionalization, or the erosion of traditions; and (3) individualization. Modern societies create more and more options, be they goods or services, lifestyles or worldviews. At the same time, traditions lose their binding meaning, their collective obligation, and become one option among others. The joy and burden of choosing between options stays with the individual who has to make up his or her mind. The traditional guideposts have vanished; to orient oneself in a pluralistic and fast-changing society with multiple life-worlds has become a lonely task. This trend can be illustrated with many examples. The traditional family, for instance, has become just one among many other ways of life. Divorces shatter the idea of lifelong relationships, more and more people live life as singles or just engage in partnerships-on-time, and in some states even homosexuals may get married now. The same pluralism applies to work. The conventional ideal of monogamous work, that is, of learning just one occupation or profession and staying loyal to the same corporation for a lifetime, as was common practice in Europe, gives way to polygamous work, to changing professions, jobs, and employers.[22] This growing pluralism in almost every area of the life-world opens up a lot of opportunities but makes people prone to crises of orientation.

According to Gross, these interlinked core processes have a tremendous power in Western societies and are hardly stoppable. If this is true, Western Europe will become more and more Americanized; the proclaimed unity of a national culture will dissolve into multiple cultural milieus as a consequence of pluralism as well as immigration, and the traditional values of solidarity will give way to a pervasive individualism. In regard to the debate on the distribution of work, this would imply that the forces of deregulation in the long run will be stronger than the concepts of solidarity. If the trend in a deregulated economy should go to-

21. Peter Gross, *Die Multioptionsgesellschaft* (Frankfurt am Main: Suhrkamp, 1995).

22. Compare Peter Gross, "Abschied von der monogamen Arbeit," *gdi-Impuls*, vol. 3 (1995).

ward a two-thirds society or anything like it, we would have to redefine work; a political solution addressing how to sustain the jobless one-third economically would have to be found as would a way in which they could make their lives count in activities of a sort beyond the economic definition of work.[23]

Predictions in social sciences have a problematic status, however. Using the framework of Gross, it proves to be of great sociological interest to empirically study the multiplicity of movements and their honored value systems. Many of them are committed to stop the process of detraditionalization. As abortion evoked the pro-life movement, the dissolution of the family evoked the pro-family movement. For an example of the outlook in Europe, Switzerland is a promising place to study such movements; a democratic society where people vote on substantial matters is a fine seismograph of what people think and feel. For Switzerland, the most important event in the 1990s was, no doubt, the vote on whether to join the European Economic Area—not the European Union, which would have been far more dramatic. The question was whether the Swiss would agree to a free trade of goods, services, capital, and people among the West European states. The outcome of the vote in 1992 was nearly half and half, with a slight majority against the treaty. While the French Swiss were clearly in favor of the agreement, a majority of German Swiss voted it down. The issue caused a schism in the country between those willing to further integrate into Europe and those who fear that Switzerland would lose its identity and become a pawn of the big European states.

Thus my former thesis that the Swiss get used to tough American-style management and to the hard reality of economic laws in the world society has to be differentiated. About half of the voting population wants to preserve the historically grown, traditional structures of economy and society. They fear that a free market with Western Europe would destroy what is dear to them. Could the small businesses of the middle class survive against the capitalist strategies of the transnational corporations? Without state subsidies, could the farmers still have cows on the meadows? Could cheese still be produced in Switzerland if production costs are much lower in the Netherlands? What if even more immigrants were entering the country, at a time when already more than 19 percent of the population consists of foreigners, nearly three times as much as in Germany or France?[24] Swiss culture, these voters are convinced, would fall apart.

Many economic experts favor an integration, while others oppose it. Both sides argue that the country would fare better economically. But the core issue is not wealth but values and emotions. Alpine herdsmen with alphorns, cows on the mountains

23. Compare Thomas S. Eberle, "Wenn uns die Arbeit ausgeht: Ueber die gesellschaftliche Bedeutung der Arbeit," *Pro Infirmis*, 50(4): 3-9 (1991); H. Hoffmann and D. Kramer, eds., *Arbeit ohne Sinn? Sinn ohne Arbeit?* (Weinheim: Beltz athenäum, 1994).

24. Swiss companies attracted many unqualified workers from abroad to keep their costs low while not taking into account the social costs of cultural assimilation.

with cowbells, and Swiss cheese of many sorts represent crucial symbols of national identity. They are not just symbols or stories; they are a lived reality, if only by a minority. In any case, they are not just a Disneyland financed by the tourism industry. There are plenty of additional local particularities that seem to be threatened by the mechanisms of unbound economic laws in a free international market, particularities that make people feel at home.

This schism is found all over Europe. No European government ever cared to ask their people whether or not they wanted to join the Common Market and the European Union. When Denmark and France finally took a vote on the Maastricht contract, the outcome was nearly half and half, too. All over Europe, there is a tension between national or local culture and economic union. This is evidenced in many instances: in the multiple special arrangements within the European Union, in the difficulty in finding a common policy toward the civil war in the Balkans, and in the discussions of people in everyday life. In addition, there is a fundamental tension in Europe between national culture and modernization, quite in contrast to the case of the United States. This schism is likely to continue far into the twenty-first century. That means that the legitimating basis of each serious question and decision remains fragile. Modernization may progress but is never safe from backlashes as dramatic as the "ethnic cleansing" in former Yugoslavia. Work dislocation policies of European corporations must always be seen in the context of this basic tension and will always have to find some sort of local, temporary compromise.

Employment Flexibility and Joblessness in Low-Growth, Restructured Japan

By KOJI TAIRA and SOLOMON B. LEVINE

ABSTRACT: Today, with the longest recession since World War II, unemployment is a growing fear among Japan's 52 million wage and salary earners. White-collar employees now outnumber blue-collar employees, and the labor force is increasingly mobile. As the structure of Japan's economy continues to change, Japanese labor markets are especially vulnerable to deterioration, without job creation sufficient to overcome job losses. Only a minority of workers have lifetime employment. Measures taken by government, employers, and worker organizations to support full employment in Japan go back 20 years. This three-way consensus successfully smoothed the way from production-first policies of the first two decades of post–World War II Japan to moderate growth, which emphasized equity and equality as well as full employment. The Japanese economy now seems to have entered a new phase, with the principal actors in the system of industrial relations, government and organized labor along with business, undergoing a restructuring that may undermine the long-standing consensus. This article examines institutions that have underpinned full employment in Japan, with an eye to changes now occurring.

Koji Taira is a professor of economics and industrial relations at the University of Illinois at Urbana-Champaign. He is engaged in international comparative research on economic institutions, human resource management, and labor markets.

Solomon B. Levine is professor emeritus at the University of Wisconsin–Madison, where he served in the East Asian Studies Program, the Industrial Relations Research Institute, the Business School, and the Economics Department. He has studied and taught in Japan on numerous occasions since 1945.

JAPAN'S official unemployment rate is considered an underestimate of the true level of labor redundancy in Japan. But it has two merits. First, the basic concepts and methods by which it is arrived at have been consistent since the labor force survey began after World War II. Second, although deficient as an indicator of the absolute level of unemployment, the consistency of its definition makes it useful for observing trends in unemployment over time. Table 1 shows the official unemployment rate for recent years along with a few other macroeconomic indicators. Employment and unemployment figures in Table 1 fluctuate in association with changes in economic conditions as, for example, represented by the growth of gross domestic product (GDP).

TRENDS IN EMPLOYMENT AND UNEMPLOYMENT

At the beginning of the 1980s, the second oil shock (1979-80) precipitated a recession in the Japanese economy. Following the Plaza Accord in September 1985, growth was again derailed, this time by appreciation of the Japanese yen relative to the U.S. dollar. In 1986, Japan suffered the so-called Yen-daka recession.

In its time, the Yen-daka recession was perceived as a major crisis, although it was at best a growth recession. Prompted by a sense of crisis, Japan resorted to massive fiscal and monetary stimuli for domestic aggregate demand and brought about a heady economic boom in 1987-91, generally called the "Bubble," on a scale not seen since the end of Japan's "miracle growth" 15 years earlier. Japan overreacted to the Yen-daka recession by boosting the economy too much in the short run at the expense of long-term health.

An acute labor shortage developed during the Bubble. If the unemployment rate's decrease from 2.8 percent to 2.1 percent seems unimpressive, more sensitive indicators such as the rate of employment growth or the ratio of job offers to job seekers (see Table 1) show dramatic changes in labor markets. The growth rate of employment more than doubled during the boom as compared to the pre-boom years. After the boom, it quickly dwindled to zero. Before 1987, job offers were far below job seekers, but during the Bubble the relationship was sharply reversed. The worsening labor shortage during this period even brought about a wholly unexpected development, the illegal rush of foreigners into Japan.[1]

At the end of 1990, the business cycle peaked and the recession of 1991-93 began. The recession officially ended in October 1993, but GDP growth has since been so sluggish that many doubt that the economy is on the mend. A great majority of observers of the Japanese economy forecast recession-level growth for 1995. The Japanese economy will then have stagnated for four years, another unprecedented experience for Japan. Even in 1995, stock prices staggered along at a level about half as high as their 1989 peak. The unemployment rate rose from a low of

1. Haruo Shimada, *Japan's "Guest Workers": Issues and Public Policies*, trans. Roger Northridge (Tokyo: University of Tokyo Press, 1994).

TABLE 1
SELECTED MACROECONOMIC INDICATORS OF JAPAN, 1984-95

Year	Gross Domestic Product (Real growth rate)	Employment (Growth rate)	Labor Productivity (Growth rate)	Unemployment Rate	Job Offers/ Job Seekers	Consumer Price Index (Rate of change)	Wages (Nominal growth rate)	Wages (Real growth rate)*
1984	4.3	0.57	3.7	2.7	0.65	2.3	3.6	1.4
1985	5.0	0.71	4.3	2.6	0.68	2.0	2.8	0.7
1986	2.6	0.79	1.8	2.8	0.62	0.6	2.7	2.3
1987	4.1	0.99	3.1	2.8	0.70	0.1	1.9	2.2
1988	6.2	1.69	4.5	2.5	1.01	0.7	3.5	3.0
1989	4.7	1.95	2.7	2.3	1.25	2.3	4.2	1.9
1990	4.8	1.97	2.8	2.1	1.40	3.1	4.7	1.5
1991	4.3	1.92	2.4	2.1	1.40	3.3	3.5	0.2
1992	1.1	1.05	0.05	2.2	1.08	1.6	1.7	0.1
1993	−0.2	0.22	−0.4	2.5	0.76	1.3	0.7	−0.5
1994	0.6	0.05	0.5	2.9	0.64	0.7	1.7	1.2
1995	0.3†	nil†	0.3	3.2‡	0.65‡	−0.2‡	1.6‡	1.8‡

SOURCES: Ministry of Labour, *Yearbook of Labour Statistics*, 1993; *Monthly Labour Statistics and Research Bulletin* (June 1995).
*Technically, this should be equal to nominal wage growth rate less consumer price index rate of change. The figures cited here show some discrepancies for reasons unknown.
†First quarter, preliminary.
‡May 1995.

2.1 percent in 1991 to more than 3 percent in April and May 1995.

The trend in unemployment is upward since full employment under rapid economic growth before the first oil shock. During the 1960s, the official unemployment rate was slightly above 1 percent. The oil shock and subsequent stabilization at lower economic growth rates raised unemployment above 2 percent in the late 1970s and early 1980s. As Table 1 shows, during the Yen-daka recession, unemployment rose toward 3 percent. In 1995, it rose even above 3 percent. The trend toward higher unemployment tempts many to anticipate 4 percent fairly soon and 5 percent early in the next century. A popular rule of thumb to translate the official figure into a truer unemployment rate is to double it.

However, what the unemployment rate will be in the future depends on the interplay of demographic, economic, and technological factors. A consensus speculation that emerges from several simulations we have seen is that a GDP growth rate of 3-4 percent per annum sustained several years would be necessary for keeping the unemployment rate from rising and that if other favorable factors—such as restraints on wage increases—reinforce GDP, the unemployment rate might be rolled back toward 2.1 percent, which was the lowest rate reached at the peak of the Bubble.

Table 1 also shows that Japan seems to have achieved absolute price stability and even shows signs of deflation—a rare achievement by international standards. Another remarkable quality shown by Table 1 is a sustained modesty of real wage increases, generally lagging behind increases in labor productivity. This indicates that wage earners have not gained as much as the growth of labor productivity should have justified. The relationship between wages and GDP has many serious macroeconomic implications. One is that the growth of domestic aggregate demand is held down by the weakness of mass purchasing power relative to aggregate supply capability. Because aggregate demand does not sufficiently absorb aggregate output, domestic economic balance and growth must depend on foreign markets. Strong exports, weak imports, a large current account surplus, and a strong yen follow. The use of foreign demand to keep Japanese production in high gear conflicts with economic policies of foreign countries.

Japan's chronic foreign trade surplus smacks of a beggar-thy-neighbor trade policy, and one source of it is a beggar-thy-worker practice: paying workers a low or decreasing share of their productivity. An understanding of this relationship would certainly give rise to a demand for more rapid wage increases than Japanese workers have obtained. However, Japanese workers have not paid much attention to the implications of the observed wage-productivity relationship. By forgoing justifiable wage increases, Japanese workers inflate profits and encourage businesses to expand production and exports further.

This beggar-thy-neighbor pattern of balance and growth is supported by the beggar-thy-worker wage-productivity relationship. A crucial question, then, is why Japanese workers' demand for higher wages is weak relative to their productivity. Because the rate of change in wages predictably rises or falls in association with changes in economic conditions, it superficially appears that the labor market is working as flexibly as it should from time to time. But over time, as Table 1 shows, these changes cumulatively make the real wage level fall further below the real productivity level than was the case at an earlier time. We suspect that long-term constraints hold workers' normal share of output low, or bias labor-management relations in favor of employers. These constraints are institutional and structural characteristics of Japanese employment practices and relationships.

POLITICAL RESTRUCTURING AND REFORM

In the past decade, the Japanese government took several important steps affecting labor markets and labor relations. By the mid-1980s, the government had privatized large publicly owned enterprises, notably the telecommunications company, the railway company, and alcohol and salt monopolies; it had adopted an equal employment opportunity law for women; and it had enacted a law regulating the supply and hire of "dispatched" employees (usually part-time workers). By the early 1990s, it had further revised the Labor Standards Law, including plans to reduce the standard workweek to 40 hours and to raise minimum wages; it had integrated the special labor relations commission for government-owned enterprises with the commission for the private sector; it had promoted improvements in the supply and training of labor for small and medium-sized firms; it had enacted controls over the inflow of illegal immigrant workers; it had instituted a national policy for child-care leave; it had regulated employment of part-time workers; and it had extended the retirement age for receiving full benefits under the social security law. Many of these measures aimed at increasing labor supply as severe shortages developed, especially in the skilled categories. They tended to be pro-employer.

The keystone government policy for preventing unemployment is the Employment Insurance System, enacted in 1974 following the first oil crisis and accompanied later with related legislation. While the courts have long held that discharge from employment must be the "last resort," the aim of this program is to stabilize employment within enterprises rather than, as in the case of unemployment insurance, only to support the jobless. (Japan's unemployment insurance system began in 1947.) Layoffs are to be avoided.

All employees outside the primary sector are covered, although the insurance is optional for firms with fewer than five workers each. Both employers and employees contribute premiums based on wages, while the government pays the expenses of the system. The great bulk of the funds paid out are for employment adjustment costs, including transfers and retraining redundant employees for new jobs. Special efforts are made to employ senior workers and the handicapped. The Ministry of Labor designates which industries are depressed according to established standards, and individual firms within them apply for wage subsidies, which vary with firm size for employees subject to employment adjustment measures. (Subsidies are either one-half or two-thirds of wages.) In the 1991-93 recession, dozens of industries were declared depressed and thousands of enterprises applied for assistance. One estimate placed the number of workers supported under these programs in October 1993 at 4 million.[2]

Continuing the practice developed in the 1960s and 1970s, the government closely consulted leading employer groups and labor organizations regarding national labor policies and remained noninterventionist in private sector collective bargaining. In general, this approach resulted in reducing the size of government, eliminating government regulations, promoting full employment and employment security, and increasing reliance on market competition. Welcoming the unification of organized labor in the late 1980s as a means for strengthening union-management cooperation, it especially advocated establishing mechanisms for joint consultation and information sharing as well as collective bargaining in both large and small firms.

Labor disputes continued to decline in number, dropping from about 7000 a year in the early 1980s to below 1300 a decade later. Work stoppages in these disputes also fell, from more than 900 a year to fewer than 300.[3] This reduction is attributable in part to the breakup of the militant railway unions on the heels of privatization. Also, no longer was there the threat of general strikes, as often appeared in the rash of walkouts that occurred in earlier years at the time of the annual wage offensive (*shunto*). Joint consultation and collective bargaining usually ended in peaceful settlements between employers and unions, much to the government's approval. The institution called Sanrokon, or Industry and Labor Conference, continued to bring together employer, union, and government leaders, along with experts, for frequent discussion of major economic and labor questions. While Sanrokon does not engage in collective bargaining, it sets a tone of moderation for similar bipartite and tripartite exchanges at the industry and enterprise levels.

Ironically, even though the conservative Liberal Democratic Party (LDP) government earlier led the way from a conflictual to a cooperative system of industrial relations in Japan, the liberal opposition had grown in strength by the late 1980s. In the summer of 1989, the LDP's control of the government began to unravel when it lost its majority in the upper house and a labor-sponsored group of 11 representatives, collectively known as Rengo, held the swing votes. LDP's defeat followed a revelation of financial misdoings by conservative political leaders and adoption of a 3 percent "consumption" tax on all sales.

The big surprise came in the summer of 1993, when, for the first time since 1955, in a general lower house election, the LDP lost control of the government as defections occurred within its ranks and no coalition with

2. *Japan Labor Bulletin*, 1 Nov. 1993, pp. 4-5.
3. Ibid., 1 Apr. 1995.

the LDP appeared possible. Led by Morihiro Hosokawa, formerly of the LDP, the new government was a complex of LDP splinter groups, the two socialist parties, and others such as the Clean Government Party (the Communists were excluded). This dramatic turn seemed to signal a definitive shift toward loosening government controls and regulations. In the eyes of the new leadership, it appears, the old LDP was too enmeshed in the established web of bureaucratic and big-business interests to achieve the liberalization desired by most Japanese and, for that matter, much of the world.

Japan is still in the midst of remaking its political configuration. The Hosokawa government actually fell in April 1994 due to the revelation of financial irregularities on the part of the prime minister. The successor coalition government, led by former LDP member Tsutomu Hata, but this time without the left-wing socialists, lasted only until June of that year, when Hata resigned on the brink of a no-confidence vote in the Diet. Paradoxically, the next government was a coalition of the remainder of the LDP, the leftist Social Democratic Party (SDP), and New Party Sakigake, one of the defector splinter groups from the LDP. The new prime minister, Tomiichi Murayama, SDP chairman, succeeded in obtaining spending cuts for the self-defense forces and an expansion of social welfare benefits. Although the SDP suffered a setback in the upper house elections of 23 July 1995, the coalition retained its majority position. For the time being, the government appears to be stuck on dead center, awaiting new lower house elections by 1996. To stimulate the economy, however, at long last the government recently announced an expanded spending program on public works and infrastructure, although it has been criticized, especially by the U.S. government, as too little and too late to bring about sufficient consumption spending to reduce Japan's enormous trade surplus.

It is too soon to know the outcome of these developments. In all likelihood, Japan will have to wait until political restructuring underway is completed and a stable government has taken power. Whatever eventually emerges, it appears that a major challenge lies in reaching a renewed consensus on policies for maintaining a flexible and fair employment system and in minimizing unemployment, official and disguised.

EMPLOYER RESPONSE
TO ECONOMIC CHANGE

The Japanese employment system, which is best known for so-called lifetime employment, is also known for its flexibility.[4] The Japanese firm's ability to adjust quantity, quality, and organization of labor inputs to changing needs of the product market gives the lie to the common perception of lifetime employment as a lifetime guarantee of employment for every employee. There is no such guarantee for any employee in the Japanese firm.

Business cycles, technological changes, and competition in product markets force companies to adjust

  4. Ronald Dore, *Flexible Rigidities: Industrial Policy and Structural Adjustment in the Japanese Economy 1970-80* (Stanford, CA: Stanford University Press, 1986).

input levels and structures. The basic human resource strategy of the Japanese firm is a multilayer internal labor market by which a small core of highly capable employees is maintained until mandatory retirement at a fixed age (formerly 55; recently more often 60), buffered by groups of workers with easily terminable employment contracts—casual, temporary, seasonal, part-time workers as well as dispatched or loaned workers from other firms. Core workers are more commonly called "regular" employees. They identify with the firm and often organize an enterprise union. The enterprise union's insistence on employment security, which implies a willingness for concessions on other conditions of employment such as hours, wages, and work rules, is an important constraint on the firm's adjustment strategy. On the other hand, nonregular workers are adjusted at will according to changes in the firm's workforce level and structure.

Management of regular employees contains considerable built-in flexibility. The core of regulars (standard workers) comprises individuals with maximum adaptability and trainability who are hired at the time of graduation from high school or college. The firm means to keep them until retirement by offering them well-structured internal career paths. But there is attrition even among them that the firm must take into account in its workforce planning: only about a third of the original cohort stays until retirement. The attrition is flexibly made up by mid-career hires, that is, workers at life stages other than school graduation and with varieties of job experience. They are also incorporated into the regular workforce and kept until retirement, subject to their own rate of attrition. The hierarchical structure of the personnel corresponds to the career progression of these carefully selected regular employees. Considerable quantitative flexibility can be attained by hiring more or fewer standard or mid-career employees, given their predictable attrition rates.

Nonregular workers are hired with fixed-term employment contracts terminable or renewable at will. Long-term employment may result from many consecutive renewals of these contracts. Some long-term nonregular workers with proved competencies are often reclassified and taken into the regular workforce. Many, however, stay nonregular no matter how many times their contracts are renewed.

The relative number of regular and nonregular workers depends on the firm's perception of cyclical fluctuations in human resource needs. Given the priority of employment security for regular workers, the firm limits the size of the regular workforce to the level that it can maintain during the slack phase of the business cycle. In return for employment security, regular employees accept rotations and reassignments to different jobs, departments, affiliates, or subsidiaries. Cyclical swings in human resource needs are also absorbed by changes in the size of the nonregular workforce. Employment adjustment due to more fundamental market and technological changes is essentially similar to cyclical adjustment.

An added consideration is how to avoid disruptive conflicts with regular employees and their unions when longer-term adjustment requires cutbacks in the regular ranks. Out of the desire for a conflict-minimizing strategy to reduce labor inputs emerged so-called Japanese-style employment adjustments.[5] The strategy was successful in that it reduced and restructured the workforce while minimizing conflict as well as maintaining productivity growth.

By the time the unprecedented boom arrived in the late 1980s, the human resource structures of Japanese firms had become fairly lean. The great expansion of demand induced keen competition among firms for more workers, resulting in an acute labor shortage. Firms apparently made a mistake in their perception of the durability of the ongoing boom. This exhilarating boom, coming after nearly 15 years of low growth, affected Japanese firms in a peculiar way: however contradictory it may sound, they may well have believed that the boom would last forever.

Due in part to this illusion, the ranks of regular employees expanded substantially, and new graduates enjoyed several job offers per person to choose from. Because regular employees should not be dismissed in principle, in the depth of the post-Bubble recession, firms ended up harboring 3-5 million redundant employees (intrafirm unemployment). This type of unemployment is about twice as large as official unemployment—another reason to doubt the efficacy of the official figure as an index of the absolute level of unemployment. Many firms quit hiring new graduates, swelling youth unemployment captured by the official labor force survey as unemployed.

The logic of employment adjustment is well-known. The firm's objective is to cut the total labor cost, which can be done by cutting total hours worked or by lowering labor compensation per hour or both. The strategy is to start with measures meeting the least resistance. Among adjustment measures, by far the most popular one is reducing overtime. Regular working hours per day and regular working days per month can also be reduced. Holidays and vacations can be increased. The hiring freeze is also a measure that invites no resistance from existing employees. Reduction of mid-career hires is a popular measure. The once-a-year hiring of standard employees can also be cut, which saves future labor costs as well as immediate recruitment expenses. Reduction of the current workforce must be avoided, for which useful measures are internal transfers and transfers to affiliates and subsidiaries. To increase the work of the existing workforce, outsourcing can be cut and internalized.

Firms suffering exceptionally severe downturns may have to do something that Japanese firms generally hate to do: lay off or even terminate regular employees. There is a distinct Japanese style here, too. As mentioned, wages during a temporary

5. Koji Taira and Solomon B. Levine, "Japan's Industrial Relations: A Social Compact Emerges," in *Industrial Relations in a Decade of Economic Change*, ed. Hervey Juris et al., Industrial Relations Research Association Series (Madison, WI: Industrial Relations Research Association, 1985), chap. 8, pp. 247-300.

layoff are guaranteed up to two-thirds of regular earnings with the help of government subsidies out of the Employment Insurance Fund. When some regulars have to be let go, the firms target senior employees, for example, 50 years old or older, and ask for voluntary early retirement by promising to sweeten the severance pay. When the target number is not reached by volunteers, certain individuals are discreetly tapped on the shoulder and asked to volunteer for retirement. Dismissals of regular employees by this method are rather rare.

Finally, major items contributing to labor costs are base pay and bonuses. These are subjects for collective bargaining and should not be tampered with lightly. Bonuses are paid twice a year, and bargaining over them is more frequent than that over base pay, which is the subject of bargaining once a year in the spring through the well-known *shunto*. The result of the bargaining is unpredictable, but, given the pressures of recession and the unions' "enterprise consciousness," firms recently won large union concessions on the wage and bonus issues. Even during the Bubble, firms used the strong yen as a reason for moderate wage increases. The argument was that by the exchange rate, the Japanese labor costs were already too high. Labor had no effective argument against that.

There is no doubt that Japanese human resource management is subtle, sophisticated, and on the whole successful. Resort to outright layoffs and discharges is rare, and the employment security of regular employees is high. From this, however, one should not conclude that Japanese human resource management contributes to low unemployment for the Japanese economy as a whole. In the first place, Japan's reputation as a low-unemployment country is founded on an uncritical acceptance of official labor force statistics. Second, although Japanese human resource management is internally commendable, it has negative externalities that raise economywide joblessness by creating a sharp labor market segmentation and by tending to limit entry into the internal labor markets of major firms.

THE LABOR MOVEMENT REORGANIZES

Already alluded to is organized labor's unification, finally achieved in 1989. Throughout the postwar era, the labor movement—which initially was strongly encouraged under the drastic reforms of the Allied occupation—for the most part was torn by ideological differences and organizational rivalries. The chief competitors at the national level were left-of-center Sohyo, heavily dominated by government workers, and moderate democratic socialist Domei, made up almost entirely of private sector unions. By and large, in both central federations, the predominant form of unionism was organizations of regular blue- and white-collar wage and salary earners together at the enterprise level. Although Sohyo and Domei both advocated industrial unionism and, for the most part, their affiliated enterprise unions together formed such industry-level bodies, in fact organized labor's locus of power lay within the enterprise. These enterprise-level unions, concentrated heavily in large-scale companies and government agencies, had financial resources and staff to carry on collective bargaining—including strikes—and joint consultation. They tended to be little interested in organizing the unorganized, a task left to the industrial and central federations. (About one-fourth of Japan's more than 12.7 million unionists belong to unions that have no affiliation with "upper-level" organizations.)

It was long the dream of most Japanese union leaders to unify organized labor, but all efforts to do so failed from the time unions were first born in the 1890s. However, once Japan began to reach the stage of an advanced mature economy on the heels of the "miracle growth" of the 1960s and 1970s, for the first time unification appeared possible. The private markets of capitalism had triumphed, and, for the unions, collective bargaining and joint consultation, especially in protection of employment security, won out over political protest and the goal of political control. Most workers by this time considered themselves members of the middle class.

The first steps toward formal unification began in the early 1980s, when key private sector union groups with more than 5 million members from both Sohyo and Domei formed Zenmin Rokyo. In 1987, private sector unions only—from Sohyo, Domei, and two small national federations—established Rengo with more than 5.5 million members in expectation that, as in other leading countries, there would be separate central organizations for public and private sector unionists. Domei and the smaller federations disbanded with Rengo's formation. Two years later, however, Rengo embraced the great bulk of the public sector unions to become a single, unified, national center for organized labor. The telecommunications workers, formerly in the public sector and led by the energetic Akira Yamagishi, paved the way to this grand merger. Rengo's membership soon reached above 8.6 million, the largest labor federation in Japanese history and one of the largest national trade union centers worldwide. Sohyo was disbanded. There were some protests against the merger. Smaller federations were formed by left-wingers, mostly government employees, who favored a separate center for public sector unions, and by former national railway workers opposed to the breakup and privatization of the government-owned lines.

Union membership in terms of numbers of employees reached a peak in 1975 with almost 12.6 million and has remained at about that level ever since. In 1975, union density (the percentage of all wage and salary earners organized) stood at almost 35 percent, a level that had been sustained through the years of rapid growth. With the drop in Japan's growth rate and continued expansion of the labor force, however, union density slipped gradually, dropping to 24.2 percent by 1993. Rengo aims to reverse the decline and regain a 30 percent level of organization.

Several reasons seem to explain the fall in union density. One is the decline in the creation of new large-scale enterprises, in which workers are likely to organize by themselves. Also, numerous large-scale firms slimmed down in face of technological and structural changes, shedding through employment adjustments regular employees who otherwise would be members of the enterprise-level union. Another reason is the failure of organized labor to gain increases in wages and benefits for union members superior to those obtained by the unorganized. *Shunto* and bonus bargaining were successful in spreading annual increases throughout the economy, benefiting organized and unorganized alike.[6] The decline was not due to stepped-up hostility to unionism by either government or employers. Many of the unorganized have their informal organizations, which negotiate and consult with employers over wages, benefits, and working conditions as required by law. One estimate shows that, if these informal unions were counted, union density in Japan would double.[7]

Another aim of Rengo is to merge and consolidate industry-level federations into large multi-industrial units such as all metalworkers, transportation workers, energy employees, and the like, along the lines of the Deutscher Gewerkschaftsbund (DGB; German Trade Union Federation). With such concentrations, it believes that industrial unionism will be more efficacious, especially as enterprise-level unions lose influence with the weakening of labor markets internal to firms and increase in interfirm labor mobility as expected in the future. Expanded industry-level federations would also be more effective in organizing the unorganized. The main challenge for organizing new unions lies in the expanding service sector, where most firms are small and many workers are female, part-time, and other nonregular employees. These are not promising areas for unionization. Organized labor needs to find new appeals and methods for organizing if it is to resume growth.

Given the political realignment under way since 1989, Rengo has been heavily involved in behind-the-scenes maneuvers that took place even though it had announced that economic activity would be its primary function. Yamagishi, as Rengo's president, was especially active in negotiating the formation of the Hosokawa government and its successors, but following the coalition of the leftist social democrats with the LDP in the summer of 1994, he resigned from his position in Rengo, alleging reasons of poor health. Throughout this period, there was considerable debate within Rengo over whether political interests were displacing the economic functions of the unions.

Yamagishi was succeeded by Jinnosuke Ashida, who had been elected to the newly created post of deputy president a year earlier and serves as president of the former Domei-affiliated textile workers' union, considered a mainstay of the right-wing

---

6. Tsuyoshi Tsuru, "Why Has Union Density Declined in Japan?" *Japan Labor Bulletin*, 1 Nov. 1994, pp. 5-8.

7. Kazuo Koike, "Workers in Small Firms and Women in Industry," in *Contemporary Industrial Relations in Japan*, ed. Taishiro Shirai (Madison: University of Wisconsin Press, 1983), pp. 103-4.

democratic socialists. In addition, disbanded in 1993 were the Rengo-affiliated politically oriented organs for former Sohyo, Domei, and neutral groups to pursue their respective political interests. It now appears that Rengo will return to a primary emphasis on collective bargaining and joint consultation as it awaits the emergence of a two- or three-party political system.

THE OUTLOOK

Prospects for Japanese employment and unemployment depend in part on forces of demand and supply surrounding human resources. The supply side is broadly determined by trends in total population, working-age population, and labor force. The observed relationship between decreasing fertility and increasing life expectancy suggests that the Japanese population is increasing at a decreasing rate and will peak in about 2020, decreasing thereafter. At the same time, the proportion of Japanese aged 65 or older will rise to more than 25 percent of the total population by 2020. The working-age population of 15-64 years of age was already tapering off in 1995. Because of the increasing labor force participation of women, the labor force may keep increasing for some more years, but it will probably begin to decrease about the turn of the twenty-first century.[8]

Other things being equal, a decreasing supply of labor should reduce unemployment. Changes in economic structure induce changes in employment structure. It is expected that, proportionately, agriculture and manufacturing will decline while construction and services will rise. The Ministry of Labor expects an especially rapid expansion of employment in health care, education, information, and environment. On the other hand, retail and wholesale trade, already overcrowded, will shed some of its workers as restructuring takes effect in this sector. Otherwise, services are generally considered good absorbers and stabilizers of employment. How much employment the economy will absorb depends on the level and growth of the aggregate demand.

Japan's widely misunderstood lifetime employment will have little to do with long-term prospects for employment and unemployment. The long-tenure core employees as a percentage of the total workforce of a firm or an employing organization will, on the average, probably decline, implying the employer's greater dependence on contingency workers. Services depend much more on certified or proven skills, specialties, and qualifications than they do on experience in internal labor markets. Even in manufacturing, the hotbed of lifetime employment so far, the importance of internal labor markets will diminish because of increasing technological maturity, which reduces the idiosyncrasy or firm specificity of technology or process. Increasing use of computers in manufacturing reduces the need for unskilled routine manual workers but retains a small group of

8. Naohiro Yashiro and Akiko Oishi, "Japanese Employment Practices under Changing Economic Circumstances," *Monthly Journal of the Japan Institute of Labour*, 37(6):38-47 (June 1995).

computer-happy problem solvers. Routine unskilled jobs are also exported to other countries through foreign direct investment.

Upward-spiraling career paths within large firms or organizations will be fewer, while specialized competencies will be in great demand everywhere. This implies that vocational and professional training will expand and that trainers will be in great demand. Individuals will have to be more responsible for occupational choice and upgrading. Japanese labor markets will then be much more diversified, open, and mobile than they have been. But all this will require considerable coordination between government, employers, and organized labor.

Reworking Work: Tough Times Ahead

By JOSEPH F. COATES

ABSTRACT: Business, financial, technological, economic, social, and political trends indicate an impending mass wave of structural unemployment rivaling that of the Great Depression within a decade. In this article, a dozen prophylactic and therapeutic remedies are suggested, all of which require a rethinking of socioeconomic policy, reevaluation of goals for the long-term future, and recognition that new policies must be approached as continuing, open-ended social experiments.

Joseph F. Coates is the president of Coates & Jarratt, Inc. (formerly J. F. Coates, Inc.), a policy research organization specializing in the study of the future. He has worked as a futurist in business, industry, and government for more than thirty years. He is an adjunct professor at George Washington University. His most recent book is Future Work *(1990).*

ECONOMICS is not one of the helping professions. The strength of economics lies in post hoc explanation rather than in anticipatory policy guidance. Therefore we must step outside the conventional economics framework to look at what potential radical changes may be occurring in the workforce.

The evidence developed in this article points to massive technological unemployment within the next decade or so. The remedies are numerous and may, in concert, deal with the situation for the nation's collective benefit. The core goal linking remedies should not be the creation of jobs, although that may be part of it. The core goal should be putting a fair share of the gains in productivity into the pockets and purses of everyone in order to keep the machinery of the market economy both working and providing a better life for us all.

THE EMERGING SITUATION

In a more or less traditional economic analysis, we would have little to fear about the future of the nation's prosperity were the workforce to enjoy a 2.0 or 2.5 percent per capita increase in gross domestic product annually. That increase would put enough money in the hands of the people that they would find ways to spend it and we would find new jobs created as old jobs decline or disappear. This has been the American experience from 1945 to 1975. The increasing prosperity of the country created hundreds of occupations employing millions of people doing things that were simply unthinkable as paid employment a half century earlier. The trouble with that argument is that the economic payoffs associated with productivity gains today are decreasingly likely to fall into the hands of the generality and much more likely to fall into the hands of the top-income quintile, decile, or centile. There are no good social mechanisms for distributing the benefits of improved productivity when people are unemployed.

The only way we all can enjoy an increase in our individual well-being is by increasing our national productivity. A per capita annual productivity increase of 2.0 to 2.5 percent would double our individual real income in 25 to 35 years. Such a growth is well within the framework of technical, economic, and social plausibility. To achieve that, however, we are likely to follow the route of productivity improvement that has been so astonishingly successful in agriculture and so visibly successful in manufacturing. That route is to replace people with knowledge embodied in machines, devices, and equipment and at the same time to drastically reduce the number of workers in those sectors.

Today, about 80 percent of the workforce is in the service sector. About 60 percent of that is made up of information workers, and the rest are blue-collar service workers. The productivity of the service sector has been more or less static for the last twenty years. Therefore, as business and industry continue their relentless pressure for improved productivity, they will turn to the service sector and begin to replace workers with automation or, in the case of white-collar workers, bring in newer levels of automation that raise the productivity of those employed and dismiss the surplus workers.

In about two generations, 1920-90, the portion of the workforce employed in agriculture fell from 40.0 percent to 1.8 percent. That change occurred while the United States was becoming the most productive agricultural region in the world. We replaced people and human labor with knowledge embodied in machines, soil treatments, better crops, and so forth. This in turn led to the aggregation of firms and further reduction in the need for workers.

We are witnessing a parallel development now in manufacturing, the only sector of the economy in which there is a significant increase in productivity. As we increasingly replace people with knowledge embodied in high-tech machines linked and assisted by computers in coordination and operation, productivity skyrockets and workers are replaced. If all goes well, the current 16 percent of the workforce in manufacturing should decline to 4-6 percent by 2005, which, incidentally, would be essential to our increasing global competitiveness. This runs directly counter to the current administration's notion of increasing employment in the manufacturing sector. More people in manufacturing is anticompetitive and contrary to the long-term interests of the economy.

Turn now to the 80 percent of the workforce that is in the service sector. One cannot expect real income growth for service workers or the nation as a whole unless there are improvements in productivity. Income growth without improvements in productivity is an invitation to disastrous inflation. Improved productivity, which we anticipate will sweep over the service sector in the next decade, will, as it did in agriculture and manufacturing, depend on replacing large numbers of people with knowledge embedded in devices. Whether those devices are in the grocery store or in the bank, whether they are robots where blue-collar assembly-line workers used to be or intelligent machines at the local health club, the service sector will be traumatized.

For the future of the service and information sectors, we assume less drastic declines than have shown up in agriculture but greater than those that have occurred in manufacturing. By 2000-2010, there may be a 30 percent cut in the white-collar workforce and perhaps a 25 percent cut in the blue-collar nonmanufacturing workforce.

The evidence pointing to massive structural unemployment flows from several semi-independent developments. Hence the argument is powerful in that it is convergent and does not depend on a single line of argument or a single development.

TRENDS

Other trends aggravate the situation. One is the impending entry of the baby-boom echo into the workforce beginning around 2005-10. Another concerns the high probability of continuing immigration, running today around 800,000 people per year. By and large, immigrants are at the lower end of the economic scale unless they are educated. This builds toward a larger rural and urban proletariat, those in the society but not of the society. Among Mexican immigrants, for example, 38 percent of those of high school age currently drop out. In dropping out, they are also dropping out of hope for long-term steady incomes. In the past decade, high school dropouts' real income decreased 10 percent and those with only high school diplomas have seen their real income decline by about 3 percent.

A third aggravating factor is that the current government policy is slowly moving the age of retirement up from 65 to 67 to improve the economic viability of social security. That means more older workers competing against a floodtide of younger workers, depressing each other's wages.

Fourth, a factor of marginal importance, except for those involved, is that a percentage of the population—to a large extent, overlapping school dropouts—is weak in symbolic, oral, or written skills. Members of this group are at a greater disadvantage in the job market in the information society.

Finally, the current practice in large corporations has been to heave the burdens of restructuring their workforces onto the worker. The current corporate passion is for downsizing and outsourcing. Those two programs go hand in hand as fundamental mechanisms for throwing onto the back of workers the economic burden of satisfying the stockholders with increasing dividends. The simple result is the lower-paid temporary and contingent worker.

Downsizing has displaced large numbers of workers in the last decade and has had particularly dramatic effects on middle managers. This practice will surely continue and is entering a new phase of anticipating downsizing, which prepares the corporation for future contingencies.

Outsourcing, within the country and overseas, seeks cheaper sources for equivalent-quality goods and services, thereby reducing labor rates domestically.

A consequence of outsourcing and downsizing has been the creation of a large and growing contingent workforce. Aside from the fact that the goal of outsourcing is to reduce the direct labor package and the benefits burden, it has the effect of politicizing the work situation. After all, the contingent worker increasingly finds himself or herself hanging by a thread, with a totally unreliable employer holding the other end of that thread.

Another development of some importance is distributed work, that is, work off-site in unconventional locations—at home, on the road, in a vendor's or a supplier's facility, or at a customer's base. It has the effect of reducing any power of the workers to organize and collectively act for their own benefit. While about 3.5 percent of the workforce today is in distributed work, as present trends continue and corporations desire to cut costs and workers press for increases in flexibility, the portion of the workforce that is in distributed work could easily rise to 20 percent by 2005 and perhaps 40 percent by 2020.

THE ABUSIVE CORPORATION

The core of the antiworker practices of the corporation, which are not limited to antilabor measures, lies in the corporation's increasingly sharp focus on a single factor: the stockholders, more recently called by the softer term "shareholders." The stockholders driving corporate misbehavior are not primarily individuals. They are mutual funds and pension funds. They constantly press for increases in their stock value and are relentless and ruthless in applying pressure to corporations for quarterly and annual profits. Therefore the chief executive officers (CEOs) and the executive suites are pressured to be merciless in meeting the objectives of the large stockholders. One of the side effects is that the CEOs in U.S. corporations are now rewarded out of all balance with CEOs in other industrialized nations. This excessive compensation is balm to salve a ruffled conscience about the abuse to which they are subjecting workers and their families.

No science has ever taught us to kill Jews, to murder gypsies, to dispose of the handicapped, or to eliminate the lame, the blind, and the psychotic. Yet we know that, when ideology takes hold of a country, those things do happen, and science and technology are brought in to make the process more efficient, more effective, more socially acceptable, and less visible. In the same way, when conservative economists talk about the goal of the corporation as maximizing return to the stockholders, that is not a scientific statement coming out of economics; it is unadulterated ideology. It is no less ideology than some Communist fantasy, and yet, once one unquestioningly accepts that ideological statement masquerading as science because it is put forward by prestigious, professional economists, all the rest of the analytical capability of economics turns out to show how to accomplish that ideological objective. Fundamentally, the confusion between ideology and science, insofar as economics is a science, is the intellectual underpinning of our present worsening situation. Remedies include a direct confrontation with that ideology, calling it what it is and demanding a public review. A new ideology must lie at the core of any remedy to future structural unemployment.

Foreign competition has added to the pressure that the corporation feels. It has not been a powerful factor in the depression of labor rates, however, because most of the imported foreign products come from relatively high-labor-rate countries such as Germany and Japan. In the future, however, the situation is likely to be far different as the scientific and technical workforce around the world steadily swells in number and technical capability and what we now consider newly industrialized countries become direct and effective competitors in low-, mid-, and high-tech products and services.

To some extent, the misbehavior of the corporation is accompanied by a shift in attitude; the result is in sharp contrast to the situation in Germany or Japan. The American corporation has abandoned any sense of patriotism, that is, any sense of primary duty to the home country. The shareholders' contentment is held above all other considerations. Accompanying this absence of sense of duty to the country is the decline in sense of duty to the community, to its own managers, to its workers, and to any other group to which it reasonably could expect to have some obligations. The only obligations, other than to stockholders are those forced on it by law.

Accompanying this absence of corporate sense of duty are two additional factors directly affecting the economic health of the citizenry. First is the steady fall in the wages for new jobs. That decline has most sharply hit high school dropouts and those who have only high school diplomas. These drops reflect the move away from a world in which muscle counts to a world in which information capabilities count. The blue-collar world is history. Those who have trained and worked and expected to be employed and paid handsomely in middle- and low-skill blue-collar functions are in for the greatest disappointments.

On the other hand, the information worker is not in any great shape for the future. There is a widespread myth that the knowledge worker is creative and uses analytical skills at the workplace. Consider that 60 percent of the workforce who are information workers. The reality is that the bulk of them are not involved in any theoretically or analytically demanding activities. Most knowledge workers are just pushing buttons and working prefabricated programs. They are information workers largely because they are engaged in some kind of data entry, data processing, or machine handling. The next wave of information technology will make them redundant by the millions. The percentage of information workers combining theoretical, analytical, and information technology skills is quite small and is unlikely to ever exceed 25 percent of the workforce because of the simple limitations on native ability.

Information workers have generally felt more or less insulated from foreign competition, particularly those at the upper end of information work—those involved with software production or those involved in using sophisticated information technologies in consulting and related services. Both of those groups are whistling in the dark. There has been a dramatic increase in the exportation of data-entry work. That market will disappear in both domestic and overseas work as new information technology allows direct data entry with no human intermediary.

In the more technically demanding field of software production, we already see the emergence of world-class software capabilities in India, Eastern Europe, and China. The American software specialists' argument that those countries are only doing the easy stuff, the simple-minded stuff, may be true. But they have to start somewhere. Software development is not physical-capital intensive but is intellectual-capital intensive, and it is straightforwardly learned and perfected by the Ph.D.'s and their equivalents in India, Eastern Europe, and China. The software people sound as dismissive as the auto industry people did when the first Volkswagens arrived in America.

A social and economic byway of the problem is the turn in the polity to questions of welfare and welfare abuse and a strong pressure to get those on welfare into responsible jobs. Insofar as that is successful, it will create further pressures to depress wages. Whatever value there may be in terms of self-respect and self-regard for those welfare recipients who are pushed into traditional employment, it cannot relieve structural unemployment. More people chasing fewer jobs will by itself depress wages.

In putting the numbers together and anticipating a nominal workforce of 153 million people in 2005, it is by no means unthinkable that we would have 20-25 percent of them structurally squeezed out of the workforce, that is, unemployed (see Table 1).

As most readers remember, the stock market broke 1000, then 2000, then 3000, then 4000, and is now eagerly anticipating breaking 5000. Looked at through the cold eye of reality, there is no substantial basis for that growth in the value of stock. It rather reflects a mentality characteristic of the tulip mania that led to an economic disaster in Holland. The growth of the present system is fed largely by the pressures and the behaviors of the large investment funds. Aside from all other factors at play, that bubble must eventually burst if it continues to swell, and it may burst sooner than any of us would care to see. That, of course, would put the labor force problems front and center in the public agenda in the worst possible circumstances, disaster.

REMEDIES

Some social thinkers write about solving the unemployment problem. That already misleads in that it assumes that unemployment is bad or a problem and that definitive actions can be taken to solve it. The assumption that definitive actions can be taken is a technical issue rather than a result of a structural transformation in the society. To illustrate with a metaphor, one would not think of solving the rainfall problem of the Sahara. That falsifies the issue. Rather, one would look for ways to adapt to circumstances, to the climate.

The concept of solving the so-called unemployment problem has the additional negative social consequence of bifurcating the population: one class that is mostly employed and another that is mostly un- or underemployed, the educated and the uneducated, the competent and the incompetent.

The effectiveness of remedies depends on how reliably the problem is framed. The politically and socially attractive family of remedies directed at providing jobs skirts the core issue. The core need is to put money in the hands of individual citizens so that they can acquire the things that they need and can, at the same time, keep a market economy functioning and productive in delivering goods. At the same time, they must enjoy a satisfying degree of self-respect, have the awareness and reality of a satisfying life, and be effective participants in our democratic process. Work has traditionally been the most important way to achieve

TABLE 1
EMPLOYMENT AND UNEMPLOYMENT IN THE YEAR 2005

Distribution of Work	Year 1995 Percentage of Workforce	Year 1995 Number of Workers (Millions)	Year 2005* Number of Workers (Millions)	Year 2005† Assumed Percentage of Job Loss	Year 2005† Number of Workers (Millions)	Year 2005‡ Assumed Percentage of Job Loss	Year 2005‡ Number of Workers (Millions)
Agriculture	2	2.8	3.1	20	2.5	0	3.1
Manufacturing	16	21.0	23.1	60	9.2	28	16.6
Information	60	78.8	86.6	25	65.1	20	69.2
Other services	22	28.9	31.8	20	25.4	10	28.6
Total employed		131.5	144.6		102.2		117.5
Unemployed		7.6 (5.5%)	8.4 (5.5%)		50.8 (33.2%)		35.5 (23.2%)
Total workforce		139.1	153.0§		153.0		153.0

SOURCE: Coates & Jarratt, Inc.
*Assume same percentages of workforce as in 1995.
†Assume that present trend accelerates.
‡Assume that present trend declines.
§Bureau of Labor Statistics estimate.

these aims. The future calls for broader remedies including, but not limited to, work for pay and pay for work.

There has been a sharp skewing in the distribution of income as productivity has increased. Without putting a fair portion of the gains resulting from productivity into the hands of the multitude, that skewing can go in only one direction: to further favor the top decile to centile. Those with the most money will not spend proportionately as much as will those with less money.

Shortening the workweek or work life would be compatible with the long-term trends in this century. A mandated drop from 40 to 36 hours of work a week would create 10 percent more jobs. While those jobs would not necessarily match the skills of the surplus labor, there would be some close fits. The longer-term strategic approach of shortening work life would imply keeping young people in school longer and retiring people from the workforce earlier. A related strategy would be to intersperse the forty-year work life with nonwork or other hiatuses.

Shrinkage in the life cycle of work is surely plausible when it is realized that within this century, the workweek has been shortened from 60 hours to 40 hours and the work life has become shorter, starts later, and ends earlier. The work life used to begin at age 16 and end at age 70; it now begins at 20 and ends at 62 for most workers.

Reduction of the workweek need not be on a fixed schedule or by fixed amounts. Imagine legislation setting up a workweek control board operating much the way Alan Greenspan now controls interest rates—a board that would control the workweek not weekly but over periods of three months to a year. Incidentally, it is worth noting in this connection that the propaganda that one so frequently hears about the extended workweek of the average American simply does not stand up to the data from the best available research, the time-budgeting work of John P. Robinson of the University of Maryland.

Legitimating welfare could be a powerful remedy. Frequently when I lecture before business groups, I ask audience members to raise their hands if they have ever been on welfare, relief, or the dole. Hands never go up. I immediately follow that with the question of how many of them are graduates of state universities. There is usually a forest of hands, and almost simultaneously they recognize the connection and laugh. Legitimization of the dole requires that public expenditures to individuals be seen as a legitimate, honorable, and valuable part of the work life cycle.

We might acknowledge socially that unemployment must be a necessary part of each of our lives and therefore take aggressive steps to recognize that as an honorable phase it will hit us two, three, or four times in our working lives. Making unemployment a life-cycle phase is almost a necessity, with public largesse to provide income.

Make-work strategies rarely, if ever, have worked in the last fifty years, although the United States did have successful make-work programs with the Civilian Conservation Corps, the Work Projects Administration, and the Public Works Administration in the Great Depression of the 1930s. Crucial to successful make-work is that the assignment be not merely make-work. It must be patently, tangibly, and unequivocally socially useful. Further, it must provide some capability that is useful after the make-work assignment is over. Notice the careful selection of the pejorative terms in these remedies. In many cases, it is necessary to overcome the pejorative language and find positive language reflecting positive concepts and positive programs.

Extending education fits the generally recognized trend toward lifelong and continuing education that millions of people are already involved with. It need not be the case, however, that extending education as a remedy to structural unemployment be focused only around work skills and competence. Traditionally, public education has had three functions: preparation for work, preparation for citizenship, and furnishing the mind. All three of those objectives should be part of an extended, lifelong education program.

Melding working and leisure could again become significant. Corporate goals in the past 15 years have been to squeeze out anything that is nonproductive at the workplace. Yet, for the 20 years before that squeeze occurred, there was a steady increase in activities unrelated to productivity at the workplace, such as time donated to charities or collection of funds for the United Way or other socially significant activities. Various forms of volunteerism could be undertaken under the rubric of the employer's sponsorship, such as reconstruction of buildings; training and teaching; maintenance of artwork; being a docent at a museum; providing chauffeuring services for the ill, the old, or the handicapped; teaching English to foreign speakers; or teaching reading or writing to the illiterate.

The growth of two-income households in the United States in the last 15 years has not been particularly out of necessity. The principal area of growth in two-income households has been in the upper middle class, where the small family size of well-educated women drove them, out of ennui, into the workforce. This growth pattern is reflected in the skewed distribution of the nation's income, showing a relatively high increase in family income in the top quintile in the population. If incomes are depressed as a result of structural unemployment, the two-income household with two marginally paid workers may become necessary rather than discretionary for greater numbers of households.

Self-employment is widely touted as desirable. This is to a large extent an overblown myth basically serving the corporate passion for downsizing and outsourcing. Self-employment is extremely chancy. Most of us are simply not entrepreneurial, that is, most are not ready to start a business with the drive and incentive to continually grow, expand, and become dominant in one's field. Most self-employed people are not even small businessmen in the sense of the dry cleaner or the restaurateur but are self-employed largely as a way of creating jobs for themselves. The economic reality is that in a period of recession, depression, or labor surplus, self-employment becomes merely one step short of the bread line. The price elasticity of demand for labor is very steep.

Letting the workers own the modes of production surely has a somewhat obsolete, socialist ring to it. However, there are two opportunities that do relate to that which may be partial remedies. One is the employee stock ownership plan (ESOP), which implies that one is or was an employee of an organization and that there is the opportunity to buy into its ownership and hence become particularly attuned to its productivity and health and development. ESOPs often have been a desperate strategy for saving mismanaged, faltering companies. The concept, however, does have merits, and numerous ESOPs have been successful. An alternative concept proposed by an analyst at the then National Bureau of Standards came out of his anticipation of technological unemployment. He proposed that automated machinery, specifically robots, be owned by the workers and leased to companies. Obviously, one would not store the robot in one's garage and tow it to the factory. The concept implies that there be intermediate organizations as the go-betweens.

Restricted immigration and even sterner measures to deport illegal immigrants is a mechanism for reducing the internally competitive, non-American workforce.

Taxes as a means of discouraging the replacement of people by machines could be a powerful brake on the corporate passion for downsized efficiency in the workplace. Such policies are already under way in Europe for environmental reasons; there they are meant to discourage the movement toward more environmentally challenging devices.

Taxes may also have a protectionist effect by discouraging overseas use of low-cost labor. One might anticipate high taxes on would-be imported products coming from countries that have extremely low labor rates.

Collective solutions—group living, group farming, group houses, group activities—will always have an appeal to the tiny percentage of the population that is ideologically driven. Such groups will never be large enough or numerous enough or durable enough to be significant in the economy, however. Collectivism simply does not fit the American ethos unless religiously motivated.

Work as a privilege is not untenable. If the social functions of work were seen as income, status, respectability, and self-worth, there surely would be many kinds of jobs in the society that could be allocated or rationed on a priority basis. Priority could be given to those who have performed well in certain tasks or functions, have special qualifications, or are being rewarded for some other activity.

The Third Sector is often spoken of as the group of nonprofit activities distinct from government and distinct from business. The role of the Third Sector in the economy has been to deal with activities that seem inappropriate for government and that do not find a ready business market. One might look at the Third Sector as filling the gaps created by market failures. By no means is the Third

Sector or the nonprofit sector without prosperity, high incomes, and high prestige. Everything from the Heritage Foundation and the Brookings Institution to a local settlement house falls into the Third Sector. The Third Sector also has the capability of recruiting large numbers of volunteers in socially useful activities. Former president Carter has made famous those groups in home reconstruction. Religious organizations involve themselves in church building on a voluntary basis. The Girl Scouts, Boy Scouts, and related organizations are well known and well regarded.

The Third Sector, therefore, may have the opportunity to orchestrate and recruit people to engage in socially useful activities. At what point the money flows, and to whom it flows, is the crucial open question. In both government and business, one can see money funneled, as happens now, into the Third Sector to pay for its organizational structure and managerial work. On the other hand, one can envision that practice carried further, paying the people who "volunteer" for various tasks.

A dual system of money and scrip could well come into being. Scrip would be issued to people who performed select functions. It would be exchanged for fundamental maintenance items—food, clothing, and shelter—whereas money would be required for all the other goods and services of the society.

As the massive workforce outside the industrialized nations swells over the next decades, workers may find themselves in most aggressive competition for jobs and in a continually economically depressed global environment. International commerce may make the workforce of the advanced nations increasingly noncompetitive. For the United States, that raises the long-term strategic possibility of raising protectionist walls and becoming insulated. The advanced nations could keep out products that result from the absolutely depressed wage rates of the rest of the world. This could maintain high wages at home. The net long-term effect is likely to be a substantial reduction in the rate of economic growth. Growth, of course, is not so necessary to those nations that have already achieved high levels of socioeconomic development.

Many women, and to an increasing extent men, are now homemakers, spending a large portion or all of their time in domestic chores, primarily framed around raising families. It is clear from twenty years of feminist research and advocacy that, by anybody's standards, that is real work. It may be practical, therefore, to tie that work to a compensation program. The numerous ifs, ands, and buts would have to be dealt with, but there is no reason to believe that homemakers could not be compensated for their labor. Payment might be based on the size of one's family, the level of one's education, the conditions under which one works, and so forth. Ironically, the concept might also appeal to conservatives who are so enthusiastic about promoting so-called family values.

The beginning of this article attributes a great deal of the present corporate abuse of workers to business's sole concentration on stockholders and the concomitant relentless pressure for enhanced stock value. A primary long-term strategic reform that would minimize the intense short-term concentration on stockholders and begin to focus attention on other constituents of the corporation would come from stock market reform. The shape that the reform might take is uncertain, but perhaps measures that simply reduce the rate of the turnover of stock might go a long way toward remedying the situation. Related solutions might include mandated representation of broad constituent groups on the boards of all stock companies capitalized at more than $20 million.

The potential remedies are there. The earlier we get ready to use them, the more capable we will be to prevent, squelch, or minimize the effects of any impending structural unemployment.

We must seek as our national goal the accomplishment of three things: (1) improvement in productivity, (2) broad distribution of the benefits of that productivity, and (3) respectable work for all through most of their lives.

It is obvious that there is no clear route to dealing with the impending structural unemployment, and one can surely not expect the wisdom of the economist, the legislator, or the White House to offer a definitive response. However hard they might try, they are simply unable, because of the complexities of the situation, to develop definitive, clear, unequivocal solutions. Consequently, one of the policy elements that should be central to dealing with this impending structural unemployment is to recognize that incapacity for definitive solutions and to approach a multifaceted strategy as a frank nationwide continuing experiment. We can learn from this experiment how to deal more effectively with the problems that confront us.

This brief article has not dealt with the problems of the other advanced nations or with the larger problems, in all senses, of the developing world. Those problems call for a palette broader than this article could accommodate.

Computers Don't Kill Jobs, People Do: Technology and Power in the Workplace

By CHARLEY RICHARDSON

ABSTRACT: New technologies are increasingly common in America's workplaces. The pace of technological change can be expected to increase in the future. The impacts of technological change include job loss, changes in skills, and health and safety effects, among others. These are of great importance to the workforce. From a social policy perspective, however, the most important impact of technological change is its effect on the power relationships between workers and managers in the workplace. Many of the traditional sources of union or worker power or leverage are undermined as new technologies are designed, developed, and implemented. Effective technology policy needs to go beyond dealing with the symptoms of technological change to taking on the core issue, which is precisely the loss of power that the workforce experiences.

Charley Richardson is the director of the Technology and Work Program at the University of Massachusetts, Lowell. The program provides unions with training, technical assistance, and strategic planning support concerning new technology, new forms of work organization, and labor-management programs. Richardson spent 10 years as a shipfitter (heavy steel fabricator) in three shipyards, directly experiencing the impact of changing technology on skilled work. Following a back injury at work and the closing of the third yard, he earned an MBA.

THE American workplace is undergoing massive change. *Business Week* speaks of a "revolution in America's workplace," invoking the law of the jungle and warning that only some will prosper, only the strong will survive: "It's getting positively Darwinian. The American workplace, once a protected habitat offering a measure of prosperity in exchange for a lifetime of dedicated work, is now a dangerous place."[1]

In calling up the ghost of Darwin (and social Darwinism), *Business Week* manages to avoid, for itself and for its readership, any responsibility for the outcomes of the "revolution": "There are no villains at work, just the inexorable forces of economic and technological change. The remaking of the world of work is but a means to one end—boosting productivity."[2]

Even *Business Week*, though, has to admit that the changes in the workplace are hurting people: "If there are no villains, there are certainly victims. . . . These are difficult times for many working people in America."[3]

Many others have detailed the disaster that is becoming the daily experience of working Americans.[4] In this article, I examine one central aspect of the changes that are occurring in the workplace: new technology. I argue that, rather than an "inexorable force," technology is a critical, socially defined component of the move to reorganize America's workplaces. This reorganization has among its goals achieving massive increases in productivity, quality, and market sensitivity and flexibility, but it also seeks to vastly increase the power of management in relation to the workforce. Understanding the transfer of power that technology enables is critical to understanding and improving the future prospects for American workers.

Descriptions of technology as an independent and uncontrollable force—defined as progress—reflect the author's comfort with the social impact of technology or, at a minimum, with the general nature of the transfer of resources and power. Meanwhile, those who write with concern about the impacts of technological change but ignore the role of technology in transferring power risk directing attention away from the critical issue and providing an inappropriate foundation for policy prescriptions.

New workplace technologies are being introduced at an ever increasing rate. At the same time, the scope (breadth of impact) and penetration (depth of impact) of technological change are growing rapidly. In the course of this change, the boundaries of skill and geography that placed

---

1. "Revolution in America's Workplace," *Business Week*, 17 Oct. 1994, p. 252.
2. Ibid.
3. Ibid.
4. See, for example, Jeremy Brecher and Tim Costello, *Global Village or Global Pillage: Economic Restructuring from the Bottom Up* (Boston: South End Press, 1994); Jeremy Rifkin, *The End of Work: The Decline of the Global Labor Force and the Dawn of the Post-Market Era* (New York: Putnam, 1995); Juliet Schor, *The Overworked American: The Unexpected Decline of Leisure* (New York: Basic Books, 1991); Donald Bartlett and James Steele, *America: What Went Wrong?* (Kansas City, MO: Andrews & McMeel, 1992); Bennett Harrison and Barry Bluestone, *The Great U-Turn: Corporate Restructuring and the Polarizing of America* (New York: HarperCollins, 1990).

limits on management and provided leverage to the workforce are being broken by the move toward workerless factories, expert systems, and distributed activities linked by an information superhighway. Social regulation and labor-management interaction designed for a static and geographically constrained workplace are proving ineffective in protecting workers in the workplace of the future.

While our social fascination with technology often focuses on what it can do in technical terms—how many millions of instructions per second, for example—or what an individual could do with it, technology's true significance lies in the choices that it provides within society and to whom it provides them. A laptop computer and global positioning system used in the woods to guide a hiker and keep a journal have primarily an individual significance. The same pieces of technology when placed in a tractor trailer and used to continuously monitor a driver's activities, without the consent of the driver, are highly socially significant and represent a loss of power or control by the driver.

The discussion of the technical aspects of technological change and the analysis of the changing workplace and its negative impacts on the workforce remain disconnected and insignificant without the link of social power. Like technojunkies, people are forced not only to take the new technologies that are offered to them but also to like them enough to call them progress and to call for more. They become convinced that the increases in productivity and quality that the dealers of technology promise will somehow solve the poverty, pollution, displacement, and disempowerment that accompanied the last round of technological change.

The real question that must be answered is being ignored or missed. Before asking what we are going to do about the loss of jobs due to technology and the poverty that accompanies it, we need to be asking, Why does a massive increase in the productive capacity of people lead to a decrease in the quality of life for the vast majority? Only by answering that question can we take aim at the cause rather than the symptoms.

New technology does not kill jobs; people do. Technology provides the means and allows job loss to be named progress. But people decide what kinds of technology to develop and how and when to use it. It is to the social dimensions of technological change and, in particular, to its impact on power relations in society that we must ultimately turn our attention.

TECHNOLOGICAL CHANGE IN THE WORKPLACE

The impacts of technological change in the workplace are a product of the social process of design, development, and implementation. New workplace technologies emerge from a system that is generally unresponsive to the needs of the broad populace and over which the broad populace exerts little or no control. This system is staffed by people who speak in a different language from that of most people, who live in different communities, who work in different worlds, and who, in many ways, are taught to ignore, demean, and eliminate the workforce.[5]

While much of the research and development is controlled by the private sector (obviously out of reach of the public and the workforce), even public intervention and funding do little to improve the situation. The Advanced Technology Program (ATP) of the National Institute of Standards and Technology (NIST) has over the last two years been holding meetings to discuss the technologies that need to be developed for the future, with the purpose of guiding government funding. The attendees at these sessions are a clear indication of who makes the decisions about technology.

One such meeting was directed at technology in health care. But who was in attendance? It was not nurses. It was not dietary aides. It was not nurse's aides. It was the big hospitals, but it was also McDonnell Douglas, IBM, and Digital Equipment Corporation—large corporations looking for new markets in which to push their technologies, large corporations that are known for their recent downsizing and lack of concern for the workforce.

Technologies are designed, developed, and implemented with little or no attention to the needs of the workforce or the impact that the technologies might have on the workforce. In fact, they are often designed and developed with a disdain for the workforce. Technologies are then used to increase control over and decrease reliance on the workforce, and it is from here that the impacts of technological change emerge.

Much of the discussion about technology's social impact has focused on the effects on jobs and skills. The great debates over whether technology is a net destroyer or net creator of jobs and whether it increases or decreases skills have been endless. While interesting, these debates miss the core point; net impacts are not the issue. The real questions are not how many jobs and how much skill but who has them, what kinds of leverage they provide, and what they mean in a social context.

Surely people do seem to lose their jobs due to new technology. But more bluntly put, and more accurately described, they are no longer needed by those who have the power to decide. The process can be done without them, and so they no longer have any value.

Technology also changes the skills that are needed to complete the production or service delivery process. For those possessing the no-longer-needed skills, it matters little whether or not the net effect is "upskilling." Who has access to the new skills? At what cost? Are the new skills connected to the power base of the workforce (the union), or are they held by people who have been legally and/or culturally tied to management? These are the questions that need to be explored.

Even those who survive technological displacement do not avoid the negative impacts of technology on the workplace. New technologies have

---

5. Harry Braverman, *Labor and Monopoly Capital: The Degradation of Work in the 20th Century* (New York: Monthly Review Press, 1974); David Noble, *Forces of Production: A Social History of Industrial Automation* (New York: Knopf, 1984).

been used to create workplaces where people are continuously monitored, where processes are increasingly lean, where repetitive strain injuries (RSIs) are commonplace, where stress is increasing, where new chemical hazards are introduced daily, and where dull and dead-end occupations reign.

The negative impacts of technological change on the workforce are rarely accidents. There are certainly thousands of examples of technologies that were built and implemented without allowing for the operator. But even these can hardly be called accidents, for the decision to ignore and demean the workforce was taken consciously decades ago and is still built into the education of engineers and the systems of technology design and implementation.

The vast majority of problems connected with technological change are in fact the result of intentional design. The designs were intentional, the outcomes were desired, and the impacts on the workforce were either ignored or depersonalized to the point that they became irrelevant. No one particularly wanted to create joblessness in society, but some did want to eliminate certain jobs. No one particularly wanted to eliminate people's skills, but some did want to make them irrelevant to the production and service delivery process—which is essentially the same thing. No one wanted to cause stress-related illness, but some did want to monitor and measure, to increase demand and decrease control—all of which contribute directly to stress.

No one wanted to increase the incidence of RSIs, but some did want to intensify work, eliminate downtime, and, in the process, increase repetition—all of which help create RSIs.

We can look at RSIs and stress as examples. There are four basic risk factors for RSIs: force, awkward posture, repetition, and lack of rest or recovery time. Force and awkward posture are mistakes. They could be called accidents of design. Somebody forgot to think about the person who is actually doing the job. The current focus on the redesign of work stations according to ergonomic principles is aimed at fixing some of the force and awkward-posture issues.

Repetition and no rest are different matters, however. Repetition and no rest are, in fact, design goals of a technology design, of workplace design. Just-in-time (JIT) systems and lean production are aimed at eliminating rest and increasing repetition. It is perhaps ironic, and perhaps sinister, that even some of the so-called ergonomic improvements that are being made, while eliminating force and awkward posture, are increasing lack of rest and repetition and may therefore be having a net negative impact on RSIs.

The stress resulting from computer monitoring of the workforce is another example of an impact that is the direct result of conscious design. It is no accident that in most workplaces, some form of computer monitoring is occurring. Despite this, there have yet to be any real analyses of the impact of computer monitoring on the workforce.[6] We do know that lack of control and increased de-

6. U.S., Office of Technology Assessment, *The Electronic Supervisor: New Technology, New Tensions* (Washington, DC: Government Printing Office, 1987).

mand, both of which can result from continuous monitoring, are key sources of stress and causes of stress-related illness.[7]

Those who have never been monitored at work should think about what it is like to drive a car with a police officer behind you, even if you routinely obey the traffic laws. Computers are the officer that is always behind you when you are at work.

Technologies have a significant impact on the conditions under which people work. Of that there is no doubt. Further, it is clear that many of the negative impacts of workplace technology grow directly out of a technological system that tends to ignore the needs of the workforce. While it would seem that technology would provide the basis for improving conditions for the workforce, the opposite seems to be the case in most instances. It is to the question of power—of why the system can ignore the vast majority and how technology ultimately affects power relations—that we must now turn our attention.

TECHNOLOGY AS AN INSTRUMENT OF POWER

If the impacts of technology can be connected to a social process of design, then the questions of who controls the decision making and in whose interests decisions are being made rise to the top. While this analysis is relatively straightforward, we must now turn our attention to the ways in which decisions about technology affect power rela-

tions within the workplace. The main and most significant impact of technological change is not RSI, is not stress, and is not job loss. These are in fact merely symptoms of an overwhelming loss of power on the part of the vast majority.

If the workforce had the power to demand or take breaks or to slow the work down, RSIs and stress would be much less of a problem. If the workforce had the power to refuse weekend work or 12-hour shifts, their lives would be less harried and more controlled. If the workforce had the power to share productivity gains, wages would rise and the workweek could be shortened. If the workforce had the power to stop displacement, retraining for new technologies and new skills would become part of what employers do. If the workforce had the power to just say no to harmful technologies, the development process would change to reflect their needs and concerns.

On 3 July 1995, the *New York Times* published an article titled, "The New World of Work, Where Employers Call All the Shots." The article describes the declining ability of the workforce to have a say in the workplace, pointing to weaker unions, global competition, and new technology as the key ingredients leading to increasing insecurity for the workforce. It also notes that along with diminished job security, workers have experienced diminished bargaining power. They are losing the ability to negotiate, for example, for higher wages and improved health benefits.[8]

7. Robert Karasek and T. Theorell, *Healthy Work: Stress, Productivity and the Reconstruction of Working Life* (New York: Basic Books, 1990).

8. Peter T. Kilborn, "The New World of Work, Where the Employers Call All the Shots," *New York Times*, 3 July 1995.

Rather than being one of three factors, technology needs to be seen as a key to all the changes in power in the workplace. Certainly, the decline of unions has been supported by technological changes that have eliminated traditional skills, automated union jobs, and allowed work to be moved easily to nonunion plants, nonunion areas, and even other countries. Technology, in making it easier to move work around, has created much of the competition that we now complain about.

To understand the impact of technology on power in the workplace, we need to examine the sources of that power. For the workforce, power comes fundamentally from management's reliance on a certain set of workers to produce a product, provide a service, and, ultimately, make a profit. Management's power comes from the fact that it owns or controls the organization, the process, and the technology and from the fact that the workforce is dependent on the workplace to earn a living.

Technology can be seen as knowledge that is embedded in a production or service process, in a piece of equipment, in a material, or in a piece of software. Changes in technology therefore can affect whose knowledge and effort are necessary to production. Technology is often designed to capture knowledge and experience (or to make them irrelevant), and thus it changes the leverage of those with control over traditional skills. Expert systems, computer monitoring, statistical process control (SPC), and computer numerical controls (CNC) are examples of technologies that are designed specifically to capture and/or displace the knowledge of the workforce, thereby making the existing workforce less necessary.

Technology is also developed with the purpose of exerting control over effort and providing access to an increased effort pool (labor market). Computer monitoring and machine-paced processes are examples of technologies that help to control effort, while the information superhighway and electronic controls are designed and implemented specifically to enhance the transferability of work, thereby expanding the available effort pool to encompass the entire world population.

In these days of empowerment rhetoric, it is probably unfashionable to talk about disempowerment, but specific analysis of workplace technologies shows the workforce to be suffering from a massive erosion of bargaining power. Technology's "power to . . ." can generally be translated into "power over . . ." and the workforce is, first and foremost, on the short end.

The mantra "workforce involvement," which dominates much of the management literature, implies synergy—that both parties gain more from the relationship than from the lack of a relationship. Workers are told that new technologies will benefit both parties and that therefore it is in the interest of the workforce to help implement technological changes.

Technology undoubtedly contributes to productivity, which should, of course, make more available to all. But buried (not too deeply) in the very innovations that increase the productive capacity of the workforce are factors that serve to deny the workforce the bargaining power to gain their share of the output. Realization of synergy assumes a balance of power between the workforce and management that does not exist now. In fact, the imbalance of power is increasing with technological change. Like a breeder reactor that makes its own fuel, technology, developed and implemented by and in the interest of those with power, in turn enhances that power and helps to undermine the countervailing power of other groups in society, particularly the workforce.

Management can produce a product or provide a service without relying on traditional skills of the workforce. What does that do to the bargaining power of the workforce?

On a tour of a sheet metal shop in 1992, the owner of the shop told how, 10 years earlier, he had done $5 million worth of business and he had 14 cutters. Cutters do layout and are the most highly skilled sheet-metal workers. At the time of the tour, he did $25 million annually and he had 1 cutter.

Even that one cutter was isolated from the main production process. The core design and layout were being done on a computer, with instructions automatically sent to a computer-controlled cutting machine. Bar-code labels were generated for each part so that they could be tracked. The sheet-metal workers were essentially reduced to doing assembly work. A job that had been a very skilled craft job had been deskilled. The result is a loss of bargaining power for those more easily replaceable workers.

The transition to plastic from steel pipe by gas companies is another example of the change in bargaining power that accompanies new technology. Plastic pipe comes in long rolls that are attached to each other using an automated plastic welding process. Thus the skills of pipe fitting and pipe welding are no longer needed by the gas company. The street workers no longer have the power that they had because they cannot deny the company the ability to put pipe in the ground anymore, at least not as effectively as before.

Computer numerical controlled machine tools are used to cut pieces of metal into precision shapes. Prior to their introduction, the machinist had a great deal of control over how a part was cut. Even when there was a formal process sheet that told the machinist how management wanted the piece made, the tacit knowledge of the machinist was crucial to successful machining. In fact, many machinists will say that the first thing they did when making a part was to take the process sheet out of the envelope, rip it up, and throw it away. Then they made the part. "Work to rule," doing exactly what management said to do, was one of the strategies employed by workers and unions to highlight their leverage, proving that without their brains, the system produced junk.

But when the instructions are electronic, when they are directly transmitted to the machine, workers cannot rip them up and throw them away. Someone else is doing the programming, someone else is controlling the process, and that someone else, in most cases, is not in the union. Control over the production process has effectively been separated from the traditional power base of the workforce.

Production takes place and services are provided without significant human effort. What does that do to the bargaining power of the workforce?

The gas company in Boston uses an automated meter-reading system called ENSCAN. With it, the company no longer needs meter readers, whose job was to go into basements of buildings and read the gas meters. Now there is a van that drives up and down the street and takes the readings. The van sends out a radio signal, which activates the meter, which then transmits a reading directly into a computer in the van. The van can drive 35 or 40 miles an hour down a street, picking up all the readings as it goes. The bargaining power of the meter readers no longer exists.

The production process can be located—and relocated—anywhere. What does that do to bargaining power?

Much of the technology that is being applied today is designed to break the ties of geography, giving companies access to a much wider labor market, thereby undermining the bargaining power of the workforce. In 1994, Fleet Bank in Boston moved back-office jobs from Boston to Utica, New York, where wage rates (and rents) were lower. The bargaining power of the Boston workforce was completely undercut by the ability of the bank to use information and telecommunications technology to move the work at will. The bargaining power of the remaining workers at the bank was also diminished by this effective demonstration of their distensibility.

Construction is a sector that is often ignored in the discussion of technological change. One of the key aspects of technological change in construction is the transfer of work off-site and the consequent industrialization of craft work. Prehung doors and windows are a good example of this trend. Instead of being custom constructed on the building site, windows and doors, with frames, are premanufactured as commodity items. Construction workers become installers as the core work is moved into a factory and industrialized and thereby deskilled.

There are larger examples of off-site work as well. A tunnel is currently being built to carry automobile traffic under Boston Harbor. Actually, the tunnel itself was built in Baltimore, Maryland. It was delivered by barge and dropped into place in Boston.

The tunnel was built not by construction workers but by industrial workers. They happen to be unionized in this case, but the fact remains that they could do the work off-site, away from construction union contracts, and away from construction work rules, work organization, and pay scales. The expansion of the labor market seriously undermines the bargaining power of the local construction workforce.

At a very basic level, we can see how technology affects the tools of workforce and union leverage. Picket lines, designed to deny management the knowledge and effort of the existing workforce and to prevent the knowledge and effort of others from replacing it, have traditionally been a key symbol and important instrument of trade union power. However, if technology is used to make much of the information necessary to production and service delivery available in electronic form, instantly accessible from databases controlled by management, then a picket line may be ineffective at denying critical skill or knowledge. If the work can be transported over the information superhighway to another location with similar equipment, then a picket line will also be ineffective in controlling effort.

The laws, contracts, and culture governing labor-management interaction, while they have traditionally supported (in limited ways) the exercise of union power over current conditions, have also helped to exclude unions and workers from the technology discussion and have therefore supported the disempowering process of technological change.

The legal structure supporting bargaining in this country, meanwhile, does not recognize technology as a mandatory subject of bargaining. Although management is required to bargain over the impacts of technological change, this exercise has been described, particularly in the recent past of downsizing, as negotiating the terms of a funeral.

In any case, laws and regulations, while important as sources of leverage, are reflections of power rather than fundamental sources of power. As technology is used to remove power from the workforce at the workplace, regulatory mechanisms that have supported the application of worker bargaining power can be expected to be dismantled. The current Congress's plans to severely weaken the Occupational Safety and Health Administration (OSHA), the National Labor Relations Act (NLRA), and other regulatory mechanisms are examples of this trend.

The three-year contract is the basic form of agreement between management and labor, although this has been changing somewhat recently. But with technology changing constantly, the contract, which once gave some security to the union and its members, can actually turn into a chain around their neck. Under most contracts, a management rights clause leaves technological change as the exclusive domain of management. Thus the contract is used to exclude the union from this very important area.

The issue of culture, while it is perhaps more difficult to define, may be the most important of all. It certainly deserves more attention and study. People feel disempowered by technology because it is discussed in a different language, because it is new and different, and because workers particularly have been convinced that they have neither the right nor the ability to effectively comment on technology issues. The result is that workers are often excluded from the discussion of technology simply because they feel that they should not ask to be included.

THE FOLLY OF IGNORING THE POWER QUESTION

The literature is full of nice solutions to the problems raised in the course of technological change. Retraining; shorter workweeks; better competitiveness: a high-skill, high-wage path; free trade; trade barriers; and building new sectors are all discussed in the literature on dealing with the changing workplace.

It is interesting that just saying no—that is, stopping technology or particular technologies—is seen as a backward response to the problems created in the course of rapid technological change. Yet many other responses that hold little or no promise receive praise. The idea that retraining can solve the problem of joblessness and poverty ignores the reality of systemic unemployment. The "high-skill, high-wage approach to competitiveness" may sound appealing, but it becomes difficult to imagine how it will work when every other industrialized country is pointing in the same direction and when the technologists are actively seeking ways to avoid reliance on skills. The new-sector solution, based on the agriculture-to-manufacturing transition, does not deal with ongoing change and suffers from the fact that its flagship sectors have not come anywhere near to producing the jobs that are needed. The biotechnology industry is held up as an important new sector, and yet that industry has created fewer than 97,000 jobs in the last 10 years. It is also true that biotech processes are being developed in part to replace more traditional—and more job-intensive—processes. Thus, for each biotech job created, several others may be directly destroyed.

The basic problem is that too few of the policy prescriptions are based on a real understanding of the power issues involved and therefore on an understanding of what it would take to make the desired changes. In the end, ignoring power means conceding power.

There are very few people who would not like a shorter workweek. Certainly the increases in productivity from automation should allow us to produce the same amount of goods and services while working fewer hours. But *Fortune Magazine* sees the trend going in the other direction: by the year 2000, instead of working fewer hours and having more leisure time, half of the current workforce will be working more hours and the other half will be unemployed.[9]

We can say that other countries have shorter working hours. Vacation times in most other industrialized countries are two to three times the average in the United States. We can say how nice it would be. We can even argue that it would be better for the country as a whole. But all of these distract us from a discussion of the real issue, which is how people might go about forcing a shorter workweek on those who make the decisions. This is about power.

The problem is power, and while there may be many scenarios that we think will solve the problem of technological displacement and disruption, none of these scenarios could come to pass unless those who want them have the power to make them happen. And while the discussion of the impact of technological change continues, the power imbalance continues to increase.

9. William Bridges, "The End of the Job," *Fortune Magazine*, 19 Sept. 1994, p. 62.

POLICY IMPLICATIONS

To the extent that technology plays a role in the distribution and application of power, discussions of technology policy need to be focused on how technology disrupts or changes the balance of power—or the imbalance of power—between different groups in society. The key policy issue is how to build and support effective countervailing forces. To the extent that technology is used to undermine the traditional mechanisms of power of the workforce, the key policy issue is how to develop and provide new mechanisms.

If one believes that workers should have a say in their workplace, then government initiatives supporting the development of technologies (such as the information superhighway) that would, for example, make it easier for a company to transfer work or to end reliance on the traditional skills of the workforce should be counterbalanced by mechanisms—through law, regulation, or direct support—that either would make work transfer more difficult or would give alternative sources of power to the workforce. In the absence of this, attention to the impacts of technological change can be compared with putting a Band-Aid on cancer.

The proposed OSHA ergonomics standard is perhaps the most important piece of technology policy that has been written in the recent past. It was not generally recognized as such, but it was avidly and unanimously opposed by business precisely because management understands the voice it would give to the workforce in designing and implementing workplace technology. Strengthening the NLRA to include technology as a mandatory subject of bargaining and to make it more difficult for companies to avoid union contracts through technologically mediated means would also be very sound technology policy. The OSHA ergonomics standard has been put on hold because of business and congressional opposition, and the NLRA is being weakened rather than strengthened.

Dealing with technological change would require addressing several key areas of policy. One is a technological right to know. The health and safety and environmental movements fought long and hard for the right to know about the chemicals that are being used in the workplace. In many ways, this was a fight for the right to know about technologies—in this case, materials technologies—and their impact in one particular area, health and safety. The principle of the right to know should be expanded to the full range of technologies and the widest scope of impacts. There need to be mechanisms whereby the workforce and the general public have significant access to information about the technologies that are being developed. Full knowledge is the first requirement of democracy.

A second area has to do with social impact statements. While access to information is important, so too is access to expertise and analysis. Technologies that are going to be introduced into the workplace should be analyzed for their impact on a whole list of issues including power. We have come to accept the concept of environmental impact analysis;

technological impact analysis should be no less acceptable.

A third policy area is the rebalancing of power. Policy must pay particular attention to fixing the power imbalance. The policies of the government should be designed to rebalance power so that the voice of the workforce in determining its future grows rather than shrinks.

We have a long history in this country of exerting control over technologies, either by pushing them forward or by standing in their way. It is not that we cannot exert social control over technology; rather, exerting that control is a question of will and power. Nuclear power has been placed under severe limits. Drugs are subjected to long periods of testing before they are allowed on the market. Biological and chemical weapons were internationally banned because their negative impacts were seen as uncontrollable.

Workplace technology is being pushed forward, designed, developed, and implemented according to the needs and wishes of a small minority. Workplace technology, from the perspective of the workforce, is out of control because it is beyond their control. Those who wish to deal with the impacts of technological change need to look at and confront the core issue of power.

Performing Work without Doing Jobs

By DANIEL MARSCHALL

ABSTRACT: Plant closings and the widespread disappearance of industrial jobs have severely strained the American labor movement. To successfully recruit the millions of workers in service and other expanding occupations, some observers have proposed that unions adopt a form of occupational unionism that would seek to unite members around the sort of broadly conceived work that they do rather than the narrow job duties they perform at a specific work site. This article looks 10 years into the future. It presents an interview with a fictional labor leader who has embraced the model of occupational unionism, contributing to a dramatic revival of union size and influence. It is impressionistic and suggestive, not comprehensive. It is a blending of fact and fiction based on the author's projections of how advanced technology, skill-related initiatives, and research findings in cognitive science could contribute to a resurgent labor movement. The two government programs cited, skill standards and the school-to-work initiative, are real, in their early stages of evolution.

Daniel Marschall is special assistant to the executive director of the Human Resources Development Institute, the employment and training arm of the AFL-CIO, and chief liaison with the National Skills Standards Board. Previously, he worked for the Working Women Education Fund, the Ohio State Building & Construction Trades Training Foundation, and the state of Ohio as planning coordinator for the Dislocated Worker Program. He is a member of the Cement Masons Union and the Society for Applied Learning Technology and a director of the National Institute for Metalworking Skills.

NOTE: This article represents the personal views of the author and his interpretation of current affairs. It does not necessarily reflect the views of the AFL-CIO or its affiliated unions.

Special to *Los Angeles CyberTimes Magazine*

CENTURY CITY, California (7 May 2005)—For us baby-boomers drifting into our golden years, it is practically a dim memory: the traditional 9-to-5, full-time, single-office-or-factory-location, commute-to-work-every-morning job. The last decade has witnessed a radical transformation in how work gets done, not to mention the role that working plays in our daily lives. Thousands of industrial factories have closed their doors, decentralizing into multiple agile business units networked with fiber optics and coordinated by chip-resident intelligent agents. Telecommuting is the norm. The integrated entertainment industry has bloomed into the major sector of the economy. Government statistics show that 62 percent of the labor force now works part-time, is self-employed, or qualifies as contractors or contingent workers. The number of persons with full-time jobs, primarily top-level corporate managers, continues to dwindle.

All of this, of course, is old news, the culmination of global workforce and economic trends that accelerated at the end of the Cold War. The digital libraries of the two major telecable networks are filled with interactive stories about the difficulties individuals have had dealing with these vast trends. Most interesting these days is how various institutions are coping with these changes, struggling to adapt and survive in one form or another. In this context, nothing is more striking than the revival of organized labor. From a stressed-out institution in the 1980s, under sustained attack by outside political enemies and suffering from the loss of millions of industrial jobs, the unions have come roaring back to life. Who would have thunk it?

While the roots of labor's resurgence remain a hot topic of debate, observers agree that the organization and rapid spread of occupational networks was an important factor. Central to this development has been Cynthia Morovcek, currently executive coordinator of a network of retail employees. We caught up with Morovcek the day before what may be her crowning achievement: the founding convention of a diversified federation of occupational network unions, the United Network of Professionals (UNOP). Exhausted but invigorated, barely holding back a stream of demands for decisions from anxious aides, Morovcek gave us an hour to review the past and contemplate the future.

Q: The last time we talked in any depth, two or three years ago I think, you were smarting from criticism by certain political activists and other union leaders who were still charging that your retail network was not a real union, more of a social service agency to give benefits to low-wage workers and prop up little firms always on the verge of bankruptcy. Now those critics are silent and you are looked on as the new-wave leader of a postindustrial labor movement. How does it feel to beat out your opponents?

MOROVCEK: Well, I don't really see it as one side beating out the other side. You've got to view these things in historical perspective. The structure of the American economy, actually the whole global economy, has changed profoundly in the last, say, 150 years. Work performed according to particular crafts was dominant when early unions were founded. Unions of craft workers were the mainstays of the early labor federation, and the barons of growing manufacturing industry were dead set against their factories being organized, at least until the depression, the upsurge of mass production workers, World War II, and the growing power of central federal government authority. At that point, and for a number of decades, industrial unions were the powerhouses. It was understandable, you know; many of my union sisters and brothers saw these two models of unionism, craft unions and industrial unions, as the principal vehicles for defending the interests of their members. Our disagreements were based on sincere concern for our members, differences about how to cope with rapid economic transformation.

Q: Looking back, how do you explain the unfolding of those trends?

MOROVCEK: As usual, there were a number of factors—economic, social, technological—that came together. One was the rise of the service sector. Health care, retail, business services, computer software, education, maintenance of telecommunication networks, government services—all of these industries grew and absorbed more and more workers. Simultaneously, manufacturing firms adopted advanced technology at a faster and faster pace. They reengineered, restructured, and right-sized—and displaced millions of blue-collar workers accustomed to their narrowly defined, traditional jobs. Those were the scary days. It was not that long ago that serious observers of economic trends saw a time when jobs would almost not exist, when massive numbers of people would be unemployed and unemployable because high technology and computer-mediated processes and paperless offices were doing everything. Now we can see what was going on. Sure, traditional *jobs* were disappearing. But massive *work* still needed to be done, partly to repair the destruction wrought by the abuses of an industrial society.

Another big factor was social: the movement of women back into the workforce in huge numbers, along with their determination to balance the demands of work and family, the home front and the work front. That meant flexible work schedules and bouts of temporary employment, while retaining the right to make significant contributions to their chosen organizations. For men, especially your baby-boomer types, it was being fed up with the hierarchical, dictatorial, bureaucratic way most organizations were run. They were thirsty for greater autonomy, with self-employment and the creation of microbusiness ventures as a realistic alternative.

Then the real impact, I think, was made by young people, those baby-echo kids who saw few permanent jobs available and managed to adapt with the help of some creative government programs. They are the first generation to be truly comfortable with computers and interactive media. To them, mastering the technology and moving from employer to employer, while still cultivating an occupational identity, was no big thing. Occupational unionism was a natural fit for them.

Q: I never have grasped this "occupational identity" thing and the emphasis you put on it. Really, these are kids working in tiny shops where there is a great deal of turnover. How important could occupational identity be at this stage of their lives?

MOROVCEK: Listen, I've spent many years working closely with the kids who still don't get the proper respect for the sort of work they're doing. I am constantly amazed at how well they have been able to adapt and mature in a chaotic society where change is perpetual, morals and values are constantly shifting, and technology leaps forward at a rate that no one can understand. We've had a great deal of success recruiting young people in high school, presenting our program to them in understandable—and respectful—terms, and hooking them up with mature role models in the industry. They start working part-time and have access to adults who care about them and are sincerely interested in conveying the cultural richness of our industry.

What's most exciting to me is how our training programs, the ones that combine work experience with industry knowledge and positive social and interpersonal skills, have been able to compete and provide a real-life option instead of going straight to college. I know of many students who graduate from the university and flounder around for years trying to decide what to do with their impressive-sounding degrees. Our young members get started on an honorable career in a growing industry where they make decent entry-level wages and the salary potential, long-term especially, is excellent.

We've also had good success in our COP Centers, our Community of Practice Centers, where young people can hang out and talk with their peers about work experiences and even trade information about job openings and what's happening with this or that store. Multimedia reports are available there on a variety of current issues. They can easily access our Organizational Memory Archive. Considering that the media still look down on retail work, you would be amazed at the sophisticated stories that get swapped at these neighborhood centers, most having to do with how to improve customer service or get a handle on the latest inventory tracking software. There is a tremendous body of knowledge and expertise among these kids. And worldliness: they don't hesitate to move to another store if the boss mistreats them or they see the opportunity to advance their skills.

Out of all the services that our members receive for their monthly dues—the usual occupational network benefits of health care coverage, insurance, credit cards, travel, Web access—I think the COP Center environment is the most popular with our young members. We call it "cultivating occupational identity." Our young members find it cool and comfortable, a place where their ideas are listened to and where they can gather information that can have an immediate impact on their lives. It's also where many of our training programs are held.

Q: I understand that you recently shut down several of your COP Centers and that you've been experimenting with some new technology. What's going on?

MOROVCEK: For a few years now, we've had a COP Center in every major city. Actually, those centers were mainly administrative hubs, the location of our Web servers and a few desks for mobile staff, along with the hangout space. For a center director, a big part of his or her job was facilitating community-of-practice exchange among the members in many locations, you know, cybercafes and shopping malls and various community centers. In essence, a center was a hub of often dozens of little groupings formed by friends or corresponding to different segments of the industry and different neighborhoods. Center directors don't *control* these activities. Instead, they *enable* them to happen and provide services when needed. In several areas, the autonomous groupings are where the action is, so we closed the centers and are servicing the groups at a state or regional level. We are very flexible about the evolution of the centers and are constantly evaluating and assessing the structure.

The technology thing is really interesting. All of our members have their career subnotebooks with the usual array of multimedia capabilities, lots of flash memory, and a UHS [ultra high-speed] modem to jack into the Web from anywhere they can access the NII [National Information Infrastructure]. They have their training and skill upgrading MO [magneto-optical] mini-disks they can use to download and store material. Their personal Web sites sit on our COP Center servers, often in automatic interaction mode. (It's their choice whether to be in automatic interaction or passive mode.) They leave video messages for one another constantly. We've been testing this software that sits on the server and pops up as a kind of virtual hangout space, a more realistic, super-3D version of the Shared Virtual Space tools pioneered by Enterprise Integration Technologies in the late 1990s.

So, we have these virtual spaces that members can enter from remote locations, check out who else is there, interact while in video mode, catch up on union announcements or notices from the hiring hall, leave questions for staff, and so on. These are like virtual COP Centers and are becoming more and more popular, especially among suburban members. Considering our odd working hours, these virtual hangout spaces are essential for some members to keep in touch with their associates and the entire occupational network. We're looking closely at the role that this virtual space will play in the future, even having electronic union meetings.

Q: Going back for a moment, back to your big-picture trends, you mentioned technology as one of the driving forces for occupational unionism. Did that have a big impact?

MOROVCEK: Of course it did, although I think of technology more as a force that enables things to happen, changing people's consciousness along the way about the full range of possibilities. (Let's not get deterministic here!) Anyway, there were the economic trends in the growth of the service sector, social developments in the movement of women into the workforce, and baby-boomer rejection of oppressive structures—and then the fuel that advancing technology spread on the fire.

Once the fiber optic infrastructure was in place, videoconferencing surged in popularity and more businesses embraced telecommuting as a good tactic to hang on to their most talented employees. The traditional office environment became practically dysfunctional. People could use their subnotebooks to work from their home, car, or hotel room, exchanging information and conducting business in real time with clients and customers worldwide. Speech recognition devastated clerical jobs. Language translation software, at least once it was perfected in real-time mode, truly transcended national boundaries. There was less and less need for people to meet physically to do their jobs.

But, human nature being what it is, we still hungered for social time, time to get together with one another and socialize and enjoy that one-on-one exchange of energy. It was only logical that people working in the same broadly defined occupations would want to spend time with one another, preferably in low-stress kinds of settings. In effect, the distinction between work and play began to break down, along with the split between work and learning. Basically, the development of occupation-centered unionism, a community of interest that meets the tangible needs—personal, social, and economic—of the new service worker, emerged naturally from this confluence of developments.

Fortunately, the labor movement was flexible enough to forge new structures and adapt. We looked back in labor history to our finest traditions and went from there. It was just a matter of rediscovering our roots and actively experimenting with new programs in line with the potentials of new technology and the sensibilities of new generations of workers. Remember: we always said labor was flexible and adaptable. We've been matching reality to the rhetoric.

Q: You also mentioned government programs. What was their role?

MOROVCEK: There were two programs that made a difference. One was the so-called school-to-work initiative that took off in the mid-1990s. It was clear by that time that the vast majority of growing service jobs didn't really require a college education. In fact, a rising chorus of employers began complaining about how college grads had inflated expectations and had absorbed a lot of worthless abstractions and then needed to be retrained once they got into a real workplace with the latest technology. Yet our whole system and society—guidance counselors, parents, telecable sitcoms about the fascinating fictional lives of professionals, and so on—pushed kids to believe that unless they had a university education, they were somehow worthless. Untold thousands of young people would start college, drop out, and be even more discouraged about their lives and futures. We were heading for disaster.

It was the school-to-work movement that broke the college-only cycle. After the historic *America's Choice* report in 1990, the federal government, and then state after state, implemented creative programs to develop careers in the numerous skill areas that didn't depend on four years of liberal arts education. The programs gathered considerable momentum after a few years, and they have now become an accepted part of our education and training system. For us, school-to-work programs opened up high schools to skilled practitioners, trained through our union and joint labor-management training trusts, who could come in and demonstrate that meaningful work opportunities existed apart from college. This ended up to be a big boost to our long-range organizing.

Q: Wait a minute. I thought the unions hated the school-to-work initiative. Weren't the unions very skeptical about its chances for success?

MOROVCEK: True, there were problems at first. Once again, you had some insensitive government officials, along with some small nonprofit groups, that put these ideas forward as "youth apprenticeship," a wrong-headed term that put the building trades on edge—you know, they were thinking, "Here comes another ill-considered government boondoggle that's going to undercut joint apprenticeship." Those misunderstandings were worked out, and numerous unions at city and state levels got very involved in linking the schools to unionized, high-performance workplaces in various sectors.

After all, who has better access to highly skilled, experienced workers who can serve as the mentors that school-to-work efforts find so essential? Who has better access, if not the unions, to the advanced network technicians that keep the NII humming? In particular, once the NAMWU [North American Metal Workers Union] came together in 1999 and pointed its considerable resources in the school-to-work direction, the supply of skilled workers for advanced manufacturing systems became plentiful.

Q: What was the other government program?

MOROVCEK: The second one with big impact was skill standards. I know, the National Skill Standards Board (NSSB) has encountered some serious criticism. It took them a while to really get rolling, but once they did and certified broad skill standards in major occupational clusters, this led to a historic shift in how we view jobs in our regional trading bloc. Almost single-handedly, the skill standards initiative killed those old, divided-up, Tayloristic sorts of narrow job categories, especially when combined with O*Net data being easily available on the Web. [O*Net was the first iteration of the interactive, multimedia version of the old Department of Labor's *Dictionary of Occupational Titles*.] The Skill Standards Board set the model for effective postindustrial government programs; you know, pull together the major sectors—and don't even think about excluding unions—develop voluntary systems that meet the needs of both employees and business units, and then facilitate a wide range of strategies and experiments and organizational approaches in using the standards.

In some ways, although I would not go overboard here, our occupational networks were one of those experiments. Our retail network can be traced back to the broad skill standards developed by trade associations and unions in the commercial sector. In that sense, our roots go back to the Gingrich years. We still appreciate the work of the NSSB and strongly supported its reauthorization in 1999 and 2004.

Q: As always, I'm impressed with your grasp of history and the evolution of all these ideas and new approaches. Earlier you alluded to the labor traditions that you and other occupational unionists drew from. What were the major influences here?

MOROVCEK: Actually, I was sorting through some boxes in preparation for our unity convention and came across an old reading list that we used in the late 1990s to put together our first "Introduction to Occupational Networks" training class. Here's a copy.

What's critical, again, is to view all of this in the context of the debate in the mid-1990s about the massive destruction of jobs. People were all over the place on the supposed shape of future trends. The economy was a crapshoot; month after month, chaos seemed to rule. One corporation after another kicked people out of their jobs. In bad times, they used layoffs to save money. In good times, they used layoffs to improve their so-called competitive position. When times improved, they worked people overtime rather than take on new hires and incur the cost of benefits. Wall Street hung the sword of stock prices over everyone's heads, with slick takeover artists ready to move against vulnerable firms. This was the hostile environment we were dealing with.

Many professionals with huge personal investments in education and long job tenure—engineers in high-tech manufacturing, for example—lost their jobs and had a hard time finding comparable work. Professionals and white-collar workers thought they were secure in the middle class; they began to experience what blue-collar factory workers had gone through in the 1970s and 1980s. In many instances, women became the primary breadwinners in families. A large contingent of men and women took the opportunity to become consultants, start their own businesses, or return to school for specialized education.

At the same time, the drumbeat of personal responsibility was heard throughout the land. Democrats and Republicans, corporate leaders and media opinion makers, all picked up on this ideology that individuals had to assume personal responsibility for their careers and their work futures. The days of relying on the big-daddy corporation, or the big bureaucratic organization, for steady employment were at an end. Either you took charge of your own career or you had no employment security. None whatsoever. Some took this individualistic perspective to an extreme, not recognizing that government also has a responsibility to help bootstrap the disadvantaged and dispossessed. But all that was denounced as outmoded liberal thinking.

So, you put the movement toward self-employment together with the focus on personal responsibility, and people began to identify more intensely with a particular occupation—broadly conceived as professional work, thanks partly to the skill-standards initiative—and to look for continuous learning and upgrading opportunities. Also, the findings of cognitive science—the importance of experiential knowledge and learning in context and becoming part of a culture of common practice—became widely accepted and translated into training programs. All of this opened space for occupational unionists to begin organizing. Have I gone off on a tangent? What was the question again?

Q: Traditions, traditions. What were the labor traditions you looked to?

MOROVCEK: Right. A major one focused on women, specifically waitresses who organized and were real powers in labor from the early 1900s through the 1960s or so. Dorothy Sue Cobble of Rutgers has written some great stuff about how unionized waitresses—at one point, they had one-quarter of the workforce as members—were the superstars in the "theater of eating out." They saw themselves as a "craft sisterhood" that worked to advance the status of their occupation. A lot of restaurants went along because they realized that the waitress unions were their best assurance of a skilled, responsible labor force. Essentially, the waitress unionists managed themselves and made sure that their members met certain standards of competence. (Doesn't that sound familiar!) The unions provided training and a measure of employment stability. The members also benefited because the system allowed them to move in and out of the active workforce more easily.

It was Dorothy Cobble's studies of waitresses, and the implications she drew, that opened our eyes to a new labor typology, one that saw multiple models of unionism being applied to different segments of the workforce. In other words, basic union principles could be maintained in different structural forms, from the craft unionism of the building trades, to the industrial unionism (or what Cobble calls worksite unionism) of advanced manufacturing, to the occupational unionism of service workers and others.

Q: That experience sounds kind of old. What about some more contemporary examples?

MOROVCEK: There are modern examples, of course. Some are tied directly to our new United Network of Professionals. Again, one concerns women, this time clerical workers in offices. These jobs grew very rapidly for several decades after World War II. In the 1970s, the 9-to-5 working women's movement helped these women fight for rights and respect. But clerical jobs took a dive with the arrival of computer technology, speech recognition, and male professionals *finally* understanding that they needed to do their own word processing. Although the number of jobs dropped, there continued to be a demand for skilled staff to coordinate office functions, add hyperlinks to electronic documents, and synthesize information from the Web, Microsoft Network, and other nodes on the NII. Former clericals and secretaries rapidly dominated this emerging, broad occupation, gaining highly marketable skills they could take anywhere. Once my old friend Karen Nussbaum finished her tour of duty as head of the Women's Bureau, she moved quickly to organize the American Network of Office Coordinators and Information Technologists. We're very pleased to see it become part of our UNOP coalition.

Another interesting historical development concerned technicians, a rapidly growing part of the labor force that maintained its momentum and became pivotal to the smooth operation of the information superhighway. As I understand the history here, going back to the 1970s, outside vendors began to take more and more work from union members in hooking up telephone lines and installing networks in various companies. Some of those vendors stayed small, you know, local or regional subcontractors, but others became the giants we know of today. The unions moved to organize as many of these subcontractors as they could, integrating the new members into their locals and experimenting with the most pertinent services. This was all before divestiture in the early 1980s. Once divestiture hit, everything was up for grabs. Both AT&T and the regional Bell operating companies (RBOCs) moved to reengineer and cut costs, and that meant job loss for a lot of skilled union members.

So union leaders looked at the situation and developed some creative responses. Most notable, I think, was their hiring hall for members, coordinated with upgrading and retraining programs, and then their neo-apprenticeship program for installation, repair, and maintenance technicians. They started with those programs as experiments in a few cities, but then the programs really took off when some of the RBOCs expressed interest. Union leaders also hooked into the school-to-work initiative and designed some really sharp and innovative links with all kinds of education and training institutions. Actually, this is a good example of how an occupational unionist approach can be successfully implemented inside of existing union structures. The unions' hiring hall system is flourishing—not only in the United States but also in Canada, Mexico, and spots in South and Central America—along with their advanced technology training programs, distance learning projects, and customizable multimedia tools. We are working with them to transfer some of the COP Center technology we discussed earlier.

There are a number of other traditions that I'm not really going to have time to get into right now. An example is the garment and textile workers' unions with their aggressive promotion of quality products and industry expansion, their use of engineers to give technical assistance to small firms, and their creative multiemployer bargaining approaches.

Not to mention the building trades. I've been very pleased over the past decade or so to see how revisionist historians have gotten people to understand the insights and progressivism of the long-standing crafts; their leadership in training and skill-upgrading programs has been a constant inspiration to us. They have been very open in sharing their experiences.

And, of course, I can't neglect the arts and entertainment unions that have promoted employment security and professional recognition for their highly mobile members through flexible compensation schemes, unique dues structures, and various benefits and career advancement opportunities.

People doing all of these kinds of work, whether or not you call them jobs, have found the practices of occupational unionism to be responsive to their needs, especially when you sprinkle in some of the concepts of associational unionism that some academics put forward in the 1980s. Obviously, I could go on and on here.

Q: Okay, I know I have to let you go. So you have more than 3000 delegates gathering here tomorrow to raise the banner of occupational unionism and shake everyone up. How are you going to control all of these folks and get them moving in the same direction?

MOROVCEK: Well, you know me well enough to know that I have no intention of exercising control over all these folks. We've put a good agenda in place, with addresses by some supportive political leaders—including an interactive teleconference session with the president—and a combination of topic-oriented workshops and intensive division meetings broken down by our occupational clusters. Roger Schank and his folks from the Learning Sciences Corporation are here to record more members' work experience and add the stories to our Organizational Memory Archive.

This is really just the start of a long journey. When I think back, I'm very proud of the fact that organized labor was able to grapple with the supposed death of the job in a creative, flexible manner. I see this unity convention as absolute confirmation that there are three vital, healthy models of unionism, with our brand only the most recent. I know our structures will change as we move ahead. I'm confident that we have something for everyone. In fact, what about you high-flying freelance cyberjournalists? Our information and applied knowledge networks are second to none. I think I have an interactive magneto-optical promotional disk you might want to take a look at. . . .

The Employment of New Ends: Planning for Permanent Unemployment

By DAVID MACAROV

ABSTRACT: The search for full employment represents a societal delusion, given that the world does not need and cannot use all of the human labor available and, as time goes on, will need less and less. The pace of technologically created unemployment is increasing, and unceasing efforts to create jobs and to obscure the amount of real unemployment inevitably lead to personal degradation, societal corruption, economic disaster, and global danger. A new social paradigm, which does not posit work as its underlying and overarching value, is needed. Among other suggestions, that for a universal basic income has attracted serious international interest.

David Macarov is professor emeritus at the Hebrew University in Jerusalem. He is the founder of the Israeli chapter of the World Future Society and of the Society for the Reduction of Human Labor. His publications include Incentives to Work; Work and Welfare; Worker Productivity; Quitting Time; The Design of Social Welfare; *and* Social Welfare: Structure and Practice, *as well as numerous articles in scholarly journals.*

FULL employment has become a talismanic incantation among politicians, a mantra to economists, and an impossible dream to many ordinary people. If society has a Holy Grail that it vainly seeks, that Holy Grail is full employment. If society has a fata morgana, a beautiful mirage constantly beckoning it on to destruction, that mirage is full employment. If society constantly yearns for a fix of a drug from which it expects happiness but which will eventually destroy it, that drug is full employment.

THE SEARCH FOR FULL EMPLOYMENT

The long-continued failure of efforts to achieve full employment dates back at least to the time, more than 3000 years ago, when—at the completion of the pyramid at Gizeh—Cheops found himself with 100,000 unemployed laborers.[1] In a maneuver that has since been sanctified by countless repetitions, his solution was to begin another pyramid. There is convincing evidence that each of the later pyramids was begun when the previous one was half-completed. In short, the pyramids became make-work projects to disguise unemployment.[2] At the completion of the rebuilding of the Second Temple, Herod began a road around the Temple Mount for the same purpose. To safeguard jobs, Vespasion forbade the use of rivers and canals of Rome for ferrying building materials.[3] And so it has gone.

No nation has succeeded in achieving full employment as the nation itself defines it, except for short periods while at war. Indeed, the definition of full employment rises with the growth of unemployment. Thus, in 1930, Lord Beveridge spoke of 2 percent unemployment in Britain as being acceptable;[4] in 1951, the British government announced that it would not tolerate more than 3 percent;[5] in 1973, the American Council of Economic Advisors was willing to accept 3.5 percent;[6] the Humphrey-Hawkins bill of 1978 posited 4 percent;[7] in 1983, the same Council of Economic Advisors saw 6-7 percent unemployment as the "natural" rate;[8] and the Federal Reserve Board recently made it clear that 8 million people unemployed would be considered full employment.[9]

It should be noted that all of these levels are based on official unemployment figures. A large number of informed observers agree that these figures must be increased from 50 to 300 percent to include discouraged workers, involuntary part-time workers, unemployed persons coerced into training programs and thus labeled

---

1. Ricardo A. Caminos, "Pyramid," in *Encyclopedia Britannica*, ed. W. Benton (Chicago: Encyclopedia Britannica, 1965), pp. 792-94.

2. Kurt Mendelssohn, *The Riddle of the Pyramids* (London: Sphere, 1977).

3. James A. Garraty, *Unemployment in History: Economic Thought and Public Policy* (New York: Harper & Row, 1978).

4. William S. Beveridge, *Unemployment* (New York: Longmans Green, 1930).

5. William McGaughey, Jr., *A Shorter Workweek in the 1980s* (White Bear Lake, MN: Thistlerose Press, 1981).

6. Robert B. Reich, "An Industrial Policy for the Right," *Public Interest*, 7:317 (1983).

7. *World of Work Report*, 4:29 (1979).

8. Reich, "Industrial Policy for the Right."

9. R. Kuttner, "The Welfare Perplex," *New York Times*, 19 June 1994.

students, and other persons arbitrarily defined as out of the labor force—all of whom are ready, willing, and able to work but cannot find full-time employment.[10] With this in mind, the definition of full employment in the United States can be said to have risen from 3-6 percent unemployed in 1930 to 12-21 percent today. There are localities and countries where the figures are far greater: unemployment in some inner-city areas in the United States has been estimated at 80 percent; unemployment in Spain is nearly 20 percent; 20 percent unemployment in Newfoundland is considered full employment.[11]

Not only has the number of the unemployed increased, but the periods during which they remain without work has lengthened appreciably. There are also groups, such as African American inner-city youths, whose working lives will consist of several fitful periods; and there are others who will almost never be able to find work. Consequently, to the classic triple definition of unemployment—marginal, cyclic, and structural—a new entity has been added: the permanently unemployed.

Efforts mooted and tried to create jobs for such people include, among others, work relief (or relief work), subsidies to firms hiring people, topping off the salaries of workers, subsidies to the unemployed for starting their own businesses, tax relief, public service jobs, national service corps, public works, fiscal measures, sheltered workshops, and training and retraining courses. Evaluations of such programs indicate that although some of them manage to obscure the extent of actual unemployment somewhat, none of them, nor all of them together, appreciably reduces unemployment, which—over time—continues to grow.[12]

As a result, governments attempt to obscure the extent of unemployment in many ways. In Britain, for example, there is a waiting period before one is officially listed as unemployed, but if one remains without work for a sufficient time, one is listed as unemployable and removed from the statistics. It has been cynically pointed out that by lengthening the first period and shortening the second, unemployment in Britain could be statistically eliminated.[13] In the United States, one who works only one hour a week is no longer considered unemployed; nor is one who did not seek work during the week, although the reason for such failure to look for work might be an

10. Alvin Kogut and Sylvia Aron, "Toward a Full Employment Policy: An Overview," *Journal of Sociology and Social Welfare*, 7:85-99 (1980); Daniel Yankelovich, *New Rules: Searching for Fulfillment in a World Turned Upside Down* (New York: Random House, 1981); A. Levison, *The Working Class Majority* (New York: Penguin, 1974); Moshe Sicron, "How Many Unemployed Are There in Israel?" (Paper delivered at the annual meeting of the Israel Industrial Relations Association, Bar-Ilan University, Ramat Gan, Feb. 1986); Frank Field, "Making Sense of the Unemployment Figures," in *The Conscript Army*, ed. F. Field (London: Routledge & Kegan Paul, 1977); F. H. Gruen, "The Economic Perspective," in *The Future of Work*, ed. J. Wilkes (London: Allen & Unwin, 1981); *New York Times*, 2 July 1986.

11. Canadian Council on Social Development, *The Future of Work: Consultation Report* (Ottawa: CCSD, 1983).

12. Robert Taggart, ed., *Job Creation: What Works?* (Salt Lake City, UT: Olympus, 1977).

13. Field, ed., *Conscript Army*.

illness, a natural disaster, inclement weather, or a transportation strike.

THREE COMFORTING MYTHS

The vain search for full employment is bolstered by three myths. One is that technology creates new jobs. And indeed it does—in the short run. In the long run, it more than eliminates the jobs thus created. Take, for example, the enormous need for punchcard operators postulated at the advent of computers as well as the assumption that almost every computer user would need the services of a programmer. It was predicted that punchcard operators and computer programmers would constitute a large sector of the workforce. However, most people using computers today have never seen a punchcard and would not recognize a punchcard if shown one. Similarly, computer programs for almost every need are now sold over the counter by the millions through innumerable outlets. The fact is that technology is symbiotic—in creating new products and services, it also creates the technology to produce them, thus reducing the need for human labor.

Then there is the facile assumption that unemployment could be wiped out by rebuilding the infrastructure if the finances would just be made available. This view rests on a nostalgic and romantic notion of swarms of men (usually few women) spreading out over the countryside with tools in their hands to rebuild roads, viaducts, and so on. Unfortunately for this view, physical construction is now largely the province of huge mechanized pieces of equipment, controlled by a few people using high technology. Studies conducted in a number of countries, as well as on a worldwide basis, indicate that the number of people employed in these endeavors would hardly make a dent in the unemployment figures.

For example, a committee of the House of Lords in Britain estimated that to insulate every home in Great Britain would require only 30,000 workers and that to rebuild every sewer, tunnel, bridge, and so forth that needed it would require 68,000 workers. These jobs would have almost no appreciable effect on the 3 million unemployed in Britain.[14] Similarly, it has been estimated that it would require 8 million workers to build a house for every family in the Third World,[15] while in India alone there are tens of millions of unemployed workers. Thus it would not be wise to overestimate the number of jobs that rebuilding the infrastructure would create.

The final misapprehension in the public mind is that if the unemployed could somehow be used to fill the lacunae in the service sector, services would improve and worklessness would be eliminated. Although the former might be true, the latter is not. As regards nurses, for example, the United States has a staff-to-patient ratio that is twice that of the former West Germany and three

14. U.K., Parliament, House of Lords, Select Committee on Science and Technology, Subcommittee IIa, *Occupational Health* (London: Her Majesty's Stationery Office, 1982).

15. S. V. Sethuraman, "Basic Needs and the Informal Sector: The Case of Low-Income Housing in Developing Countries," *Habitat International*, 9:299-316 (1985).

times that of Japan.[16] Still, an addition of 300,000 nurses would satisfy current demand in this area.[17] Similarly, another 800,000 social workers are needed, and 1 million additional teachers could reduce average classroom size from the current 24 in the United States to 15.[18] Together these additions would not reduce unemployment to anywhere near a full-employment status. Indeed, even if the services were to be thus expanded, most of the jobs would be taken up by previously nonworking women,[19] primarily working part-time.

THE MORALITY OF WORK

Despite historical and repeated proof of the ineffectiveness of the search for full employment, the attempts continue because human labor continues to be seen as both necessary and desirable for the individual and for society. Since Martin Luther held that working was a method of serving God, work has been seen not only as an economic activity but also as one that is morally required. Further, political, social, and economic programs are all based on the assumption that people need and want to work and that society needs all the work that everyone capable of laboring can produce. Work as a prerequisite of existence is the cornerstone of most modern civilization.

On an individual basis, people are judged not only by the work they do but also by the manner in which they do it. People who do not or cannot work are viewed as somehow outside the mainstream of life. Work structures time, determines attitudes, shapes self- and other-images, and permeates every aspect of life including education, family, religion, and even peripheral areas such as the prison system.

Therefore, the need to provide jobs is one of the most pressing problems facing governments and is the reason why they propose and use various schemes and subterfuges to try to reduce or conceal unemployment. Enormous efforts are made to find jobs, create jobs, divide jobs, maintain unnecessary jobs, and give the illusion of jobs by ruling people out of the labor force by various means as well as obscuring the actual extent of unemployment by definitional deviousness, statistical sleight of hand, and junk jobs.

Were such efforts merely useless, they could be tolerated, if not condoned. However, full employment is a classic example of a solution worse than the problem given that efforts to achieve full employment not only end in frustration but inevitably lead to personal degradation, societal corruption, economic disaster, and global danger.

PERSONAL DEGRADATION

Full employment increasingly requires the creation of jobs with little concern for the work actually done,

---

16. David R. H. Hiles, "Health Services: The Real Job Machine," *Monthly Labor Review*, 115(11): 3-16 (1992).
17. *New York Times*, 18 Apr. 1988.
18. Ibid., 6 Apr. 1988.
19. S. Ollson, "Towards the Transformation of the Swedish Welfare State," in *Modern Welfare States: A Comparative View of Trends and Prospects*, ed. R. R. Friedman, N. Gilbert, and M. Sherer (New York: New York University Press, 1987), pp. 44-82.

workplace conditions, the features of the job, or the salary paid. Such deliberately created or maintained jobs contain little to attract or to satisfy the workers, who are driven to accept them only by inability to secure income in any other way.

It should be noted that many people in ego-satisfying, power-wielding, influential, and challenging jobs really love their work and do not believe it when told that the overwhelming majority of people, who do the mundane, banal jobs of society, get no satisfaction from their work, wish they did not have to work, and use many devices to avoid work. An example of this lack of congruence is the fact that while 93 percent of university professors would choose the same job again, only 16 percent of unskilled autoworkers would.[20] Ironically, and even tragically, those who get satisfaction from their work make the employment and social policies that govern those who do not, and often do so by projecting their own feelings concerning work onto the others.

Surveys, interviews, participant observation, and workers' behavior all bear witness to widespread unhappiness at work.[21] Satisfaction with work has been declining for the last 15 years, with the rate of decline precipitous in the last few years. Despite constant declarations concerning people's physical and psychological necessity for work and even work's morality, we indicate in many ways that we understand and share the real feelings of doubt, ambivalence, and reluctance regarding work that most people have.

For example, take all the admonitions to work hard with which people have been bombarded since biblical days—the proverbs, fables, mottos, sayings, stories, songs, and even nursery rhymes, such as "Jack shall get but a penny a day because he can't work any faster." Their very existence is proof of an underlying disinclination to work. If people wanted to work or enjoyed working, such massive socialization efforts would not be necessary. Nowhere do we find such pressure to engage in sex, for example, or to eat or play. Obviously, people do not have to be persuaded to do what they like. The constant persuasion and coercion to work to which we are all subject is tacit admission of what our real attitudes toward work are.

---

20. U.S., Department of Health, Education and Welfare, *Work in America* (Cambridge: MIT Press, 1973).

21. Chris Argyris, "The Individual and the Organization: An Empirical Test," *Administrative Science Quarterly*, 4:145-67 (1959); Lillian B. Rubin, *Worlds of Pain: Life in the Working Class Family* (New York: Basic Books, 1976); Studs Terkel, *American Dreams: Lost and Found* (New York: Ballantine, 1980); Louise K. Howe, *Pink Collar Workers* (New York: Putnam, 1977); Jerome I. Baim, *Work Alienation and Its Impact on Political Life: Case Study of District Council 37 Workers* (New York: City University of New York, 1981); Kurt Lasson, *The Workers* (New York: Grossman, 1971); Barbara Garson, *All the Livelong Day: The Meaning and Demeaning of Routine Work* (New York: Penguin, 1975); Rosabeth M. Kanter and B. A. Stein, eds., *Life in Organizations: Workplaces as People Experience Them* (New York: Basic Books, 1976); Robert Shrank, *Ten Thousand Working Days* (Cambridge: MIT Press, 1978); M. Fein, "Motivation to Work," in *Handbook of Work, Organization and Society*, ed. R. Dubin (Chicago: Rand McNally, 1976); D. F. Roy, "Banana Time: Job Satisfaction and Informal Interaction," in *Life in Organizations*, ed. Kanter and Stein.

One clear recognition of these attitudes regarding work is the fact that almost every social welfare program in the world has a wage stop built into it, limiting benefits to a proportion—often a small proportion—of what the recipient could make from working.[22] The underlying reasoning is quite clear, and most people agree with it and accept it: if people can get from any other source what they could get from work, they would choose not to work.

Take, for example, the fact that males in the United States may retire at age 62 instead of 65, but to do so they give up three years' salary and 20 percent of their retirement income for life. Since this possibility became available in 1961, the proportion taking up this option rose to 36 percent by 1970 and to 70 percent in 1994.[23] Currently, more than 90 percent of male retirees are retiring early,[24] and it is predicted that this trend will not only continue through the 1990s but accelerate between 2000 and 2005.[25] In Holland, 75 percent of males between the ages 55 and 65 were in the workforce in 1972, but in the 1980s early retirement became available, and the proportion has since dropped to 35 percent.[26]

Nor should the bulk of such retirement be seen as forced; since passage of the Age Discrimination Act in the United States, which forbids firings based on age, the number of early retirees has not dropped—it has, in fact, increased.[27] Early retirement is also not taken primarily for health reasons; 62 percent of retirees report themselves as healthy.[28]

Further, take the reduction of the workweek, from six days, to five and a half days, to five days, to four and a half days, and in some places to even less; the more numerous non-working holidays; and the increased length of vacations. In 1900, the average workweek in the United States was 53.0 hours; in 1979, it was 35.5 hours; in 1987, it was 34.8 hours; and in 1990, it was 34.4 hours.[29] That such reductions in work hours have not been achieved against workers' desires is obvious. All of this speaks of our real underlying attitudes toward work, despite the continuous brainwashing that requires us to report work as positive.

Who knows how much stress and strain, and how many emotional and behavioral problems, arise from the need to work when one would rather be playing tennis or golf, parenting

---

22. David Macarov, *Work and Welfare: The Unholy Alliance* (Beverly Hills, CA: Sage, 1980).

23. Murray Gendell and Jacob S. Siegel, "Trends in Retirement Age by Sex, 1950-2000," *Monthly Labor Review*, 115(7): 22-29 (1992).

24. David S. Hurwitz, "Retirement and Pension Plans," in *Encyclopedia of Social Work*, ed. A. Minahan (Silver Spring, MD: National Association of Social Workers, 1987), pp. 507-12.

25. Gendell and Siegel, "Trends in Retirement Age by Sex."

26. B.M.S. Van Praag and K.W.H. Van Beek, "Unemployment and the Social Security Trap," in *The Art of Full Employment*, ed. C. de Neubourg (New York: Elsevier North-Holland Science, 1991).

27. Hurwitz, "Retirement and Pension Plans."

28. Herbert S. Parnes, ed., *Policy Issues in Work and Retirement* (Kalamazoo, MI: W. E. Upjohn Institute for Employment Research, 1983).

29. International Labour Office, *Yearbook of Labor Statistics, 1989-1990* (Geneva: ILO, 1990); Eugene McCarthy and William McGaughey, *Nonfinancial Economics: The Case for Shorter Hours of Work* (New York: Praeger, 1989).

one's children, indulging in hobbies, or simply enjoying oneself? Who knows how much creativity has been stifled by the need to work, how many great works of art, literature, science, or philosophy have been lost to the world because of the time constraints imposed by work schedules? The ancient Athenians, relieved by conquest and by slave labor of the need to work, laid the basis of civilization as we know it today through their creations in literature, mathematics, drama, sports, art, sculpture, and much more. Are we any less talented than they were?

Further, our widespread endeavors to redefine, redivide, artificially create, and spread jobs result in an understanding on the part of many workers that the kind and amount of work they do is not really important—not to themselves, not to others, and certainly not to the economy as a whole. They understand that they are to pretend to like their work and to give the impression that they see it as important but that they are not expected to exert themselves or to use all their skills and abilities. An elemental dishonesty is thus required of many workers who must appear busy all the time, while in truth their work could be done in much less time and often more cheaply, better, and faster by a machine—and they know it.

SOCIETAL CORRUPTION

The artificial creation of jobs, the insistence that people work when their productivity is not needed, the tacit acceptance of informal work-regulating norms, the condoned resistance to new machinery and methods, and contractual legitimation of various forms of featherbedding all amount to moral corruption on the part of society. The corruption inherent in such a system inevitably communicates itself and spreads to the individuals concerned. Workers who sign in and then go out to take care of personal matters; those who have others insert their cards in the time clock in their own absence; those who deliberately or unconsciously stretch their work to fill in the assigned time; those who dawdle, gossip, play games, or simply idle; those who do not come in or come in late every Monday—all of these are the products of nonserious work, not its causes.

Schumacher has written that people are destroyed by an inner conviction of uselessness,[30] while Lebow is more direct in an article entitled "No Man Can Live with the Terrible Knowledge that He Is Not Needed."[31] This is what results from a system that artificially inflates the amount of human labor needed to provide everyone with a job. The myths that are necessary to maintain a full-employment system, the cheating by society and by individuals that is accepted as normal, and the self- and other-images that are thereby created constitute a socially sanctioned delusional system that is both corrupt and corrupting.

Just as laws that are obviously unenforced eventually create contempt for law in general, so unneces-

30. Ernest F. Schumacher, *Small Is Beautiful: Economics as if People Mattered* (New York: Harper & Row, 1973).

31. Eliot Lebow, "No Man Can Live with the Terrible Knowledge That He Is Not Needed," *New York Times Magazine*, 5 Apr. 1970.

sary work and artificially created and maintained jobs lead to other cons on and by society. The results of widespread societal hypocrisy regarding jobs—that they are necessary, important, and fulfilling—counterpoised with the feeling of many jobholders that what they do is basically unimportant, unnecessary, and boring, are spreading cynicism, dishonesty, immorality, and societal structures based on fraud rather than on friendships.

Not incidentally, the heavy emphasis on work that marks our society causes the unemployed to be both stigmatized and penalized even when they know, and others know, that the situation is not of their doing.

ECONOMIC DISASTER

In addition to the effects on individuals and the social world, there are the economic aspects to consider. As jobs must be divided into smaller and smaller portions to increase their numbers, the growth of part-time work and temporary jobs accelerates. In 1980, there were 400,000 part-time workers, but by 1987 this number had more than doubled, to 900,000.[32] These jobs pay less in all occupational groups, offer fewer benefits, and escape accountability, including unionization.[33] The work itself becomes less interesting as the focus becomes more narrow. Such segmentation, as Durkheim pointed out long ago, leads to alienation and anomie on the part of the worker.[34]

Perhaps more important, from an economic point of view, is the fact that the need to provide jobs leads to a bias toward labor-intensive industries. For example, governmental help on all levels is certainly more easily available to a prospective employer of several hundred people than it is for the purchase of sophisticated machinery that reduces the need for workers. Thus the move toward more and better goods and services at lower prices, available through technology, is slowed in favor of a search for more and better jobs. The ultimate result is higher prices and lower quality because machines work faster, more cheaply, and more precisely than do human beings.

It has been noted that 75-90 percent of changes in productivity are achievable through changes in methods, machines, and materials, leaving only 10-25 percent to changes in human work patterns.[35] Human labor is very inefficient as compared to machines, and an economy that depends on human labor as its base will soon find itself falling behind other, more technologically inclined economies.

Further, labor-intensive industries can succeed only if they can com-

32. Richard S. Belous, "How Human Resource Systems Adjust to the Shift toward Contingency Workers," *Monthly Labor Review*, 112:7-12 (Mar. 1989).

33. K. Hall, "How Shall We Ever Get Them Back to Work?" *International Journal of Manpower*, 5:24-32 (1984); T. Kumpke, "Works Organisation in the Post-Industrial Company" (Paper delivered at the conference "New Technologies and the Future of Work," European Center for Work and Society, Maastricht, Netherlands, 1986); A. Lewis, "Vocational Training: Education as an Investment" (Paper delivered at ibid.).

34. Emile Durkheim, *The Division of Labour in Society* (New York: Free Press, 1933).

35. James M. Rosow, "Productivity and People," in *Productivity: Prospects for Growth*, ed. J. M. Rosow (New York: Van Nostrand Reinhold, 1981).

pete with other labor-rich countries such as India, Taiwan, China, and—increasingly—African countries. To do this, they must pay competitively low wages, or, in other words, keep the workers' standard of living down to the level of that in the competing countries. That higher wages hurt exports is an important component in current efforts to achieve a protectionist foreign trade policy.

GLOBAL DANGER

The need to provide jobs for everyone blunts distinctions between necessary and unnecessary work, and—more important—between socially desirable activities and those that are polluting, dangerous, and counterindicated. The most general rationale for overlooking dangerous leaks, structural deficiencies, and ecologically damaging activities is to point out how many jobs will be lost if the enterprise is moved or closed. A trade-off is sought—explicitly or implicitly—between the amounts of physical damage being caused and the economic damage expected to ensue from correction or elimination.

Finally, there is the foreboding possibility that the blind commitment to full employment will threaten the peace of the world. Munitions manufacture, including planning, development, testing, production, distribution, sales, and so forth, makes up a relatively large portion of many nations' economies. Many jobs are dependent, directly or indirectly, on the munitions industry, including the whole area of satellites and their ramifications. Reduction in arms manufacture is heavily influenced by the expected impact on the unemployment picture.

When a manufacturing plant—including a munitions plant—is threatened with closure, the possibility of job loss plays a large part in the political decision whether or not to keep the plant open. As two examples, President Bush was reported as opposing higher-mileage cars, and thus less pollution, because they would have resulted in fewer jobs, and the Connecticut legislature refused to ban cheap handguns and automatic weapons because it would result in job losses at the Hartford Colt factory.[36]

THE NEED FOR A NEW PARADIGM

The basic reason for continued and growing unemployment, despite all the efforts made to reduce or obscure it, is almost universally ignored, resisted, or denied. The fact is that society does not need and cannot use all the human labor available and will need less and less as time goes by. Unemployment has consistently increased over the last 65 years or so, primarily because technology has increased productivity enormously, reducing the need for human labor. Whereas, in 1850, people used 13 percent of their total energy at work, today they use less than 1 percent. In 1950, every employed civilian worker in the United States produced $5000 of the gross national product. By 1975, this had risen to $16,000. It is predicted that by the year 2000, the amount will be $85,000. Were current increases to continue, by the year 2100 every worker would pro-

36. "Gun Control versus Jobs," *New York Times*, 7 July 1992.

duce $5 million of the gross national product.[37]

Due to gains in productivity, both in goods and in services, we are rapidly moving toward a society in which increasingly large segments will be permanently unemployed, a society in which the majority of jobs will be held by a minority of people. To cope with this approaching situation, a new societal paradigm will be necessary, one in which something other than work will be the overriding and controlling value and in which the distribution of technologically derived wealth will not be based on individual work activities or records.

There are historical examples of societies whose basic value was something other than work, such as the aforementioned ancient Athens. There have also been societies based on religious observance, military valor, obedience to a leader, study, and cooperation. What the future society will value as the present does work remains to be seen.

There is, of course, the question as to how resources will be distributed if people do not work. The answer will depend on the values adopted, but suggestions include redefining paid work to include housework, parenting, caring for one's parents, volunteering, community service, good neighboring, playing music, engaging in sports, dancing, and almost any activity in which people choose to engage. Another suggestion is that the means of resource creation should be owned cooperatively or collectively, as in the Israeli kibbutz.

There is also the proposal that everyone be granted a basic income regardless of activities.

The proposal for a basic income is by no means new. Thomas More made the suggestion in 1517, and Thomas Paine had the same idea at the end of the eighteenth century.[38] In our times, a guaranteed minimum income was suggested as a way to end the means test in social work[39] and then taken up by economists such as Milton Friedman, culminating in President Nixon's Family Assistance Plan, which was rejected by Congress.[40]

Although not exactly a basic income, many countries—although not the United States—pay children's and/or family allowances on a universal basis. One way of arriving at a basic income in such countries would be to change children's and family allowances to individual allowances and to raise them high enough to at least keep everyone out of poverty. In a somewhat different vein, Alaskan oil revenues are distributed to citizens without regard for work records, on the basis that the oil belongs to all of them. Further, in the Israeli kibbutz, everyone is guaranteed all the necessities and many of the luxuries of life without regard for the work, or the amount of work, done.

37. Mark W. Dumas, "Productivity in Industry and Government, 1990," *Monthly Labor Review*, 115(6): 48-57.

38. Nicole E. M. de Jager, Johan J. Graafland, and George M. M. Gelauff, *A Negative Income Tax in a Mini-Welfare State: A Simulation with MIMIC* (Den Haag, Netherlands: Central Planbureau, 1994).

39. Edward E. Schwaartz, "A Way to End the Means Test," *Social Work*, 4:3 (1963).

40. Daniel P. Moynihan. *The Politics of a Guaranteed Income: The Nixon Administration and the Family Assistance Plan* (New York: Vintage, 1973).

Throughout the world, there are a number of groups and organizations grappling with the need for a new paradigm and methods of achieving and implementing it. These include the Society for the Reduction of Human Labor, the North American Network for Shorter Work Hours, the Basic Income European Network, and Reorganisation/Reduction in Work Time. Although somewhat different in their structures and activities, all of these organizations agree that, whether based on equality or equity, some new method of distribution of resources will have to be devised and implemented as the almost-workless world approaches.

It may be, of course, that the almost-workless world will never arrive. Still, it is better to have a plan and not need it than to have a need and no plan for it.[41] Working out the details of an economic system with constantly growing numbers of the permanently unemployed may yet prove to be a useful exercise.

41. David Macarov, "Planning for a Possibility: The Almost-Workless World," *International Labour Review*, 123:629-42 (Nov.-Dec. 1985).

EPILOGUE

It remains now only to point out one last time how much more research, analysis, and constructive dialogue we need if we are to adopt proactive social policies equal to the job-change challenge.

Fortunately, 1996 marks the fiftieth anniversary of the 1946 Full Employment Act, a brilliant piece of social legislation with which we have not entirely kept faith. It was designed to reassure veterans returning from overseas that they were not returning to unemployment levels reminiscent of the Great Depression but would instead gain high-quality job training and satisfactory employment. Should the marketplace falter, the act pledged that the federal government would prop up job generation and do so with meaningful jobs.

Academics from coast to coast will attend Full Employment Act anniversary conferences and give papers this year updating our post-World War II concerns. Many will bring to bear the sort of fresh insights highlighted in this volume. Much media attention is expected and possibly even the sort of policy-shaping dialogue that the subject plainly merits. At the very least, the subject will get a reasonable airing. Better still, the spirit of the 1946 act may stir fresh recognition of the seriousness of the job-change challenge and the need to try to get out ahead of it, as we did fifty years ago.

For my part, I hope all of this attention includes certain facts that the media tend to judge too complex for bumper-sticker reportage and are therefore easily overlooked. Typical is the fact that while 21 years ago the same proportion of Americans were out of work as are out of work today (as of this writing, October 1995), 21 years ago they were out of work for a bit over half as long as are today's unemployed: 10 versus 17 weeks.[1] *Barron's* cites corporate restructuring as the reason for this trend; instead of being laid off as was the case in the past, workers today often are fired—and their jobs are permanently eliminated. People require more time to find new jobs when they have no hope that they will be called back to work by their former employers.[2]

A second fact that warrants attention is that, although the output of U.S. manufacturers grew by 2.1 percent between 1987 and 1992, jobs fell by 4.0 percent.[3]

Another relevant fact is that, during the 1980s, the United States was the only advanced country to have suffered not only major decreases in real earnings but also major increases in inequality.[4] As contributors to this volume make clear, our major competitors may be doing a better job of protecting their standards of living, even as they are enjoying faster growth in manufacturing productivity than is our country.[5]

1. *Trade Union Advisor* (Labor Research Association), 3 Oct. 1995, p. 2.
2. As cited in ibid.
3. Edward Cornish, "Outlook '96," *Futurist*, p. 1 (Nov.-Dec. 1995).
4. David R. Howell, "A Degree Doesn't Equal High Pay," *New York Times*, 3 Oct. 1995.
5. *Trade Union Advisor*, 10 Oct. 1995, p. 3.

A fourth fact worth greater attention than ever comes from a fall 1995 report of the Bureau of Labor Statistics released too late for use by this volume's contributors. The report confirms that nearly half of all the job openings between 1983 and 1993 were for jobs that required the least amount of education or training.[6] This would seem to undermine the case of those who, like Secretary of Labor Robert Reich, contend that more training is the best possible response to the job-change challenge.

Off-the-wall speculations are another component of the discussion that merit attention commonly denied, although not by some of the more imaginative contributors to the present volume.

Typical is the brow-arching contention of Hans Moravec that, by 2010, robots will be able to do relatively intricate mechanical tasks such as automobile repair, factory assembly work, and bathroom cleaning. By 2040, humans will be unable to find work because no jobs will be available for people that cannot be done better by robots. There is no need for panic, however, because when industry is totally automated and hyperefficient, it will create so much wealth that retirement can begin at birth. Corporations will be taxed and those moneys will be distributed to all the people in the form of social security payments that people receive throughout their lives.[7]

My favorite line of speculation focuses on the possibility that ongoing advances in molecular nanotechnology will soon be able to replace the entire work world with an unprecedented world of nano (super-tiny) machines. Nano operates at the most fundamental level (atoms and molecules), has plummeting costs, and may soon be able to improve just about any object we use, including our own bodies. Its proponents expect productivity gains to produce a "Horn of Cornucopia" in 50 or fewer years, complete with near-total joblessness but also with abundant wealth for distribution. They believe we can transition with minimal disturbance from our historical reliance on employment to a new world of empowering leisure.[8]

If we are to do so, it will help even now to ponder "The Leisure Party Manifesto," a 1995 declaration of independence from obsessive job concern. Its anonymous author or authors hail our ability to change our priorities and experience the joys of life as well as the many wonders of the earth and human society. In the age of thinking machines, leisure is a fundamental right rather than merely a privilege. The thinking is that, if machines and computers are able and willing to work, they should be allowed to do so. We are to realize that life involves a lot more than just work.[9]

Perhaps . . . and then again, perhaps not. Freud believed life was fundamentally a mix of "love and work," and a future without the latter would seem

6. *LRA's Economic Notes* (Labor Research Association), p. 5 (Oct. 1995).
7. As quoted in Charles Platt, "Super Humanism," *Wired,* pp. 149, 202 (Oct. 1995).
8. In this connection, see K. Eric Drexler, *Engines of Creation* (New York: Doubleday, 1986); K. Eric Drexler and Chris Peterson with Gayle Pergamit, *Unbounding the Future: The Nanotechnology Revolution* (New York: William Morrow, 1991); Ed Regis, *Nano: The Emerging Science of Nanotechnoloy: Remaking the World—Molecule by Molecule* (Boston: Little, Brown, 1995).
9. "The Leisure Party Manifesto," *Wired: Scenarios* (special ed.), p. 108 (Fall 1995).

to threaten the former. Guided, however, by the sort of advice that Macarov and others offer in this volume, we may be able to best the challenge. All things considered, we have much still to ponder and to experiment with, much that the articles in this volume illuminate.

ARTHUR B. SHOSTAK

Book Department

INTERNATIONAL RELATIONS AND POLITICS	206
AFRICA, ASIA, AND LATIN AMERICA	210
UNITED STATES	216
SOCIOLOGY	227
ECONOMICS	232

INTERNATIONAL RELATIONS AND POLITICS

ADAMS, JAMES. *Sellout: Aldrich Ames and the Corruption of the CIA.* Pp. xiv, 293. New York: Columbia University Press, 1995. $37.50.

James Adams is a correspondent for the London *Sunday Times*, a freelance journalist, and the author of several books, fiction and nonfiction, on terrorism, war, and the weapons trade. His 1992 book on the life of supergun inventor Gerald Bull was described by a reviewer as reading "like a thrilling spy novel." Now comes his first real work on espionage, *Sellout: Aldrich Ames and the Corruption of the CIA*, which one would expect to read like a spy novel but which spends as much time dissecting the weaknesses of the bureaucracy of the Central Intelligence Agency (CIA) as it does telling the tale of the notorious Aldrich Ames. This informative book is therefore much more, and much less, than a fast-paced spy story.

Adams reveals not only the deadly treachery of Ames but also the incompetence and indifference of the CIA's old-boy network, which allowed a blatant drunk with extravagant tastes and unexplained bank accounts to continue stealing shopping bags full of secret documents for years. Through numerous reports and analyses, Adams documents the slow movement toward reform in the CIA, reform that became unavoidable after Ames was arrested on 21 February 1994.

Adams quotes a Western intelligence official's description of Ames as "the most valuable asset the Soviets or the Russians have ever had in Western intelligence in modern times." This is certainly an arguable assessment, but far from unanimous in the intelligence community. Boris Solomatin, the now-retired Soviet spy master, believes that John Walker was the most valuable Soviet spy. Walker provided military strategic information and cryptography, while Ames supplied information in the field of counterintelligence, including the names of Russians working as CIA agents. Solomatin says Ames's information provided onetime benefits to the Soviets, but Walker's information helped them over time to understand how the American military thinks. The fact that Walker provided American codes and ciphers was particularly compromising. Solomatin told an American reporter, "For more than 17 years Walker enabled your enemies to read your most sensitive military secrets. We knew everything! There has never been a security breach of this magnitude and length in the history of espionage."

Adams, like many other analysts, elevates Ames's espionage to the highest level of infamy, not so much because it caused strategic damage to American security but because of the personal price paid by CIA sources, at least 10 of whom were killed as the result of Ames's treachery. Other recent books on Ames, such as Peter Maas's *Killer Spy*, are even more explicit in highlighting the bloody consequences of Ames's espionage.

Both Ames and Walker were motivated by money, not ideology. Ames's wife, Rosario, was complicitous only late in the game, but her taste for luxury was an early force that drove Ames to seek money for America's secrets. The day of the ideological spy clearly ended a generation ago.

HERBERT FOERSTEL

Columbia
Maryland

KOLKO, GABRIEL. *Century of War: Politics, Conflicts, and Society since 1914.* Pp. xx, 546. New York: New Press, 1994. No price.

The fourteenth century used to be the benchmark of human tragedy in Western history, but Gabriel Kolko, in this dense, difficult, and very rewarding book, shows clearly how our own century has surpassed it in horror and death. *Century of War*, however, is not a description or analysis of battle but a brilliantly argued condemnation of the leadership of the Western world "who invariably substituted those delusions that their domestic political interests and personal ambitions required for realistic assessments of the titanic demands and consequences that modern warfare inevitably creates."

Kolko contends that the blindness of leaders, both political and military, to the consequences of war is universal in every war of this century. None of them considered the cost in lives or the economic destruction that would occur during the conflict or the social upheaval that might occur when the fighting was over. Indeed, the second major argument of the book is that war is the engine that has driven "social upheaval and change in our era."

Concentrating on World Wars I and II, the Korean War, and the Vietnam war, although not ignoring other wars large and small, Kolko examines thoroughly the way in which modern wars grew and evolved beyond the capabilities of political and military leaders to wage them. The "romantic ideas" that inspired French and English officers before World War I, for instance, "failed to prepare them . . . for the technical and logistical complexities of prolonged conflicts." On the other hand, the "huge quantities of technology and firepower" expended by the United States in Vietnam failed to achieve victory against an enemy that "could easily hide until the initiative favored them and they could exploit the element of surprise." Robert McNamara's book *In Retrospect* might almost be a case study designed to complement Kolko's vivid dissection of the appalling failures of modern political and military leaders.

Kolko also examines the myriad changes in society and politics brought about by war. He analyzes the Russian and German revolutions and the consequences of the Nazi occupation of Europe in great detail to make clear the erasure of the difference between civilian and soldier in modern warfare. The suffering of citizens and their loss of faith in traditional leadership frequently brought about the downfall of that leadership.

An intensely rich book, *Century of War* also contains clear discussions of the downfall of communism, the pitfalls of economic liberalism, the problems of American global power, and the future difficulties of a world unable to resolve conflict without war. Great long sentences that often have to be read twice make this a difficult book, but the clarity of Kolko's vision emerges from a careful reading, as does the importance of what he has to say.

MARY BETH EMMERICHS
University of Wisconsin
Milwaukee

MLYN, ERIC. *The State, Society, and Limited Nuclear War.* Pp. xi, 241. Albany: State University of New York Press, 1995. $19.95.

With the dissolution of the Soviet Union, the chance of large-scale nuclear war has become almost nil. While worthy of celebration, the situation casts Eric Mlyn's study in an anachronistic shadow. To be sure, he writes of more than the nuclear face-off during the Cold War, but the theme of nuclear confrontation between the United States and the Soviet Union largely shapes the book.

Mlyn notes that declared U.S. nuclear arms policies varied through the post–World War II decades. The strategic objective was always to fight and win a nuclear war, but declared policy was sometimes weighted toward massive destruction, at other times toward discrete targeting. The descriptive acronym for the first approach is MAD (mutual assured destruction), while the second is NUTs (nuclear utilization theory). That our nuclear policy has swung between MAD and NUTs may be all any sane person wants to know. But Mlyn has some other instructive things to say.

He compares declaratory policies, force development policies, and action policies during three periods. The first period, the 1960s into the early 1970s, saw the MAD declaratory policy of the 1950s give way under Secretary of Defense Robert McNamara. But after pronouncing the goal of avoiding cities in a nuclear war, McNamara later slid back to declarations about massive retaliation.

The second period, the mid-1970s, saw similar confusions. Defense Secretary James Schlesinger in 1974 argued for a nuclear strategy of counterforce. Yet he maintained erroneously that this approach was much the same as declared targeting strategies since the early 1960s.

The third period began under Carter and continued through the Reagan years. Mlyn describes the Carter administration's nuclear policies as schizophrenic. Initially wanting to reduce the nuclear arsenal, Secretary of Defense Harold Brown later embraced an emphasis on nuclear war fighting strategies. The Reagan administration, Mlyn says, was "more honest at the declaratory level and more committed to NUTs at the force development level than other administrations had been."

The historical vignettes are interesting, but Mlyn's comparisons of declaratory, force, and action policies are sometimes confusing. Nor does his "statist paradigm" always clarify the web of contradictions resulting from U.S. policies. This book is for dedicated nuclear policy buffs and people who like unfamiliar abbreviations. One section is actually titled "NSDM-242 and SIOP 5." The meanings are referenced in a list of 53 acronyms that a nonspecialist must be prepared to visit frequently.

LEONARD A. COLE
Rutgers University
Newark
New Jersey

MÜLLER, HARALD, DAVID FISCHER, and WOLFGANG KÖTTER. *Nuclear Non-Proliferation and Global Order.*

Pp. xii, 258. New York: Oxford University Press, 1994. $39.95.

The book under review is the product of a successful team effort by three senior social scientists. Their project was assisted and supported by the Stockholm International Peace Research Institute and the Peace Research Institute Frankfurt.

The object of the 1968 Non-Proliferation Treaty (NPT), which entered into force on 5 March 1970, is, as the name indicates, the prevention of the proliferation of military nuclear technology. In addition to the five nuclear weapon states (NWS), 166 nonnuclear weapon states (NNWS) ratified the treaty even though they realized that they became unequal partners of the NWS. They accepted the discrimination of unequal membership because they were concerned about their own security as well as that of the world in case nuclear weapons of mass destruction fell into the hands of irresponsible governments of the so-called crazy states.

But they also expected from the NWS an intensification of the negotiations leading to nuclear arms control and disarmament. Article VI of the NPT requires that all of the parties "pursue negotiations in good faith on effective measures relating to cessation of the nuclear arms race . . . and to nuclear disarmament, and on a treaty on general and complete disarmament under strict and effective international control."

These issues dominated most of the debates during the various NPT review conferences and during the 1991 Partial Test Ban Treaty Amendment Conference. The reluctance and even resistance of the NWS, especially of the United States and United Kingdom, as shown in their rejecting any substantial changes to their nuclear deterrent policies, were greatly responsible for the failure to reach agreements.

The authors of the study under review undertook a detailed analysis of the record and results of the Third and Fourth Review Conferences (1980 and 1985, respectively) and the 1991 Partial Test Ban Treaty Amendment Conference, as well as the past implementation of the various components of the NPT regime, to assess the prospects for the NPT Extension Conference. They included in their assessment the possible impacts on the forthcoming conference of the end of the Cold War, the dissolution of the Soviet Union, and the 1991 Persian Gulf war.

The present global nonproliferation regime is also challenged by the increased number of NWS (Belarus, Ukraine, and Kazakhstan), by the stated intention of the North Korean government on 12 March 1993 to terminate its obligations under the NPT, and by the nuclear aspirations of Iraq, Iran, Algeria, and some other states. The authors assert that these developments actually demand not only the extension but the strengthening of the nonproliferation regime for the sake of universal security.

The two primary concerns of the NNWS, as expressed clearly during the various review and amendment conferences as well as at the sessions of the Conference on Disarmament, were, first, about the effectiveness of the International Atomic Energy Agency as the safeguarding instrument of the nonproliferation regime and, second, about the prospects of nuclear disarmament, that is, the demand for a Comprehensive Test Ban Treaty.

The authors emphasize that "the main problem of cohesion for the regime remains the level of progress in the area of nuclear arms control and disarmament." They believe that the prospects for negotiations on a Comprehensive Test Ban Treaty are good because of the current political climate created by the 1991 and 1993 Strategic Arms Reduction Talks, the probable continuation of the test moratorium, and the cessation of the production of fissile material for weapon purposes in the United States and near cessation in the Russian Federation. These developments might improve the chances for the extension of the NPT. (The NPT Extension Conference in New York during April 1995 voted in favor of an indefinite extension of the NPT after a prolonged debate.)

In my opinion, the authors have succeeded in the difficult task of making the complex issues of global nuclear nonproliferation and nuclear test ban policies understandable to nonnuclear experts. The appendix contains the texts of relevant documents on nuclear weapon nonproliferation, adding significantly to the usefulness of the book for students of contemporary international politics.

ERIC WALDMAN
University of Calgary
Alberta
Canada

AFRICA, ASIA, AND LATIN AMERICA

GOLDMAN, MERLE. *Sowing the Seeds of Democracy in China: Political Reform in the Deng Xiaoping Era*. Cambridge, MA: Harvard University Press, 1994. Pp. xv, 426. No price.

LIN, JING. *The Opening of the Chinese Mind: Democratic Changes in China since 1978*. Westport, CT: Praeger, 1994. Pp. xv, 186. $49.95.

Hopes for democratic reform were raised sharply in China when Deng Xiaoping assumed power in 1978. Among the People's Republic of China's long-suffering intellectuals, a mood of optimism prevailed as, one after another, traditional political taboos began to be lifted and ideological "forbidden zones" were tentatively opened to critical scrutiny. At Democracy Wall, posters boldly proclaimed that Chairman Mao had made "serious mistakes": the Great Leap Forward was a disaster; the Cultural Revolution, a fiasco.

Encouraged by the new atmosphere of ideological and political openness, a group of forward-thinking Marxist intellectuals—theoreticians, scholars, writers, and editors—set out to reshape China's ossified political institutions and humanize its shopworn Marxist-Leninist dogmas. Loosely affiliated with Hu Yaobang and the liberal wing of Deng Xiaoping's pro-reform coalition, they constituted a nascent "democratic elite." The rise—and fall—of this democratic elite is the subject of Merle Goldman's new book, *Sowing the Seeds of Democracy in China: Political Reform in the Deng Xiaoping Era*.

Goldman has long been among the most astute observers of the Chinese Communists' use—and chronic abuse—of intellectuals. In her latest work, she examines the checkered history of China's democratic elite against a backdrop of mounting intraparty conflict over the proper means and ends, scope, and limitations of democratic reform.

From the outset, the fortunes of the democratic elite were tied closely to the power and prestige of Hu. When Hu, a progressive Marxist, came under fire from Party conservatives for the alleged sin of being soft on "bourgeois liberalism," the brunt of the attack was borne by Hu's intellectual network. When Hu was finally removed from power in January 1987, the democratic elite fell on hard times; some lost their jobs, others were blacklisted, and a few were expelled from the Communist Party. Two years later, the echo of machine-gun fire at Tiananmen Square put a resounding end, for the time being, to the intellectuals' democratic optimism.

Charting the turbulent history—and ultimate failure—of democratic reform in the 1980s, Goldman tells a fascinating story; in the process, she sheds some interesting new light on the politics of the reform decade. Her account of the notorious Bai Hua affair of 1981, for example, is the best I have seen to date. (Bai was an army writer whose controversial screenplay, *Unrequited Love*, called sharply into question the Chinese Communist Party's concern for, and devotion to, the Chinese people. Criticism of Bai's work by Party conservatives resulted in the post-Mao era's first significant wave of anti-intellectualism.) The same holds true for her reconstruction of the bitter dispute over "bourgeois liberalization" that led to the sacking of Hu. Goldman's careful reconstruction of the complex, swirling political and intellectual crosscurrents of 1988, which preceded and tragically portended the 1989 Tiananmen crisis, is most compelling.

Goldman crafts her excellent narrative by adroitly interweaving documentary sources with personal interviews conducted with key Chinese participants in the events in question, including former members of Hu's intellectual network. These interview materials are an invaluable source of new information and insight; on the downside, however, they are also a source of what is arguably the book's only nontrivial shortcoming, namely, Goldman's tendency to identify a bit too closely with the aims and actions of the democratic elite and to lionize their fallen champion, Hu, while also at times maligning the motives and behavior of Hu's adversaries. Even Hu's erstwhile successor, the ill-starred Zhao Ziyang, is portrayed here—rather unfairly, in my opinion—as a petty, spiteful opportunist who took calculated advantage of Hu's misfortunes to further his own career.

In *The Opening of the Chinese Mind*, Jing Lin also examines the checkered progress of democratization in post-Mao China, but she does so from a perspective very different from that of Goldman, using a very different format. Where Goldman has fashioned an artful analytical history of China's democratic reforms and reformers, Lin, who was born and raised in China, has crafted a highly personalized account of the societal effects of Deng Xiaoping's reforms. More an extended first-person narrative essay than a detached scholarly monograph, *The Opening of the Chinese Mind* assays the "highly significant mental, psychological, and behavioral changes that have taken place among the Chinese people since 1978." Relying heavily on personal experience and opinion, augmented by survey materials gleaned from a questionnaire administered to a small, nonrandom sample of twenty Chinese citizens, Lin argues that, despite repeated policy reversals and setbacks, the social and psychological changes engendered by the reforms of the 1980s have become irreversibly entrained. A passionate believer in the transformative power of the democratic spirit, she foresees—the Tiananmen massacre notwithstanding—the imminent emergence of a genuine civil society in China. "There is no turning back," she writes. "The people are no longer passive and obedient citizens but . . . have become increasingly critical thinkers and effective participants in the processes that affect their own lives." If few of Lin's observations or conclusions are particularly new or startling, she nonetheless tells her story in a manner that is both passionate and persuasive.

While not nearly so sanguine as Lin about China's prospects for achieving an early democratic breakthrough, Goldman shares Lin's underlying faith in the power of the democratic impulse. Elaborating on the horticultural metaphor that forms the main title of her book, Goldman concludes her study on a hopeful note:

The Deng decade has demonstrated that China's soil can nourish democratic seedlings. . . . The roots of China's democracy are still fragile, the atmosphere still uncertain, and portions of the soil still unfertile. But by the end of the Deng decade, the roots had become stronger and the shoots a bit taller. (p. 360)

Each in its own way, these two fine books help bring into clearer focus the unfinished business of China's democratic reform.

RICHARD BAUM

University of California
Los Angeles

HOSTON, GERMAINE A. *The State, Identity, and the National Question in China and Japan.* Pp. xii, 628. Princeton, NJ: Princeton University Press, 1994. $85.00. Paperbound, $24.95.

This book is first of all an intellectual history of Marxism in China and Japan, much more concerned with ideas than with real historical happenings. As such, it is not easy reading, even for this professor emeritus who taught East Asian history at the University of Pennsylvania for 39 years. Germaine Hoston, a professor at the University of California, San Diego, is a Princeton- and Harvard-trained scholar and, as such, may be expected to operate in an environment somewhat more intellectual than our down-to-earth Benjamin Franklin style at Penn. But *The State, Identity, and the National Question* is above and beyond anything I had previously encountered even from Princeton and Harvard. It is, in short, stupendous—444 pages of text, 90 pages of footnotes, and 73 pages of bibliographical entries in six languages including, of course, both Chinese and Japanese sources in abundance. In need of assistance from younger, more agile minds, in writing this review, I consulted my graduate student colleague, George C. C. Chang, on China questions and referred to notes on Japan's Marxists obtained some forty years ago in extended conversations with Hagihara Nobutoshi, student-colleague of Tokyo University professors Oka Yoshitake and Maruyama Masao.

As a nonspecialist in intellectual history, my first (practical) inclination was to try to summarize what the real historical result of it all is, and I came up with the following: Marxism via Maoism won in a chaotic, disunited China, but it failed in Japan, which had a much more unified national structure. This was (or is) in spite of the fact that Japanese Marxists, at least some of them, were no less brilliant intellectually than their Chinese counterparts; in fact, some of the brightest of the Marxist ideas later used in China came out of Sino-Japanese dialogues originating in Japan. Of course, there is a lot more to the story than this.

Along the way, we learn about "the national question from Marx to Lenin," its "transformation" in the Russia of 1917, and the "dilemma" that the national question posed for Marxists in East Asia (chapter 1). Chapter 2 reviews "the national question and problems in the Marxist theory of the state." These problems arose from the "incompleteness and incorrectness" of the Marxist theory of the state and resulted in vigorous scholarly debate among Marxist scholars and activists in interwar China and Japan. Chapter 3 discusses the history of theories of the state in premodern through Meiji Japan (Shinto, *kokutai*, and so on) and premodern through Qing China (for example, legalism versus Confucianism) and shows that both of these were challenged by a Marxist ideal of "stateless communism," which was introduced via well-discussed European socialist ideas entering Japan and China around 1900. Chapter 4, entitled "Anarchism, Populism and Early Marxian Socialism," gives the European background of this and discusses how Asian anarchism started in Tokyo with "former nationalists" such as Kōtoku Shūsui, *Heimin shimbun* (newspaper), internal rivalries (for example, Katayama Sen, but no Fukuda Hideko or other women mentioned) and its suppression in Japan. Noteworthy is that the

Meiji oligarchs had encouraged and used nationalism in Japan while the alien Qing were unable to do so in China, and anarchism moved from Tokyo to Peking, but it died there, too, with the arrival of Bolshevism in 1917. Chapter 5 discusses "nationalism and the rise of Bolshevism" and how Li Da-Zhao's nationalism prevailed over Chen Du-Xiu's internationalism to lead to Mao and how Takabatake Motoyuki's nationalism portended the ultimate collapse of the Japan Communist party.

Part 3, "History, the State and Revolutionary Change," takes us into the 1920s and the emergence of the Rōnō (labor farmer) versus Kōza (lecturers on capitalism) split in the Japanese Marxist movement, which occupied—one might even say preoccupied—Japan's brightest minds (for example, antimilitarist professors of economics, law, and politics at Japan's major universities) in the 1930s as militarism took over the Japanese government. In China, it was Mao's building up the Communist challenge to Nanking. "A profound problem for Chinese Marxists" had been what Edward Said has called "Orientalism as imperialism" or, as Hoston writes, "by accepting Marx do Chinese subject themselves to Western domination?" Mao's genius was to solve this.

The chapters in part 3 are fascinating, but let us move on to "Outcomes: The Reconciliation of Marxism with National Identity" (part 4). Here we find the Japanese synthesis in "*Tenkō*: Emperor, State and Marxian National Socialism" (chapter 8) and "Mao and the Chinese Synthesis of Nationalism, Stateness and Marxism" (chapter 9) with "Conclusion and Epilogue" (chapter 10). The essence of the problem was that radical thinkers in both China and Japan were drawn to Marxism "as a medium of liberation from painful subordination to the West as well as from domestic sources of oppression." But the national question complicated this. Mao's "solution" was "sinified Marxism." The problem was "less tortured" in Japan, but then it did not bring a revolution there, with Marxism remaining pretty much an intellectual exercise—as "real" history tells us. Into this Hoston incorporates a fascinating discussion of what nationalism is, using European precedents and theories—the Enlightenment, the French Revolution, German romantics, Sorel, Nietzsche, Barrès, Déroulède, Hobsbawm, Herder, and so on—and, referring to nationalism scholars such as Hans Kohn, Geoff Eley, and A. D. Smith, coming up with two principal types of nationalism, "organic-irrational" and "voluntaristic-political." These complicated Marxism in various ways in both China and Japan "in circumstances which were not without their ambiguities."

Finally, there is an epilogue, "Nationalism and Statism in Postwar China and Japan," which finds the national question continuing to be of "singular significance to the Marxist movements in the two societies"—another fascinating chapter.

This is a brilliant book, no doubt about it. Can I think of any criticisms? A minor one (inspired by hurt feelings?): Hoston, despite her magnificent bibliography, missed my only serious foray into the national question, an article entitled "Japanese Nationalism and Expansionism" published in the *American Historical Review* (volume 60, number 4) way back in 1955 (before she was born?). Therein I found three types of Japanese nationalism—*minzoku shugi*, *kokumin shugi*, and *kokka shugi*—that she might consider in their relationship to Marxism. (I did not.) A larger question might be whether the collapse of the Soviet Union and the general malaise of Marxism worldwide have made it somewhat retroactive to spend so much time and effort tracing its ideological labyrinth. Of course, many of the ideas that have "made history" could fall into that category, and it may well be that only scholars as brilliant as Hoston can begin to deal with this as a problem in historical presentation.

HILARY CONROY with
GEORGE C. C. CHANG

University of Pennsylvania
Philadelphia

MACKERRAS, COLIN. *China's Minorities: Integration and Modernization in the Twentieth Century*. Pp. viii, 355. New York: Oxford University Press, 1994. $79.00.

For many years, the subject of China's ethnic minorities, comprising 56 different groups and nearly 100 million people, has received scant attention despite pioneering research by Owen Lattimore. Recently, however, perhaps because of the role of ethnic minorities in the breakup of the Soviet Union and Eastern Europe, there is renewed interest in the ethnic groups of China, with the obvious research question of whether these groups have the potential to cause a similar breakup of China. One recent book that deals with this subject is Doak Barnett's *China's Far West* (1993), and the University of Washington Press promises a forthcoming series. The volume under review, then, can be seen in the light of this renewed interest.

After a brief introduction, which looks at China's minorities before 1900, the bulk of the book is divided into two sections: the period between 1900 and 1949 and the period after 1949. Mackerras concludes that China's minorities in general have fared better under the People's Republic of China than they have under the Guomindang, even though both regimes shared the goal of keeping China united, because the Communists were willing to allow a certain degree of autonomy—with the exception of the Cultural Revolution period—while the Nationalists stressed assimilation.

One of the highlights is a discussion of the role of foreign powers in the development of minority border regions: Britain and Tibet, Russia and Xinjiang, Japan and Manchuria. These foreign connections were beneficial, Mackerras contends, in assisting in the modernization of minority areas, while at the same time raising the potential for secession from China—witness the Russian role in the secession of Outer Mongolia. Because minority areas in China are generally sparsely populated and relatively less well developed than is the rest of China (with some notable exceptions such as the Korean area in Yanbian), the People's Republic of China adopted as a matter of policy that new "outside" help, in the form of Han Chinese in-migration, was necessary to assist with modernization. The result is that while contemporary China has less to fear from foreign intervention, especially since the breakup of the Soviet Union, there is a perception of Han Chinese domination in minority areas. "Affirmative action" policies favoring minorities in university admissions, taxation, and birth control, however, lead Mackerras to conclude that, while ethnic tension does exist in some areas (Tibet is the most notable example), China's minorities currently do not represent a threat to break up China.

While it would appear to be a daunting task to deal adequately and comparatively with so many differing groups, Mackerras has succeeded. It is regrettable that the book's list price will place it out of the reach of most readers.

WAYNE PATTERSON

St. Norbert College
DePere
Wisconsin

RUBIN, BARNETT R. *The Fragmentation of Afghanistan: State Formation and Collapse in the International System.* Pp. xix, 378. New Haven, CT: Yale University Press, 1995. $35.00.

RAIS, RASUL BAKHSH. *War without Winners: Afghanistan's Uncertain Transition after the Cold War.* Pp. xi, 286. New York: Oxford University Press, 1994. $27.00.

The problem of state survival and legitimacy in the postcolonial, post–Cold War world continues to challenge politicians and scholars. Turmoil from the Balkans to Central Asia confronts old assumptions of national identity with the realities of ethnic, linguistic, sectarian, and regional division. Two works about Afghanistan address this late-twentieth-century questioning of the state.

In Barnett Rubin's *Fragmentation of Afghanistan*, an implicit thesis emerges that the Afghan state, discredited by a decade of Soviet control and undermined by years of post-Soviet civil war, remains a focus of interest and contention. Rubin and Rasul Bakhsh Rais, in *War without Winners*, examine the political competition and the social damage that occurred in Afghanistan after the socialist coup of April 1978 and the 1979 Soviet invasion.

Rubin's meticulously researched study notes that nineteenth-century rulers in Kabul, consolidating a socially diverse buffer state defined by imperial forces, relied on foreign trade and subsidies and never developed local infrastructural ties, either to regularize revenue extraction or to solidify political legitimacy. After regional and clan-based resistance to policies of centralization and social reform led to the 1929 overthrow of King Amanullah, Afghan rulers made little effort to transform the countryside economically or politically.

From the 1950s to the 1970s, a period of Cold War competition and aid packages, a new, ideologically committed class of urban, university-trained elites developed. Democracy, socialism, and Islam attracted those opposed to the old decentralized power structure. Leftist elites led the coup of 1978 and quickly attempted to assert state authority.

The "revolution from above" failed. Both Rubin and Rais detail the narrow social composition of the revolutionary People's Democratic Party of Afghanistan and the poorly conceived and executed reform policies that generated a cycle of opposition, greater repression, and widespread revolt.

In a comprehensive discussion of the diverse elements of the resistance, Rubin analyzes the other university-trained, radical ideologues, Islamists. Reform-minded Islamists and traditional religious leaders rallied refugees and foreign patronage from bases in Pakistan and Iran. Rubin notes how the fractious, Peshawar-based resistance parties became dependent on outside arms, funding, and ideological resources. Rais also discusses a perpetual resistance disunity traceable to "doctrinal, political, and personal" differences.

Both studies—although Rais has lapses—analyze a historically grounded situation more complex than simply a traditional or feudal society opposing inevitable modernization. Rais, in particular, explores the impact of the shifting international political scene (including the collapse of the USSR) on Afghanistan. Useful for comparative reflection is Rubin's sense that contemporary Islamic militancy, ethnic conflict, and resurgent "tribalism" are often effects generated by the dynamics of the nation-state.

Rubin's story ends in late 1994, with an almost obliterated state structure in Kabul still the goal of realigned, more ethnically focused parties built around the resistance factions. Rubin's study hints that, after 100 years, the international nation-state system may not dictate the Afghan future and that any surviving Afghan state may have a chance to negotiate infrastructural ties with local social forces.

Rubin has usefully distilled and updated a mass of earlier scholarship and has integrated a wide range of research. Rais has provided a cogent overview of the Afghan tragedy and has revealed the links between domestic, regional, and international strategic and ideological interests.

Both authors return to the image of fragmentation in describing Afghan state and society of the 1990s. Questions about endless Afghan political anarchy may be increasingly moot after the March 1995 strengthening of the Rabbani government, but the authors' understanding of continued Afghan social fragmentation offers a comparative perspective for other regions struggling to end confrontation, build consensus, and accommodate diverse ethnic and social communities.

ROBERT NICHOLS

University of Pennsylvania
Philadelphia

UNITED STATES

ALESINA, ALBERTO and HOWARD ROSENTHAL. *Partisan Politics, Divided Government, and the Economy.* Pp. xiii, 280. New York: Cambridge University Press, 1995. $65.00. Paperbound, $17.95.

Alberto Alesina and Howard Rosenthal have produced a comprehensive model, with extensive empirical tests, of the connections between politics as conducted within the divided governmental framework of the United States, on the one hand, and key facets of the economy, on the other. This intellectual tour de force is based on several key assumptions, especially (1) parties polarized along a single liberal-conservative dimension and (2) fully rational voters who are distributed along the same dimension.

Three empirically based issues are the motivations for the general approach: (1) the parties are polarized but the voters are not (supported elsewhere by Keith Poole and Howard Rosenthal in their comprehensive scaling efforts); (2) the incumbent party loses seats at midterm, independently of the state of the economy; and (3) economic growth in the second year of Democratic administrations significantly and reliably exceeds growth in the second year of Republican administrations. The modeling attempts to integrate these seemingly diverse observations, and the authors deserve high praise for this.

Major facets of the model are that moderate voters initiate institutional balancing of the immoderate parties at midterm, that voters ought to be retrospective when judging the competence of an administration and not otherwise, and that the second-year growth or inflation spurt is an "inflation surprise." Both institutional balancing and the second-year inflation surprise occur solely because of uncertainty over the previous presidential election. If voters had instituted the right balance in the on-year election, they would not need to correct at midterm. In addition, the only reason that rational, unidimensional voters would fail to institute the proper balance at presidential election time would be uncertainty about the presidential outcome. Similarly, they should not be fooled by an unsustainable growth spurt, so that it would occur only when the party winning the presidential election was unexpected.

Empirical tests indicate support for the model, but also major problems. Voters pay too much attention to the past state of the economy (they should pay attention only to party positions), and the midterm loss occurs even when the previous presidential election was a fully expected landslide. The problems, which Alesina and Rosenthal discuss in some detail, are serious because they go right to the heart of a major assumption of the model: the postulate of rational, unidimensional voters.

The failure of the full-blown rational-voter assumption implies a clear need to base models of the democratic policy process on more realistic views of voters, perhaps along the lines of the work of John Zaller. Moreover, Poole and Rosenthal found systematic changes in party polarization, with decreases until the 1960s and increases afterward. Much progress could be made from a study of the causes and consequences of changes in party polarization, against the backdrop of a boundedly rational electorate, even if one would need to forgo the comprehensive modeling approach of Alesina and Rosenthal.

BRYAN D. JONES

Texas A&M University
College Station

BERG, JOHN C. *Unequal Struggle: Class, Gender, Race, and Power in the U.S. Congress.* Pp. xi, 187. Boulder, CO: Westview Press, 1994. $59.00. Paperbound, $19.95.

John Berg provides a welcome and timely alternative to traditional American political science treatments of the U.S. Congress that rest on either pluralist or institutionalist approaches, which Berg so ably critiques as lacking explanatory power for continuing class, race, and gender inequalities within Congress and perpetuated through its legislative agendas. By contrast, Berg's Marxist approach (à la Poulantzas) not only captures what Brenner has identified as "hegemonic ideology" at work, which arises from the strong identification of the most powerful members of Congress with large capital interests, but also tracks moments of and openings for "nonhegemonic" (or, in Gramscian terms, "counter-hegemonic") struggles that can produce, albeit unevenly and too often temporarily, wins for subordinated groups, especially when they have followed a protest rather than an accommodationist strategy inside and outside Congress.

Berg's treatment is timely in that it comes during a period of global economic restructuring, to which he points in his discussion of a climate of increased global competitiveness. This climate has led not only national capital but also transnational capital to exert downward pressure on wages and work regulations, thereby undermining organized labor's power base. He also notes, although too briefly, that Congress is now more beholden to finance capital and international financial institutions than it is to citizens in the context of the globalization of capital and the internationalization of the state.

Unfortunately, Berg does not carry over this analysis very well into his historical and contemporary accounts of the struggles of labor, women, and African Americans within and with Congress. His engaging case studies of individual members of Congress, past and present, who have represented and cultivated the interests of progressive social movements tend to focus on internal politicking, with little attention to changes in the international political economy that he earlier argues frames congressional ideology and limits social struggle. For example, although he speaks to the increasingly exclusionary practices of organized labor as it evolved in the United States (which, in part, accounts for its current weakness in relation to capital), Berg does not explore how it might be reorganized to recoup its losses and power base so as to be more inclusive of nonunionized workers, primarily women and minorities, who are filling the lowest-wage and most casualized jobs that are proliferating in the post-Fordist, service-oriented economy of the United States. Nor does he address the need for a more transnational labor movement to increase leverage with transnational capital and the national legislatures beholden to it. Moreover, his tendency to see patriarchy as operating rather independently from capitalism—although certainly predating it and different from it—leads him to assert that economic relations do not limit changes in household arrangements and to predict that gender equality can be achieved in Congress and by legislative action without structural change in the economy. This flies in the face of the rise of the neoconservative agenda, now firmly in place in the new Congress, that has accompanied the rise of global restructuring, which demands the reprivatization of social welfare, reshifting the responsibility for this back onto women, who, at the same time, are expected to fill low-wage, casualized jobs in the new service economy.

Finally, in his otherwise excellent discussion of the Congressional Black Caucus Alternative Budget, Berg does not add to his reasons for its failure the rise of transnational capital (and the continued power of the military) that it directly threatens. Nor does he address how that might be a new rallying point around which coalitions can be built that would make such an alternative budget a matter of high politics on the basis of interconnecting race, gender, and class oppressions perpetuated and exacerbated by U.S.-sponsored global restructuring.

These criticisms aside, Berg has provided a highly readable alternative interpretation of the U.S. Congress, highlighting individuals inside and movements outside of it that have made a difference as well as forging new ground for more thoroughgoing and interconnected gender, race, and class analyses of the U.S. Congress in the "new world order" of global restructuring.

ANNE SISSON RUNYAN
State University of New York
Potsdam

EISENSTEIN, ZILLAH R. *The Color of Gender: Reimaging Democracy*. Pp. xi, 277. Berkeley: University of California Press, 1994. No price.

MANN, CORAMAE RICHEY. *Unequal Justice: A Question of Color*. Pp. xiv, 301. Bloomington: Indiana University Press, 1993. $35.00. Paperbound, $14.95.

The Color of Gender and *Unequal Justice* challenge the conventional wisdom and method of the social sciences as they argue for the relevance of gender and race as categories of analysis. The authors urge us to reconsider democratic politics (Eisenstein) or the American criminal justice system (Mann) through the experiences of women and minorities.

Zillah Eisenstein focuses on the reconstruction of democratic theory and argues that "the radical orientation of rights discourse can be used to transform both liberalism and socialism by specifying their universal commitments to both freedom and equality in terms of sex, gender, and race." According to Eisenstein, both the "emerging male democracies" of Eastern Europe and the American political experience in the 1980s have been characterized by a patriarchal view of democracy, where the experiences of women and minorities have been ignored.

The rejection of the socialist state in Eastern Europe has been accompanied by a new traditionalism about the place of women in society. In seeking to find the appropriate balance between "individuality and collectivity," Eisenstein suggests that the hopeful start of these new democracies has begun to give way to "nationalism, racism, and sexism." But she argues that all is not lost. Feminists must work for the recognition of women's differences and "an activist state that does not intervene on behalf of patriarchal interests."

In a much longer section on the American experience, Eisenstein indicts the Reagan-Bush era as one in which the privatization of the American state was accompanied by a patriarchal intervention into the private lives of women. In chapters on the attack on affirmative action, reproductive rights, and funding related to acquired immune deficiency syndrome, Eisenstein explores the various manifestations of this "conservatized democracy," where she believes the "legal discourse of equality, which is necessary to actualizing one's freedom of choice, has been delegitimized."

Eisenstein turns finally to her theoretical enterprise: the reimaging of democracy through the "radicalizing of privacy and the discourse of rights." Liberal democracy is not to be abandoned but rather re-created in a manner that maintains a commitment to individual freedom and equality "while recognizing individual diversity." Thus equality requires that everyone be treated fairly, not that everyone be treated alike. If one imagines democracy from the perspective of a woman of color, one's view of democracy will be encompassing of diversity and variety and will thus meet the expectations of Eisenstein's democracy.

Coramae Richey Mann considers similar questions in *Unequal Justice*. Here she examines the American system of criminal justice and challenges the argument made by some social scientists that there is no racial bias in it. In a comprehensive review of the social scientific literature on the criminal justice system, Mann makes the case for a systematic bias against minorities. Her book is an indictment of both the system and the approach taken by social scientists in studying that system.

Mann contends that to discover the bias that permeates the system, one must take a historical approach that examines the experiences of minorities and considers their unequal social and economic status in American society. She begins her argument with a brief overview of the experiences of minority groups in the United States. Her focus in this historical section is the extent to which these groups have been subjected to violence by the state.

Mann goes on to consider the biases in the way criminal behavior is measured, discovered, prosecuted, and punished, finding in each area evidence of institutionalized racism that extends beyond the actors in the system to many of the social scientists that analyze the system. Each chapter ends with a section entitled "A Minority View," which seeks to demonstrate the ways in which this institutionalized racism has been discovered by minority social scientists.

Eisenstein and Mann challenge us to rethink the traditional conceptualizations of democracy and justice. While some will see the books as polemics that violate the traditional rules for how one does social science, most should find the books enlightening and troubling as they think about the place of these central concepts in our society.

KATY J. HARRIGER

Wake Forest University
Winston-Salem
North Carolina

ELLIS, RICHARD J. *Presidential Lightning Rods: The Politics of Blame Avoidance*. Pp. viii, 271. Lawrence: University Press of Kansas, 1994. $29.95.

In *Presidential Lightning Rods*, Richard Ellis presents a thorough and enlightening discussion of presidential attempts to deflect blame from themselves and onto their subordinates. Ellis's analysis clearly points out that most of these attempts to turn subordinates into "lightning rods" have been unsuccessful, failing for a myriad of reasons he lucidly points out. Presidents too openly direct the officials involved in making policies to deflect blame. Presidents are often too openly ideological or tied to unpopular positions. At times, subordinates claim the "lightning rod" label, instigate more conflict than necessary, and become liabilities instead of blame-attracting assets.

In presenting studies of various persons and administrative positions, Ellis attempts to lay the building blocks of a broader theory of blame avoidance. Instead, what he does is to attempt to create theory by generalizing from one successful case, that of Dwight Eisenhower. Ellis argues persuasively that the Eisenhower leadership style of separation from day-to-day, hands-on aspects of governing, avoiding fixed ideological positions, engaging in no ego-inflating credit claiming, and allowing the appearance of subordinate-driven policymaking is the ideal style to use if one's goal is to deflect blame and responsibility. What Ellis does not do effectively is translate this into a broader theory.

When Ellis attempts to weave a theory out of his various case studies, it becomes clear to all, including him, that only Eisenhower ever used lightning rods successfully. Rather than settle on the conclusion that Eisenhower was an exceptional case, entering office under a unique set of circumstances (no previous open party affiliation, no previous significant political involvement), Ellis chooses to argue that other presidents were just not skillful enough to be successful with these strategies.

In drawing this conclusion, Ellis underestimates several important differences in the political environment that most presidents face today. The media's coverage of the president is constant and, as Thomas Patterson has noted, increasingly negative. Political parties no longer mediate the relationship between presidential candidates and the outside world. Most presidents have long political records, including clear-cut ideological stances and policy positions that put them in a much different position from that of Eisenhower. Ellis's studies are interesting not because Eisenhower's style is likely to become the rule but because they illustrate that it may be only political amateurs, with no perceived ideology or political history, who can govern with some measure of bipartisan agreement.

RHONDA KINNEY

Eastern Michigan University
Ypsilanti

ELSHTAIN, JEAN BETHKE. *Democracy on Trial*. Pp. xvii, 153. New York: Basic Books, 1994. $20.00.

KRASNO, JONATHAN S. *Challengers, Competition, and Reelection: Comparing Senate and House Elections*. Pp. x, 195. New Haven, CT: Yale University Press, 1995. $26.00.

What do these two books have in common? They are short, inexpensive hardbacks and I am interested in them. That is about it. *Democracy on Trial*, addressed to the intelligent general reader, is a mixture of political philosophy and public policy with a moral message. It grew out of a series of lectures for the Canadian Broadcasting Corporation. *Challengers, Competition, and Reelection* is an academic treatise that is reasonably well written but will not transform its author into a media star. Jean Bethke Elshtain's book is about civil society; Jonathan Krasno's is about congressional elections. The two books do not add up to a single theme, but each provokes much stimulating thought on its own.

Elshtain, the Laura Spelman Rockefeller Professor of Ethics at the University of Chicago, is one of the most prominent exponents of communitarianism. This movement holds that Americans have lost the Tocquevillian spirit of community and need to regain it. The country is in a mess, and there is no easy way out. We have lost the self-confidence that made for American exceptionalism, the idea that, in David Potter's felicitous phrasing, we are a "people of plenty." In our nervousness, we look out only for ourselves and make nonnegotiable demands on our polity and society. Each group insists that it is special, its claims morally superior to those of others. We do not reach out to others, or join with others, as much as we used to because we are preoccupied with ourselves. Without a web of social connections, we have become a less tolerant nation. The more we simmer, the angrier we get at the injustices that may be part of everyday life. Our rage blinds us to the tolerance and moral vision that are the only way out of our morass.

This is my take on our dilemma. I think that I do no injustice to Elshtain to put these words in her mouth, too. Elshtain writes beautifully and taps a wide range of sources, from polls to poetry to Plato, to support her thesis. Yet this is less a sustained argument on value change in American society than a plea to the larger society to think about a larger purpose. Here, as elsewhere, Elshtain points her bow and arrow at radical feminists and gay rights activists who pursue their policy agenda through claims of victimization. Multiculturalism threatens the role of education as a purveyor of morals by making the schools just one more battleground in the fight over whose rights are paramount. Although the guiding spirit is the Reverend Martin Luther King, Jr., the resonating idea is Rodney King's: why can't we all get along?

Elshtain makes a compelling case for her arguments. She issues a clarion call for a greater moral background to our politics and a need for greater collective action. Yet she offers no suggestions as to how we get there (I also must plead guilty). Maybe there is no solution other than an admonition to behave better, but it would be nice to know. The argument would also be more compelling if Elshtain set out the problem more clearly. What are our most pressing problems? How did we get there? Elshtain suggests that we have lost our moral compass, but I think that she needs to tie her thesis even more closely to the loss of trust in other people, our lack of confidence in the future, and the real economic problems faced by many Americans. Finally, I agree that radical demands threaten our social fabric, but I worry whether the debates over feminism, gay rights, and multiculturalism pose as great a threat to our nation's future as does the enduring problem of race. Andrea Dworkin may be as dangerous as the politicians who fan the flames of affirmative action, but a whole lot more people pay attention to her.

And now for something completely different: *Challengers, Competition, and Reelection* breaks new ground by comparing House and Senate elections. Krasno, an assistant professor of politics at Princeton University, argues that Senate elections are more competitive than House contests because they attract stronger challengers. Once we account for the strength of challengers and the intensity of campaigns, Krasno argues, there are few differences between House and Senate contests. This is a bold thesis that may become known as the argument of the Berkeley school. Among its earlier advocates are Raymond Wolfinger (Krasno's dissertation adviser) in the

American Political Science Review in 1980 (with Thomas Mann) and Mark Westlye (another Berkeley Ph.D.) in *Senate Elections and Campaign Intensity* (Baltimore, MD: Johns Hopkins University Press, 1991).

The most novel part of the thesis is in chapters 2 and 3, where Krasno skewers two key arguments about the differences between House and Senate elections. In chapter 2, Krasno demolishes arguments (including my own) that senators pay less attention to constituency service than do representatives and pay the price for ignoring personal favors. Using data from the 1988 and 1990 Senate Election Studies, Krasno shows in a variety of ways that this is simply not the case. His arguments are compelling. Yet I cannot help wondering whether the data gathered by Bruce Cain, John Ferejohn, and Morris Fiorina in 1978 (*The Personal Vote* [Cambridge: Harvard University Press, 1987]) may tell a complementary story. When those of us holding this argument dear advanced it, the Cain et al. data supported our claims by showing very different expectations for the House and the Senate. The late 1970s and early 1980s were tough years for incumbent senators. Perhaps senators have learned a lesson and now court constituents as well as representatives do. Certainly, incumbent senators have become more electorally secure, and I can give a lot of anecdotal evidence to support my observation.

The heart of the argument is in chapters 4 through 6. Krasno develops it well and presents a lot of evidence on its behalf. Senators and representatives in hard-fought races are better known, have better contact with constituents, and receive more votes than do legislators in low-key contests. All of this is beyond dispute. I worry about circularity, however. Krasno, following Westlye, classifies Senate races as hard fought or low-key by consulting *Congressional Quarterly Weekly Report* (and later Charles Cook's reports). But *Congressional Quarterly* (and presumably Cook) makes its classification from reporters and consultants in the field—and, whenever possible, from both public and private polls. Candidates who are ahead in the polls therefore turn out to be better known and get more votes. I remain to be convinced, although the brief analysis of campaign dynamics between 1988 and 1990 (pp. 148-51) takes me a good part of the way.

Even if Krasno were to convert me, I still would wonder why some races attract good challengers and others attract poor challengers. Squire and Bond, Covington, and Fleischer have developed models to explain challenger quality in the Senate and the House, respectively. Neither is terribly successful, and so we remain at a loss. I suggest that we need to pay more attention to the partisan undertow of both House and Senate campaigns. Westlye hit the mark when he noted that hard-fought races tend to occur in competitive political environments, while low-key races are mostly confined to one-party states. The answer to why House and Senate races differ may lie in the nature of the constituencies. Such a focus would challenge Krasno's claim that campaigns make a real difference, but it need not rule them out altogether.

Even if I quarrel with Krasno, he has started an important debate. This is a well-written and well-argued book that will shape our thinking about congressional elections. Krasno states his thesis clearly, presents a wide range of evidence supporting it, and presents compelling arguments as to why alternative explanations have gone astray. Even though the price for the clothbound version is good, it should be published in paperback now.

ERIC M. USLANER

University of Maryland
College Park

HART, VIVIEN. *Bound by Our Constitution: Women, Workers, and the Minimum Wage.* Pp. xv, 255. Princeton, NJ: Princeton University Press, 1994. $35.00.

In *Bound by Our Constitution*, Vivien Hart compares the evolution of minimum wage laws in England and the United States and argues that the United States had the advantage because its Constitution established a framework for principled debate over this complex issue. She locates the origins of English and American minimum wage laws in campaigns by women activists against sweated labor around the time of World War I. Because sex-segregated labor markets stratified women into low-wage jobs, especially sweat shops and home work where there was almost no unionization, a legal minimum would have improved women's wages more than men's. Despite the relevance of these laws to women, men formally debated the arguments. English male parliamentarians and American male lawyers represented their women peers who investigated and exposed sweated labor and the low wages that characterized women's work.

Biology, the social construction of gender, and the U.S. Constitution all constrained American women in contradictory ways. Constitutional guarantees of due process, Hart argues, allowed all these aspects to be recognized and sorted out until a benchmark minimum wage was achieved. The ability to conduct principled debate within the framework of the U.S. Constitution, Hart contends, distinguishes the debate over minimum wage law in the United States from that in England. In sharp contrast to the English common law—which only allows parliamentarians to structure legal change—the U.S. Constitution provides a clear framework for testing the legality of innovations. The English Parliament established industry-specific minimum wages through local wage boards, a mechanism that helped rectify class differences but ignored problems related to women's multiple social responsibilities. In the United States, by contrast, localities initially regulated sweated industries; later states passed minimum wage laws that covered only women; and, finally, a federal minimum wage was established under the Fair Labor Standards Act of the New Deal. This latter act, argues Hart, set the critical precedent of a statutory minimum wage based on the principle of workers' rights.

By selecting key cases that both detail and outline the progress of minimum wage laws within the complicated array of local, state, and federal laws passed in the United States—and almost as frequently overturned by the courts—Hart does readers a great service. She carefully evaluates these cases within their social context not only to highlight the key arguments used to support and oppose minimum wage laws in the United States but also to explain their evolution. Finally, Hart, an English scholar, reminds readers that the U.S. Constitution established a system of competing interests that engenders continual debate and challenges citizens to assert their rights.

NANCY BREEN

National Cancer Institute
Bethesda
Maryland

McDONALD, FORREST. *The American Presidency: An Intellectual History.* Pp. viii, 516. Lawrence: University Press of Kansas, 1994. $29.95.

This is an engaging, well-researched, and readable book. It succeeds in tying together the antecedents of the American presidency that lie in English government, law, and political theory with the intentions and legacy of the Constitution's framers. It also seeks to examine significant (as well as some insignificant) contributions of the nation's best-known chief executives to shaping that office and the way in which external events have left their mark on it. The book distinguishes itself on both fronts, the historical and the functional. The result is a tour de force of the American presidency from Washington to Clinton, an erudite exposition of constitutional history and politics embracing three centuries of our republic's experience with executive authority, colonial and national.

Portions of this book traverse the literature and events already known to, and commented on extensively by, previous generations of constitutional scholars. Some of the most interesting chapters, nevertheless, are those dealing with sixteenth- and seventeenth-century legal scholars who examined the monarchy's relations with Parliament relative to lawmaking, diplomacy, and military affairs. The last half of the book provides current updates of the presidency in matters of enacting legislation, conducting diplomacy, enforcing the law, and administering the national government. Tucked away in these chapters are discussions of twentieth-century presidents' attempts, both successful and unsuccessful, to manipulate public opinion through dealings with the broadcast and print media.

That presidents have striven to make their cases in dealing with Congress in lawmaking and diplomacy, and to take their arguments to the public correspondingly, has been well known to perceptive citizens for several generations. So are the reasons for the increasing presidential centrality to these facets of the governmental process and the consequences of that centrality for the office and the country. The outcome, across time, has been a strengthened, more influential, and resourceful presidency than the Philadelphia framers of 1787 envisioned. Concomitantly, Congress has confronted the obligation continually to find ways to adjust to this changing relationship to preserve and reuse crucial constututional prerogatives. It has been the presidency's unparalleled access to expertise (including technology) in addressing public problems, with at least an intermittent success rate in managing them for a large, expectant, and influential constituency, that accounts for the lasting significance of that office. The personalities and political skills deployed by some of our best-known presidents in dealing with Congress and in cultivating public opinion are recounted with fascinating and instructive detail.

Of the book's 16 chapters, 8 deal with historical precedents of various kinds that pertain to the presidency prior to Washington's first inauguration. Only 4 chapters address the problems and growing pains of the office's evolution during the succeeding two centuries; these chapters are confined to statute lawmaking, diplomacy, law enforcement, and governmental management. The book's emphases may sate or shortchange the interest of readers in the subject of the presidency, then, depending on their bent for earlier history or more recent occurrences. The main ideas flavoring the presidency's origins and developments by and large receive satisfactory exposition.

In sum, this book is a well-written, extensively researched treatment of our nation's chief magistracy, emphasizing the ideas that gave birth to it and the exogenous forces shaping it over time. Its scope and depth are impressive; it is more readable and selective in its focus than is Edward Corwin's *The Presidency: Office and Powers*, with which (among enduring books about our chief executives) it is most likely to be compared. To me, the book's understatement of the role of ethics in the presidency's development is about the only topic or theme insufficiently addressed. A sequel to this book suggests itself, which McDonald would be eminently qualified to write; it would address the lessons that could be drawn from two centuries of experience with the presidency for our nation's broader struggle to define and refine the meaning of democracy.

          HARRY W. REYNOLDS, JR.

University of Nebraska
Omaha

PECORELLA, ROBERT F. *Community Power in a Postreform City: Politics in New York City*. Pp. xi, 232. Armonk, NY: M. E. Sharpe, 1994. $45.00.

In this study of citizen participation in New York City politics, Robert Pecorella uses what he calls a "contextual" theoretical approach to focus "on how changes in the socioeconomic conditions around cities interact with local political developments to shape urban policy over time." Building on Clarence Stone's concept of urban regimes, Pecorella develops a historical framework for his contextual analysis and identifies three successive regime changes in New York City, each of which arose out of a fiscal crisis. Periodically, as the city's finances spun out of control, bankers stepped in and forced out the regime in power. With the fall of one regime came a new one blessed by New York's economic elite.

The first regime change came with the end of the era of "gang rule." The Tweed Ring was forced out by a bankers' strike during the crisis of 1871 and was replaced by Tammany Hall. The machine politicians kept the city's finances in line for many years, but fiscal problems eventually discredited Tammany. The Bankers Agreement in 1933 and the election of Fiorello LaGuardia ushered in a reform regime. This regime was characterized by an emphasis on professional government and a growing array of welfare programs. Important for the story Pecorella tells is that reformers placed little value on citizen participation or neighborhood politics.

The third fiscal crisis came in 1975, and, again, bankers stepped in to force fiscal responsibility on the city's government. Pecorella conceives of this latest regime as "postreform" in character because it represents a reaction to rule by technocrats. The pressure on the city to facilitate participation by neighborhood activists had begun in the 1960s, and various neighborhood participation programs evolved into a citywide system of community advisory boards.

Pecorella emphasizes the inherent tension that exists between the advisory councils and the oversight organs of the city's central government, which he contends act on behalf of the economic elite. He argues that the demands of this elite are responsible for a citizen participation system that has been disappointing, producing mixed results in terms of its effectiveness.

Although the standards by which he evaluates the performance of the community advisory boards are not always clear, Pecorella's analysis of them seems cogent and fair-minded. What is troubling about his argument, however, is that he presents little evidence documenting how the economic elite has forced the city to make decisions weakening the citizen participation program. Community involvement programs are usually disappointments, and no fiscal crisis is necessary for mayors, bureaucrats, and city councillors to find ways of protecting their turf against activists who want power devolved to the neighborhoods.

Readers of *Community Power in a Postreform City* cannot help but be impressed by Pecorella's grasp of New York's history and its complex finances. For those interested in citizen participation in urban government, this is an especially valuable book.

          JEFFREY M. BERRY

Tufts University
Medford
Massachusetts

REDISH, MARTIN H. *The Constitution as Political Structure.* Pp. viii, 229. New York: Oxford University Press, 1995. $39.95.

Martin Redish has produced a surprisingly satisfying textual analysis of the structural provisions of the Constitution. The satisfaction is surprising because his approach is so unfashionably traditional. He argues that the clear terms of the Constitution obligate judges to take seriously the framers' preoccupation with a carefully delineated set of institutional arrangements. In making his case, Redish develops a thoughtful and thorough critique of many of the approaches advanced by contemporary justices and commentators with respect to issues relating to federalism, the commerce clause, the separation of powers, and the delegation of legislative authority.

Redish is impatient with those who suggest that we should be free to disregard or reconceptualize those features of the original constitutional design that we consider anachronistic or inconvenient. From his point of view, the legal obligations imposed by the text cannot be so easily evaded. For example, he points out that the national government was designed to possess only limited, delegated responsibilities, and thus he concludes that it is simply inappropriate to interpret the commerce clause in such as way as to effectively grant the government general legislative authority. (This is the same sensibility animating the recent decision of a bare majority of Supreme Court conservatives to strike down a congressional ban on gun ownership near schools in the historic case of *United States v. Lopez* [1995].) Moreover, because the constitutional text specifies in Article I, section 9, which powers are denied to the states, it is inappropriate for the Supreme Court under the so-called dormant commerce clause to add an additional limitation by denying states the authority to regulate interstate commercial activity. Redish also claims that the vesting clauses of the first three articles require us to ensure that the institutions of the federal government exercise only those powers that are appropriate under a system of divided responsibilities; this means that we need to work harder to prevent both usurpation by one branch of another branch's sphere of authority and a branch's abdication of its assigned responsibilities (as in the practice of delegating legislative power to executive branch agencies).

In the course of advancing these positions, Redish provides a careful and comprehensive review of competing conceptualizations. This makes his argument admirably systematic. It also makes this volume very useful as a way of introducing students to the existing literature on these topics. As Redish develops his arguments, one soon discovers that his commitment to textualism is not rigidly formalistic; he is willing to consider the purposes of various provisions in light of changing circumstances. At the same time, while he frequently criticizes colleagues who argue for the practical advantages of deviating from strict textual meaning, it is also true that Redish can be tempted away from the text, as when he argues in favor of reading the term "citizen" in the privileges and immunities clause to include corporations. More difficult to understand is why Redish insists on analyzing *Morrison v. Olson* (1988) (upholding the special prosecutor law) on the basis of a general theory of strict separation of powers (as did Justice Scalia in his lone dissent) rather than by looking at the textual provisions of the Constitution relating to the power of appointment (which was the focus of Chief Justice Rehnquist's majority opinion).

Still, even those of us who view the text as an inevitably contested terrain rather than as a source of positive law can take pleasure in watching a skilled neoformalist demonstrate persuasively what it means to take seriously the design of the framers' republic. Redish helps us remember the kinds of issues that preoccupied constitutional theorists before the Supreme Court relented to the New Deal and before the legal academy reacted to the influences of legal realism and the civil rights movement.

HOWARD GILLMAN

University of Southern California
Los Angeles

WEED, CLYDE P. *The Nemesis of Reform: The Republican Party during the New Deal*. Pp. xiv, 293. New York: Columbia University Press, 1995. $37.50.

In this book, Clyde Weed has provided a clear and revealing account of Republican Party actions in the critical period of 1930 through 1938. The essential story he tells is of a party that pursued a strategy of polarization, or strenuous opposition to the New Deal, for much of this period. After brief bipartisan support during Franklin D. Roosevelt's first 100 days, Republican congressional leaders and other national party spokesmen embarked on a sustained course of sharp criticism of most of FDR's policies. This response, Weed shows, was related to—and probably contributed to—increasing Republican losses in the elections of 1932, 1934, and 1936. Only after the party moderated its criticism prior to the 1938 election—a move Weed characterizes as Downsian—were the Republican losses reversed.

The basis for Weed's account is a review of the public statements and personal correspondence of leading Republicans of the period. This is supplemented by an analysis of key roll calls in the 73rd, 74th, and 75th Congresses. The latter is particularly useful for illustrating the regional and ideological divisions that plagued the Republican Party during this period and that, Weed argues, are an essential element in the explanation of why the Republicans' original response to the New Deal challenge was so ineffective.

From a theoretical perspective, the book is an attempt to explain why the Republican Party appeared to adopt the irrational strategy—in Downsian terms—of moving away from the Democrats after 1932 rather than toward them. The basic answer is that party leaders, particularly those in the dominant conservative eastern wing, believed that there was greater opposition to the New Deal policies among the electorate than proved to be the case. Just as important, these conservative leaders felt that the long-term goal of maintaining conservative control over the party was more important than a short-term attempt to appeal to voters temporarily distracted by emergency conditions.

The least convincing argument advanced is Weed's assertion that his account breaks new ground by identifying the actions of losing parties in realignments as crucial to the realignment process. This is not a fundamentally new insight, however, and scholars of realignment will not be forced to restructure their views of realignments in light of this book. Nevertheless, both they and more general readers will benefit from this careful, clearly presented case study of a losing party's deliberations and actions in the midst of a series of electoral disasters.

JOHN FRENDREIS

Loyola University
Chicago
Illinois

SOCIOLOGY

HADDAD, YVONNE Y. and JANE IDLEMAN SMITH. *Mission to America:*

Five Islamic Sectarian Communities in North America. Pp. xii, 226. Gainesville: University of Florida Press, 1993. $34.95. Paperbound, $18.95.

Among the most interesting aspects of recent waves of immigration to the United States is the increasing religious diversity that those waves bring to American society. Paralleling the development is a growing recognition of the diversity that exists within often stereotyped religious traditions. In no small way has this been true of ethnic and religious groups of Islamic background or origin. Equally interesting is the "discovery" of Islamic-influenced groups that existed within American society prior to the massive shifts in immigration patterns since 1965. *Mission to America*, in essence, deals with both the discovery and diversity aspects as it provides a brief background for five sectarian Islamic movements.

Yvonne Haddad and Jane Idleman Smith chose to study two movements of foreign origins, the Druze and Ahmadiyya; two that draw heavily on the Afro-American experience, the Ansar Allah Community and the Moorish Science Temple of America; and United Submitters, a genuine North American sect led by an immigrant Egyptian.

The study of each group is confined to a single chapter that provides a basic historical overview of the evolution of each sect with commentary on its adaptation or adjustment to American society. In the studies of the two immigrant sectarian communities, the Ahmadiyya and Druze, the issues of adaptation are posed against a background of quite different time periods given that the Druze presence dates to the last century, allowing decades of assimilationist influences, and the Ahmadiyya movement is essentially, although not completely, a recent development. The Druze, as a relatively small, widely dispersed community, obviously face the reality of similar groups in American society once patterns of intermarriage emerge. The children of such marriages rarely follow the minority ethno-religious tradition. The case of the Ahmadiyya community is much more complex; besides its immigrant South Asian elite population, it has also been an actively proselytizing influence within the Afro-American community and has a presence in every major American city due to mosque construction since the 1980s. This community's complex mix of immigrant and native-born Afro-American adherents, together with signs of the emergence of Afro-American leadership in the sect, represents a more complex dynamic and a greater potential for indigenization of the movement. A major question that remains to be explored within this sect is the interface between the immigrant South Asian, largely Pakistani element and the significant Afro-American presence. Also, because Haddad and Smith refer to the estimated 5000 Ahmadiyya—largely Afro-American—in the United States in 1940, it would be interesting to know whether there has been continuity in affiliation. This might provide some insight into the future of the Ahmadiyya movement in the Afro-American community and American society at large. Likewise, in discussing the Ansar Allah Community and the Moorish Science Temple of America, it would have been interesting to explore the issue of continuity of affiliation.

ROBERT J. YOUNG

West Chester University
Pennsylvania

KEATING, W. DENNIS. *The Suburban Racial Dilemma: Housing and Neighborhoods.* Pp. xii, 274. Philadelphia: Temple University Press, 1994. $49.95. Paperbound, $22.95.

In *The Suburban Racial Dilemma*, W. Dennis Keating addresses the continuation of racial segregation in American cities. Partly in response to the migration of large numbers of blacks to cities since World War I, the movement of whites to the suburbs—so-called white flight—spelled the erosion of the central city's tax base and often resulted in policies of racial exclusion in the suburbs. When blacks did manage to move to some suburbs, the process often repeated itself, and those suburbs experiencing an influx of blacks resegregated themselves. By examining several of Cleveland's suburbs, Keating shows how such resegregation was successfully avoided in two cases, Shaker Heights and Cleveland Heights, by what he calls "affirmative" fair housing measures. He shows how other suburbs—Parma, for instance—remained nearly all white, and still others, such as East Cleveland, became nearly all black. For this segregation, Keating faults suburbs' decisions to pursue "race-neutral policies" or their failure to acknowledge racial transition as a problem in need of public discussion and policy.

Keating attempts to demonstrate which efforts to integrate the suburbs worked and which did not. Least successful were "racial dispersal" plans to place low-income housing throughout the suburbs at the discretion of the various locales; such plans met with resistance on the grounds that lower property values and imported social problems, mainly crime, would result, and they were usually embraced only by those communities already dedicated to racial integration. More successful were grassroots and local government efforts to put controls on reckless Realtors' practices and discriminatory bank policies. Keating's descriptions of the merit of monitoring and prohibiting racial "steering," "redlining," and "blockbusting" are persuasive. Plans he favors to provide "economic incentives" such as mortgage assistance for those willing to make "integrative" moves, however, raise critical issues such as resentment and unfairness, issues he mentions but fails to resolve. The very real concerns of blacks and whites with living in neighborhoods with poor schools, falling property values, and high crime rates need more forthright discussion. In addition, it is not clear whether it is important to Keating's vision of integration that segregated neighborhoods often emerge even within suburbs with seemingly praiseworthy racial mixes.

Keating's faith that "interracial contacts will reduce racial conflict and discrimination" determines his ultimate promotion of "greater racial diversity among homeowners living in neighborhoods that otherwise are mostly homogeneous." That contact is needed is undeniable; that it will address the deep divisions in our society without attention to the economic sources for the perpetuation of such divisions, as well as the widespread doubt about the justice of special privileges, is belied by the evidence Keating gives of continuing racial hostility and neighborhood segregation even in those suburbs considered models of racial diversity.

ELISABETH LASCH-QUINN
Syracuse University
New York

McMAHON, CHRISTOPHER. *Authority and Democracy: A General Theory of Government and Management*. Pp. xiv, 307. Princeton, NJ: Princeton University Press, 1994. $35.00.

This is a provocative work in which the author addresses the dilemma that arises when otherwise legitimate leaders work against their subordinates' moral beliefs. Christopher McMahon's discussion focuses on the corporate sphere, and he examines the conditions under which an employee is justified in disobeying directives from superiors.

McMahon essentially seeks to ensure managerial accountability to employees; failing that, he seeks to justify the disobedience of the Thoreauvian employee. He concludes that "the case for democracy in nongovernmental organizations is weaker than the case for democratic government." Nonetheless, he maintains that "constitutions for nongovernmental organizations that fail to provide the employees as a whole with some sort of role in formulating *ultimate* managerial policy are problematic."

He distinguishes between different types of authority, arguing that corporate authority should be regarded not as being grounded in some promissory relationship (P-authority) but, instead, as depending on the leader's ability to facilitate mutually beneficial cooperation (C-authority) among employees and managers, all of whom may have different moral aims. McMahon's principal metaphor is that of the conscientious Nazi German railroad employee who discovers that he can permit a few prisoners to escape without his supervisors' discovering the subterfuge. Should employees not, instead, quit their jobs if they discover that they cannot remain loyal to their employers? McMahon answers no and contends that the moral commitments of the employees would certainly outweigh the programmatic goals of the employers: "the justification that establishes the legitimacy of a given de facto authority is always justification from the standpoint of the subordinates."

While there is no disputing the importance of McMahon's focus on legitimizing authority, his thesis suffers because he does not address the parallel question, What legitimizes dissent? McMahon never states clearly the grounds on which the authority of otherwise legitimate superiors can be challenged. For example, his theory does not distinguish clearly between employees' seeking a voice in running a corporation, inmates' seeking to run an asylum, and voters' initiating a recall or simply throwing the rascals out.

McMahon's thesis is predicated on the assumption that subordinates' desires are indeed grounded in some irreproachable moral vision. While the subordinate in question may be driven by such ethical concerns, so, too, may the authority figure. Thus McMahon's discussion embodies the same tension that arises when the desires and expectations of subordinates may not be perceived by their superiors as being in their best interests. When employees disagree with the programmatic goals of employers, on what grounds can the employees be said to have a legitimate basis for challenging the vision of their superiors?

While democratic theory provides a clear basis for popular sovereignty, it is not clear how McMahon translates this into the same sovereign power for employees. On what grounds does an employee have the same claim of authority as does a citizen? How can we decide when the claims of the conscientious objector are bona fide moral concerns as opposed to uninformed ones or, perhaps, the product of disingenuousness?

There exists in democratic theory a point to which the exercise of positive authority by superiors is justified a priori. Once that point is crossed, subordinates are justified in challenging their superiors. McMahon does not explain clearly where that point lies or how we would know when superiors have crossed it. Clearly, a theory grounded in moral concerns of subordinates cannot rely merely on popular discontent—or, at least, disagreement with superiors in any given situation—as the only reason to challenge otherwise valid exercises of authority.

If it can be argued that subordinates do have valid grounds for challenging their superiors, McMahon's theory provides an interesting discussion of the bases for such a challenge. However, without a clear measure for determining whether their gripes are indeed valid, his otherwise provocative work leaves the reader hanging.

MARK E. RUSH

Washington and Lee University
Lexington
Virginia

TORRES, ANDRÉS. *Between Melting Pot and Mosaic: African Americans and Puerto Ricans in the New York Political Economy.* Pp. xxi, 245. Philadelphia: Temple University Press, 1995. $49.94. Paperbound, $19.95.

As the title indicates, in this book Andrés Torres compares the economic, social, and political positions of the two largest minority communities in New York City, African Americans and Puerto Ricans. Beyond shedding some welcome comparative light on the nature and causes of continuing poverty and examining the two communities' economic and political efforts relative to each other and to others, Torres raises several important questions concerning the complex relationships between class, race, and immigration. While the result provides useful insights into the two communities and makes for interesting reading, the reader looking for systematic answers to the larger questions will be frustrated.

The analysis is framed within a neo-Marxist, segmented labor market perspective and is unabashedly political. The final two chapters are devoted to a critique of the Reagan and Bush years and the conservative agenda for solving problems of poverty and race—for example, workfare and school reform based on competition—and call for a variety of programs generally supported by the Left including job training, the strengthening of public education, community economic development, and a national training system as well as changes in the overall approach to overcoming the marginalization of minorities including antipoverty measures not based on enlarging the middle class, a challenge to prevailing market-driven criteria and to taking democracy seriously. Finally, Torres calls for a collaborative research agenda involving both researchers and community groups in a common endeavor to overcome social inequality and political powerlessness.

While the first two theoretical chapters and the concluding "what should be done" chapters are predictable and do not cover new ground, chapters 3 and 4 are more interesting. In these chapters, Torres discusses the different historical legacies of the two communities. Shared conditions of poverty and marginalization have given rise to some differences in economic positions (for example, African Americans have higher median family incomes and greater access to public employment), political power, and community infrastructures (for example, more complete and active social and religious institutions and organizations, more concentrated residential patterns) that have placed African Americans in a somewhat better political position.

Despite differences between the two communities and the built-in competition for jobs fostered by the capitalist economy (which depends on class, race, and gender hegemony), African Americans and Puerto Ricans have employed similar strategies, including insurgency, to attempt to combat hegemony and overcome their marginalization. Despite the threat to interethnic solidarity, the two minority groups have also worked together to elect African American politicians such as Mayor David Dinkins and Jesse Jackson.

BARBARA SCHMITTER HEISLER

Gettysburg College
Pennsylvania

WHITE, MERRY. *The Material Child: Coming of Age in Japan and America.* Pp. xvii, 256. Berkeley: University of California Press, 1994. Paperbound, $12.00.

The term "material child" refers to adolescents in two of the world's most consumer-oriented societies—Japan and the United States—societies in which youths are drawn to possess the material objects promoted by consumer industries and the media and societies in which youth identities are shaped in part by that market. The same youths are also "material" to the survival of these societies because they are these societies' future.

Enriched by interviews with media and marketing researchers and other experts on youths as well as with 50 Japanese and 30 American adolescents, Merry White focuses on the impact of culture on adolescence experience in Japan, using the experience of American adolescents as a mirror to provide further illumination. In so doing, she focuses on differences she finds in these two groups of adolescents, differences that lie "in the meanings they attach to growing up, to family, school, sexuality, friendship, and the wider world, and in the expectations that adults have for them in all these arenas of life." Although her comprehensive view of the experience of adolescence in Japan (the main focus of her research) recognizes the diversity of Japanese adolescents, she tends to overgeneralize about the experience of American adolescents, and this weakens her use of American adolescence as a mirror to reflect on adolescence in Japan.

White views adolescence in Japan as a time of promise in which teens are preparing for their own as well as society's future, in which friendships and peer associations provide training for social relations in adult life. By contrast, she sees America as viewing adolescence as a limbo period, a time in which youths are at risk to themselves and others, a time in which peer pressure can lead to additional risks. She explains these differences as culturally based. The mixed messages given to American youths are confusing and lead American adolescents to question the hypocrisy of adults. Conflicting messages in Japan, however, are viewed as "complementary contradictions" and as providing an acceptable area of freedom in the gap between the ideal and the real. Thus, in Japan, different or even deviant behaviors that are done in private can coexist without conflict along with correct behaviors done in public.

It is this concept of complementary contradictions that illuminates White's analysis of the impact of culture on the development of Japanese adolescents in the chapters on family, school, the material child, friendship, and sexuality.

JEAN E. BROOKS
Jackson State University
Mississippi

ECONOMICS

GRAVELLE, JANE G. *The Economic Effects of Taxing Capital Income.* Pp. xv, 339. Cambridge: MIT Press, 1994. $35.00.

This book provides a comprehensive economic analysis of capital income taxation. Jane Gravelle, whose own research has contributed to the vast body of scholarly literature on the subject, uses the conventional economic performance benchmarks of efficiency and equity to assess both present capital income taxation and alternatives for possible improvement. Although presented from the perspective of the professional economist, the book is clearly written so as to make its contents understandable to the noneconomist who has a special interest in the taxation of capital income. It thoroughly describes existing capital income tax law within the framework of the ongoing political debate concerning the subject.

Following the introductory chapter, which provides an overview of the book, chapter 2 considers the fundamental question of whether capital income should be taxed at all. Assuming an answer of yes to this question, chapters 3 through 9 systematically examine the present mechanism for taxing capital income in relationship to the efficiency and equity criteria, a discussion that interfaces with an insightful review of the literature. Specific topics include accelerated depreciation, capital gains taxes, the alternative corporate minimum tax, the passive loss restriction, the investment tax credit, and the exemption of income for retirement savings. Chapter 10 extends the analysis beyond the domestic American economy to capital income taxation in the setting of an open international economy. The final chapter recommends greater uniformity in the taxation of investment within an income tax structure while arguing for the integration of the corporate and personal income taxes.

Among the many contributions of the book are the critical evaluation of the conventional wisdom that links lower capital income tax rates to increased rates of savings, a discussion of the lock-in effect associated with capital gains taxation, and an assessment of the relationship between the level of capital income taxation and international competitiveness. Meanwhile, the two appendixes provide an excellent summary of the history of capital income taxation in the United States and a detailed description of the calculation methods and data sources used in the book, respectively. The reference section offers an extensive listing of bibliographical citations. Overall, the book makes an important contribution to the capital income tax literature by addressing this complex subject in a well-organized and competent fashion that distinguishes the forest from the trees.

BERNARD P. HERBER

University of Arizona
Tucson

HECKSCHER, CHARLES. *White Collar Blues*. Pp. ix, 224. New York: Basic Books, 1995. $23.00.

The central development addressed in this monograph is the decade-long effort of U.S. corporations to downsize middle management. Based on extensive case studies, Charles Heckscher critiques alternative organizational strategies that firms have pursued in implementing these policies, and he suggests ways in which both firms and middle managers can successfully respond to emerging employment environments. Heckscher argues persuasively that the old moral contract between firms and middle management, based on complementary corporate paternalism and employee loyalty, is no longer viable because, in the highly dynamic contemporary marketplace, flexibility and cost containment are at a premium. The era of the "organization man" is over.

Indeed, Heckscher argues convincingly that firms endeavoring to deal with their middle-managerial turmoil by patching up recent breaches invite the worst consequences; the contradictions between loyalist regimes and the new competitive marketplace are simply too intense. Significantly, Heckscher includes among these failed initiatives most recent attempts to introduce greater levels of participatory management, suggesting that the sharing of top management's visions and concerns with middle managers falls short of the degree of inclusion that can effectively respond to the structural changes taking place.

Curiously, Heckscher also finds that middle managers, despite the rocky road they have been obliged to travel in recent years, are at least as wedded to the loyalty paradigm as are their employers. This loyalty, along with the self-censorship it entails, renders it difficult if not impossible for managers to successfully execute the new responsibilities imposed by the more competitive marketplace.

What must be done, according to Heckscher, is to transform the traditional relationship between middle managers and their employers, displacing the moribund structures of paternalism and loyalty with a new professionalism where the managers are committed to their own personal skills, goals, and professional affiliations rather than to particular organizations and where firms provide an environment in which middle managers can develop these attributes and share in the formation as well as the execution of the corporate objectives as long as such a relationship meets the needs of both parties. This "community of purpose" paradigm is exhibited by the firms that have responded most successfully to recent competitive challenges.

The reader can be convinced that a new implicit contract is required under these new circumstances without being convinced of Heckscher's sanguine evaluation of the consequences, however. Indeed, only continuing employees were interviewed for his research, essentially ignoring the fate of legions of middle managers who have found themselves without portfolio in recent years. With firms reporting a tripling and even a quadrupling of revenue per employee over this period, the relevant analogy is musical chairs, where greater flexibility and generalized professional commitment cannot invariably translate into a successful sequence of employment opportunities.

Heckscher realistically evaluates alternative responses to the continuing assault on middle management but is less successful in convincing the reader that the imperatives of the impersonal marketplace are also in the best interests of the individuals who bear its brunt. Middle management is inexorably losing its privileged status and becoming increasingly generalized and commodified as firms are compelled to seek ever new realms of cost-cutting in pursuit of competitive advantage.

ALEXANDER M. THOMPSON III

Vassar College
Poughkeepsie
New York

VIETOR, RICHARD H. K. *Contrived Competition: Regulation and Deregulation in America.* Pp. 436. Cambridge: Harvard University Press, Belknap Press, 1994. $35.00.

Richard Vietor has produced a valuable scholarly treatment of the impact that regulation and deregulation have had on the performance and conduct of the American airline, telecommunications, natural gas, and banking industries. The beauty of the book is the author's ability to evaluate the evolution of four industries over more than a sixty-year period. Beginning with the surge in federal regulation during the New Deal, Vietor traces how these industries have been affected by government regulators and, in turn, how the business strategies of these corporations have influenced their own markets.

Vietor addresses each industry by using material from government publications, the trade press, business archives, and interviews with some key players in each industry. He uses this information to evaluate such hypotheses of government regulation as the public choice and regulatory capture models. In part, because he considers such a broad period, he finds that none of the often discussed models of regulation and deregulation fares well at explaining the evolution of the four markets. Vietor argues that regulation should be viewed "as an evolving system of market governance, embedded in the changing macroeconomic and political context." The nature of regulation changed not only because of the fluctuations in the performance of the economy but also because of new technologies, the evolution of academic theories of market and government behavior, political entrepreneurship, and ineffective government policies.

Vietor's work is especially stimulating where he tracks the forecasts made by proponents of regulation or deregulation. For example, he notes that to the surprise of many proponents of regulation, pricing mechanisms became more complex once government controls were reduced. Rather than moving on to cost-based pricing, as some economists had predicted, many of these markets exhibited an increased level of price discrimination because firms used prices to segment customers and establish customer loyalty.

Perhaps because of the period of time and the range of industries covered by the book, the chapters on each industry are not equally balanced. Vietor's analyses of the banking and airline industries are stronger than his discussions of the gas and telecommunications industries.

Vietor's work is an important addition to the contributions made by business historians at the Harvard Business School on the broad factors that are affecting the evolution of American industry.

DAVID GABEL

Queen's College
Flushing
New York

OTHER BOOKS

ABEGAZ, BERHANU, PATRICIA DILLON, DAVID H. FELDMAN, and PAUL F. WHITELEY, eds. *The Challenge of European Integration: Internal and External Problems of Trade and Money.* Pp. xiv, 316. Boulder, CO: Westview Press, 1994. $59.95.

ACHINSTEIN, SHARON. *Milton and the Revolutionary Reader.* Pp. xiv, 272. Princeton, NJ: Princeton University Press, 1995. $35.00.

ALMAGUER, TOMAS. *Racial Fault Lines: The Historical Origins of White Supremacy in California.* Pp. xii, 281. Berkeley: University of California Press, 1994. $40.00. Paperbound, $15.00.

AUSTIN, BETTY, comp. *J. William Fulbright: A Bibliography.* Pp. xx, 189. Westport, CT: Greenwood Press, 1995. $65.00.

BACHARACH, SAMUEL B., PETER BAMBERGER, and WILLIAM J. SONNENSTUHL. *Member Assistance Programs in the Workplace: The Role of Labor in the Prevention and Treatment of Substance Abuse.* Pp. vii, 88. Ithaca, NY: ILR Press, 1994. Paperbound, $10.95.

BANDOW, DOUG. *The Politics of Envy: Statism as Theology.* Pp. xix, 338. New Brunswick, NJ: Transaction, 1994. $34.95.

BAR-SIMAN-TOV, YAACOV. *Israel and the Peace Process 1977-1982: In Search of Legitimacy.* Pp. xi, 338. Albany: State University of New York Press, 1994. $21.95.

BATTAGLIA, DEBBORA, ed. *Rhetorics of Self-Making.* Pp. vii, 147. Berkeley: University of California Press, 1995. $30.00. Paperbound, $14.00.

BECKMAN, PETER R. and FRANCINE D'AMICO, eds. *Women, Gender, and World Politics: Perspectives, Policies, and Prospects.* Pp. xi, 248. Westport, CT: Bergin & Garvey, 1994. $59.95.

BENNETT, W. LANCE and DAVID L. PALETZ, eds. *Taken by Storm: The Media Public Opinion and U.S. Foreign Policy in the Gulf War.* Pp. xvi, 308. Chicago: University of Chicago Press, 1994. $40.00. Paperbound, $15.95.

BLUMBERG, ARNOLD, ed. *Great Leaders, Great Tyrants? Contemporary Views of World Rulers Who Made History.* Pp. xiv, 354. Westport, CT: Greenwood Press, 1995. $49.95.

BORDERS, REBECCA and C. C. DOCKERY. *Beyond the Hill: A Directory of Congress from 1984 to 1993.* Pp. xv, 215. Lanham, MD: University Press of America, 1995. $46.50. Paperbound, $19.50.

BUDGE, IAN and DAVID McKAY, eds. *Developing Democracy.* Pp. vi, 346. Thousand Oaks, CA: Sage, 1994. $85.00. Paperbound, $26.95.

BUGAJSKI, JANUSZ. *Ethnic Politics in Eastern Europe.* Pp. xxvi, 493. Armonk, NY: M. E. Sharpe, 1994. $75.00.

BUNDY, BARBARA K., STEPHEN D. BURNS, and KIMBERLY V. WEICHEL, eds. *The Future of the Pacific Rim: Scenarios for Regional Cooperation.* Pp. xv, 263. Westport, CT: Praeger, 1994. $59.95. Paperbound, $18.95.

CALLARI, ANTONIO, STEPHEN CULLENBERG, and CAROLE BIEWENER, eds. *Marxism in the Postmodern Age: Confronting the New World Order.* Pp. xxiii, 560. New York: Guilford, 1994. $49.95. Paperbound, $19.95.

CAPLOW, THEODORE. *Perverse Incentives: The Neglect of Social Technology in the Public Sector.* Pp. 164. Westport, CT: Praeger, 1994. $49.95. Paperbound, $15.95.

CARLIN, DIANA B. and MITCHELL S. McKINNEY, eds. *The 1992 Presidential Debates in Focus.* Pp. xxi, 274. Westport, CT: Praeger, 1994. $55.00.

CLOSE, DARYL and NICHOLAS MEIER. *Morality in Criminal Justice:*

An Introduction to Ethics. Pp. xvi, 604. Belmont, CA: Wadsworth, 1995. Paperbound, no price.

COLEMAN, CHARLES J. and THEODORA J. HAYNES, eds. *Labor Arbitration: An Annotated Bibliography.* Pp. viii, 269. Ithaca, NY: ILR Press, 1994. $35.00.

COOK, TERRENCE E. *Criteria of Social Scientific Knowledge: Interpretation, Prediction, Praxis.* Pp. x, 151. Lanham, MD: Rowman & Littlefield, 1994. $59.50. Paperbound, $21.95.

COOKE, EDWARD F. *A Detailed Analysis of the Constitution.* Pp. ix, 203. Lanham, MD: Rowman & Littlefield, 1994. Paperbound, $17.95.

COOKE, JAMES J. *The Rainbow Division in the Great War.* Pp. xii, 271. Westport, CT: Praeger, 1994. $55.00.

CRELINSTEIN, RONALD D. and ALEX P. SCHMID, eds. *The Politics of Pain: Torturers and Their Masters.* Pp. xvi, 195. Boulder, CO: Westview Press, 1995. $54.95.

CROSS, SHARYL and MARINA A. OBOROTOVA, eds. *The New Chapter in United States-Russian Relations: Opportunities and Challenges.* Pp. xiv, 227. Westport, CT: Praeger, 1994. $57.50.

CUTHBERTSON, IAN M. and JANE LEIBOWITZ, eds. *Minorities: The New Europe's Old Issue.* Pp. xii, 322. Boulder, CO: Westview Press, 1994. $39.85.

DANFORTH, JOHN C. *Resurrection: The Confirmation of Clarence Thomas.* Pp. viii, 225. New York: Viking, 1994. $19.95.

EDENS, JOHN A., comp. *Eleanor Roosevelt: A Comprehensive Bibliography.* Pp. xvii, 506. Westport, CT: Greenwood Press, 1994. $75.00.

FOLEY, MICHAEL, ed. *Ideas That Shape Politics.* Pp. vii, 232. New York: Manchester University Press, 1995. $69.95.

FREEDMAN, ROBERT O., ed. *Israel under Rabin.* Pp. xiii, 255. Boulder, CO: Westview Press, 1995. $55.00. Paperbound, $19.95.

FRIEDMAN, MILTON. *F. A. Hayek: The Road to Serfdom.* Pp. xlvi, 274. Chicago: University of Chicago Press, 1994. Paperbound, no price.

FRUCHTMAN, JACK, JR. *Thomas Paine: Apostle of Freedom.* Pp. xii, 557. New York: Four Walls Eight Windows, 1994. $30.00.

GARBY, CRAIG C. and MARY BROWN BULLOCK, eds. *Japan: A New Kind of Superpower?* Pp. 209. Baltimore, MD: Johns Hopkins University Press, 1994. $35.00. Paperbound, $13.95.

GEBREMEDHIN, TESFA G. and LUTHER G. TWEETEN. *Research Methods and Communication in the Social Sciences.* Pp. x, 167. Westport, CT: Praeger, 1994. $45.00.

GEORGE, STEPHEN. *An Awkward Partner: Britain in the European Community.* Pp. x, 277. New York: Oxford University Press, 1994. No price.

GILL, MARY LOUISE, and JAMES G. LENNOX, eds. *Self-Motion: From Aristotle to Newton.* Pp. xxi, 367. Princeton, NJ: Princeton University Press, 1994. $45.00.

GOLDSTEIN, ROBERT JUSTIN. *Saving "Old Glory": The History of the American Flag Desecration Controversy.* Pp. xv, 263. Boulder, CO: Westview Press, 1994. $29.95.

GRUSKY, DAVID B., ed. *Social Stratification: Class, Race, and Gender.* Pp. xv, 750. Boulder, CO: Westview Press, 1994. $69.50. Paperbound, $29.95.

GUILLEN, MAURO F. *Models of Management: Work, Authority, and Organization in a Comparative Perspective.* Pp. xiii, 424. Chicago: University of Chicago Press, 1994. $57.50. Paperbound, $18.95.

HAAS, MICHAEL. *Improving Human Rights.* Pp. viii, 254. Westport, CT: Praeger, 1994. $55.00.

HAGGARD, STEPHAN and STEVEN B. WEBB, eds. *Voting for Reform: Democ-*

racy, Political Liberalization, and Economic Adjustment. Pp. xv, 519. New York: Oxford University Press, 1994. $19.95.

HALLER, MAX and RUDOLPH RICHTER, eds. Toward a European Nation? Political Trends in Europe—East and West, Center and Periphery. Pp. x, 274. Armonk, NY: M. E. Sharpe, 1995. $60.00.

HAMRIN, CAROL LEE and SUISHENG ZHAO, eds. Decision-Making in Deng's China: Perspectives from Insiders. Pp. xlviii, 255. Armonk, NY: M. E. Sharpe, 1995. $65.00. Paperbound, $25.00.

HARRISON, ELIZABETH. Andrew M. Greeley: An Annotated Bibliography. Pp. xvii, 389. Metuchen, NJ: Scarecrow Press, 1994. $49.50.

HELD, JOSEPH. Dictionary of East European History since 1945. Pp. x, 509. Westport, CT: Greenwood Press, 1994. $59.95.

HEPER, METIN and AHMET EVIN, eds. Politics in the Third Turkish Republic. Pp. xi, 270. Boulder, CO: Westview Press, 1994. $59.00.

HIPPLER, JOCHEN. Pax Americana? Hegemony or Decline. Pp. xii, 212. Boulder, CO: Westview Press, 1994. $61.95. Paperbound, $17.95.

HOBERMAN, SOLOMON, and SIDNEY MAILICK, eds. Professional Education in the United States: Experiential Learning, Issues, and Prospects. Pp. xii, 222. Westport, CT: Praeger, 1994. $55.00.

HOFFE, OTFRIED. Political Justice. Pp. vii, 351. Cambridge, MA: Polity Press, 1995. $54.95.

HOWARD, MICHAEL, GEORGE J. ANDREOPOULOS, and MARK R. SHULMAN, eds. The Laws of War: Constraints on Warfare in the Western World. Pp. vii, 303. New Haven, CT: Yale University Press, 1994. No price.

HOYLES, MARTIN. Gardeners Delight: Gardening Books from 1560-1960. Pp. 214. Boulder, CO: Westview Press, 1994. $43.95.

JACOBSOHN, GARY JEFFREY. Apple of Gold: Constitutionalism in Israel and the United States. Pp. viii, 284. Princeton, NJ: Princeton University Press, 1993. Paperback, $14.95.

KING, ROY D. and MIKE MAGUIRE, eds. Prisons in Context. Pp. 159. New York: Oxford University Press, 1994. Paperbound, $19.95.

KITCHEN, HELEN and J. COLEMAN KITCHEN, eds. South Africa: Twelve Perspectives on the Transition. Pp. xii, 203. Westport, CT: Praeger, 1994. $55.00. Paperbound, $18.95.

KLEIN, MICHAEL, ed. An American Half Century: Postwar Culture and Politics in the USA. Pp. viii, 301. Boulder, CO: Westview Press, 1994. $59.95. Paperbound, $19.95.

KRUMHOLZ, NORMAN, and PIERRE CLAVEL. Reinventing Cities: Equity Planners Tell Their Stories. Pp. xvi, 250. Philadelphia: Temple University Press, 1994. $49.95. Paperbound, $22.95.

LAPIDUS, GAIL W., ed. The New Russia: Troubled Transformation. Pp. viii, 280. Boulder, CO: Westview Press, 1994. $57.00. Paperbound, $19.95.

LASHLEY, MARILYN E. and MELANIE NJERI JACKSON, eds. African Americans and the New Policy Consensus: Retreat of the Liberal State? Pp. xii, 246. Westport, CT: Greenwood Press, 1994. $55.00.

LAVER, MICHAEL and KENNETH A. SHEPSLE, eds. Cabinet Ministers and Parliamentary Government. Pp. ix, 318. New York: Cambridge University Press, 1994. $59.95. Paperbound, $21.95.

LEVITE, ARIEL E., BRUCE W. JENTLESON, and LARRY BERMAN, eds. Foreign Military Intervention: The Dynamics of Protracted Conflict. Pp. xvii, 334. New York: Columbia University Press, 1995. Paperbound, $16.50.

LILLA, MARK, ed. *New French Thought: Political Philosophy.* Pp. xii, 239. Princeton, NJ: Princeton University Press, 1994. Paperbound, no price.

LIPOVETSKY, GILLES. *The Empire of Fashion: Dressing Modern Democracy.* Pp. x, 276. Princeton, NJ: Princeton University Press, 1994. No price.

LIU, NANCY, PETER RAND, and LAWRENCE R. SULLIVAN, ed. *Deng Xiaoping: Chronicle of an Empire.* Pp. xxi, 288. Boulder, CO: Westview Press, 1994. $69.95. Paperbound, $19.95.

LUNDESTAD, GEIR, ed. *The Fall of Great Powers: Peace, Stability, and Legitimacy.* Pp. xviii, 414. New York: Oxford University Press, 1994. $35.00.

LUTTWAK, EDWARD N. *The Endangered American Dream.* Pp. 365. New York: Touchstone, 1994. Paperbound, $14.00.

MADDEN, FREDERICK and JOHN DARWIN, eds. *The Dependent Empire, 1900-1948: Colonies, Protectorates, and Mandates.* Pp. xxvi, 876. Westport, CT: Greenwood Press, 1994. $125.00.

MAINGOT, ANTHONY P. *The United States and the Caribbean.* Pp. xi, 260. Boulder, CO: Westview Press, 1994. $52.00. Paperbound, $18.95.

MANENT, PIERRE. *An Intellectual History of Liberalism.* Pp. xviii, 128. Princeton, NJ: Princeton University Press, 1994. No price.

MANN, THOMAS E. and NORMAN J. ORNSTEIN, eds. *Congress, the Press, and the Public.* Pp. vii, 212. Washington, DC: Brookings Institution, 1994. $36.95. Paperbound, $16.95.

McPHERSON, HARRY. *A Political Education: A Washington Memoir.* Pp. xix, 495. Austin: University of Texas Press, 1995. Paperbound, $19.95.

MILLER, ARTHUR H. and BRUCE E. GRONBECK, eds. *Presidential Campaigns and American Self Images.* Pp. xi, 306. Boulder, CO: Westview Press, 1994. $55.00. Paperbound, $19.95.

MOLEN, THOR. *Thought Splinters: Fiction Today, Reality Tomorrow.* Pp. xiii, 63. Pittsburgh, PA: Dorrance, 1994. $25.95.

MONTGOMERY, TOMMIE SUE. *Revolution in El Salvador: From Civil Strife to Civil Peace.* 2d ed. Pp. xv, 344. Boulder, CO: Westview Press, 1994. $69.00. Paperbound, $19.95.

MULCAHY, KEVIN V. and MARGARET JANE WYSZOMIRSKI, eds. *America's Commitment to Culture: Government and the Arts.* Pp. xiv, 235. Boulder, CO: Westview Press, 1995. $49.95.

NANDY, ASHIS. *The Illegitimacy of Nationalism.* Pp. xii, 94. New York: Oxford University Press, 1994. Paperbound, $8.95.

NEUHOLD, HANSPETER, PETER HAVLIK, and ARNOLD SUPPAN, eds. *Political and Economic Transformation in East Central Europe.* Pp. xviii, 357. Boulder, CO: Westview Press, 1995. Paperbound, $54.95.

PASSAS, NIKOS. *Organized Crime.* Pp. xxix, 579. Brookfield, VT: Dartmouth, 1995. No price.

PETTAVINO, PAULA J. and GERALYN PYE. *Sport in Cuba: The Diamond in the Rough.* Pp. ix, 301. Pittsburgh, PA: University of Pittsburgh Press, 1994. $49.95. Paperbound, $19.95.

POPA, OPRITSA D. and MARGUERITE E. HORN, comp. *Ceausescu's Romania: An Annotated Bibliography.* Pp. x, 153. Westport, CT: Greenwood Press, 1994. $59.95.

RAPOPORT, ANATOL. *The Origins of Violence: Approaches to the Study of Conflict.* Pp. xxvi, 620. New Brunswick, NJ: Transaction, 1995. Paperbound, $24.95.

REMINGTON, THOMAS F., ed. *Parliaments in Transition: The New Legislative Politics in the Former USSR and Eastern Europe.* Pp. vii, 246. Boulder, CO: Westview Press, 1994. $49.95.

RENSHON, STANLEY A., ed. *The Clinton Presidency: Campaigning, Govern-*

ing, and the Psychology of Leadership. Pp. ix, 261. Boulder, CO: Westview Press, 1994. $64.95. Paperbound, $19.95.

ROBERTS, JOHN W., ed. Escaping Prison Myths. Pp. xii, 212. Washington, DC: American University Press, 1994. $58.50. Paperbound, $24.50.

RUGMAN, ALAN M., ed. Foreign Investment and NAFTA. Pp. xii, 340. Columbia: University of South Carolina Press, 1994. $39.95.

SATTERWHITE, JAMES H., ed. The Crisis of Modernity: Karel Kosik's Essays and Observations from the 1968 Era. Pp. xi, 237. Lanham, MD: Rowman & Littlefield, 1994. $43.50.

SCHERVISH, PAUL G., PLATON E. COUTSOUKIS, and ETHAN LEWIS. Gospels of Wealth: How the Rich Portray Their Lives. Pp. xi, 284. Westport, CT: Praeger, 1994. Paperbound, $19.95.

SEGERS, MARY C. and TIMOTHY A. BYRNES, eds. Abortion Politics in American States. Pp. viii, 279. Armonk, NY: M. E. Sharpe, 1995. $55.00. Paperbound, $19.95.

SHARER, ROBERT J. The Ancient Maya. 5th ed. Pp. xxxii, 892. Stanford, CA: Stanford University Press, 1994. $24.95.

SHEA, DANIEL M. and JOHN C. GREEN, eds. The State of the Parties: The Changing Role of Contemporary American Parties. Pp. xi, 395. Lanham, MD: Rowman & Littlefield, 1994. $57.50. Paperbound, $21.95.

SHTROMAS, ALEXSANDRAS, ed. The End of "Isms"? Reflections on the Fate of Ideological Politics after Communism's Collapse. Pp. 234. Cambridge, MA: Basil Blackwell, 1994. Paperbound, $17.95.

SHUMAN, MICHAEL. Towards a Global Village. Pp. x, 189. Boulder, CO: Westview Press, 1994. $66.50. Paperbound, $17.95.

SIEGELBAUM, LEWIS H. and RONALD GRIGOR SUNY, eds. Making Workers Soviet: Power Class and Identity. Pp. xiii, 399. Ithaca, NY: Cornell University Press, 1995. $49.95. Paperbound, $19.95.

STINE, JEFFREY K. Twenty Years of Science in the Public Interest: A History of the Congressional Science and Engineering Fellowship Program. Pp. xiii, 192. Washington, DC: American Association for the Advancement of Science, 1994. Paperbound, $15.95.

TEMPLETON, MALCOLM. Ties of Blood and Empire: New Zealand's Involvement in Middle East Defence and the Suez Crisis 1947-57. Pp. xi, 278. New York: Oxford University Press, 1994. $32.00.

TIEFER, LEONORE. Sex Is Not a Natural Act and Other Essays. Pp. xvi, 232. Boulder, CO: Westview Press, 1994. $49.95. Paperbound, $19.95.

TOLLEY, GEORGE, DONALD KENKEL, and ROBERT FABIAN, eds. Valuing Health for Policy: An Economic Approach. Pp. xiv, 422. Chicago: University of Chicago Press, 1994. $55.00.

WACHMAN, ALAN M. Taiwan: National Identity and Democratization. Pp. xvi, 294. Armonk, NY: M. E. Sharpe, 1994. $55.00. Paperbound, $19.95.

WALSH, ROBERTA W. and JOHN G. HEILMAN, eds. Energizing the Energy Policy Process: The Impact of Evaluation. Pp. x, 244. Westport, CT: Quorum, 1994. $59.95.

WRIGGINS, W. HOWARD, ed. Dynamics of Regional Politics: Four Systems on the Indian Ocean Rim. Pp. xiv, 338. New York: Columbia University Press, 1995. Paperbound, $16.50.

ZERNICKE, PAUL HASKELL. Pitching the Presidency: How Presidents Depict the Office. Pp. viii, 175. Westport, CT: Praeger, 1994. $49.95.

INDEX

Adler, Paul, 61-62, 63-65
Affirmative action, 39
Aronowitz, Stanley, 10, 14
  ARONOWITZ, STANLEY and WILLIAM DiFAZIO, High Technology and Work Tomorrow, 52-67
Austin, Texas
  labor market, 85-87
  school-to-work system, 89-94
Automation, 115, 155-56, 173

Boyd, Lawrence, W., 11, 14
BOYD, LAWRENCE W., JR., The End of Hawaii's Plantations: Back to the Future? 95-110
Braverman, Harry, 60-62, 63-65

Career development, 73, 74, 79-80
Coates, Joseph F., 12, 14
COATES, JOSEPH F., Reworking Work: Tough Times Ahead, 154-66
Collective bargaining, and technology, 176, 178
Computer monitoring of workers, 171-72, 173
COMPUTERS DON'T KILL JOBS, PEOPLE DO: TECHNOLOGY AND POWER IN THE WORKPLACE, Charley Richardson, 167-79

Deskilling, 60-62, 63-64, 74, 174-75
DiFazio, William, 10, 14
DiFAZIO, WILLIAM, see ARONOWITZ, STANLEY, coauthor
Dislocated workers, 111-26
DISLOCATION POLICIES IN THE USA: WHAT SHOULD WE BE DOING? Ross Koppel and Alice Hoffman, 111-26
DISLOCATION POLICIES IN WESTERN EUROPE: PAST, PRESENT, AND FUTURE, Thomas Samuel Eberle, 127-39
Downsizing, 113, 114, 157, 163

Eberle, Thomas Samuel, 12, 14
EBERLE, THOMAS SAMUEL, Dislocation Policies in Western Europe: Past, Present, and Future, 127-39

Economic redevelopment, community-based, 40-41
Education
  and global economic competition, 47-51
  see also Vocational education
Employee stock ownership plans, 164
Employment Act of 1946, 29
Employment at will, 39-40
EMPLOYMENT FLEXIBILITY AND JOBLESSNESS IN LOW-GROWTH, RESTRUCTURED JAPAN, Koji Taira and Solomon B. Levine, 140-53
Employment, full, 192-93
  human rights, 32
  inflation, 30-31
  morality, 195
  U.S. Conference of Catholic Bishops, 32
EMPLOYMENT OF NEW ENDS: PLANNING FOR PERMANENT UNEMPLOYMENT, THE, David Macarov, 191-202
END OF HAWAII'S PLANTATIONS: BACK TO THE FUTURE? THE, Lawrence W. Boyd, Jr., 95-110
Ergonomics, 171, 178

Firestone Tire and Rubber Company, 128-30
France, shortened workweek, 20

Geography, and work, 175-76
  see also Global economic competition
GERMAN APPRENTICESHIP SYSTEM: LESSONS FOR AUSTIN, TEXAS, THE, Robert W. Glover, 83-94
Germany
  apprenticeship system, 84
  workweek, shortened, 20, 133, 134-35
Global economic competition, 115, 130-32, 156, 158, 159
  and education, 47-51
Glover, Robert W., 11, 14
GLOVER, ROBERT W., The German Apprenticeship System: Lessons for Austin, Texas, 83-94
Gross, Peter, 137
Gutek, Barbara A., 10, 14

GUTEK, BARBARA A., Service Workers: Human Resources or Labor Costs? 68-82

Hall, Jack, 100-101, 102
Hawaii
  displaced workers, 95-110
  housing for plantation workers, 102-3, 105-7
Hershberg, Theodore, 10, 14
HERSHBERG, THEODORE, Human Capital Development: America's Greatest Challenge, 43-51
HIGH TECHNOLOGY AND WORK TOMORROW, Stanley Aronowitz and William DiFazio, 52-67
Hoffman, Alice, 11, 14
HOFFMAN, ALICE, see KOPPEL, ROSS, coauthor
Human capital, 43-51, 83-94
HUMAN CAPITAL DEVELOPMENT: AMERICA'S GREATEST CHALLENGE, Theodore Hershberg, 43-51

Immigration, and unemployment, 156-57, 164
Inflation, 30-31, 33
Information Age, 17-18
Information workers, 159
International Longshoremen's and Warehousemen's Union (ILWU), 98-103, 106-109

Japan
  employment trends, 141-43, 152-53
  human resource management, 147-49
  lifetime employment, 40, 146, 152
  organized labor, 145, 149-52
  unemployment, 141-43, 144-45
  wage-productivity relationship, 143-44
  workweek, shortened, 144
Job retraining, 104, 106, 107, 110, 111-26, 177
Job satisfaction, 78
Job Training Partnership Act, 117-18, 126
JOBS: NEW CHALLENGES, NEW RESPONSES, Sumner M. Rosen, 27-42

Knowledge, 62, 63-64, 71-72
Koppel, Ross, 11, 14
KOPPEL, ROSS and ALICE HOFFMAN, Dislocation Policies in the USA: What Should We Be Doing? 111-26

Labor displacement, 54-55, 61-63, 65-67, 95-110

Labor productivity, 53, 59, 78, 81, 136, 143-44, 200-201
  see also Wage-productivity relationship
Levine, Solomon B., 12, 14
LEVINE, SOLOMON B., see TAIRA, KOJI, coauthor

Macarov, David, 13, 14
MACAROV, DAVID, The Employment of New Ends: Planning for Permanent Unemployment, 191-202
Managed health care, 70, 80
Marschall, Daniel, 13
MARSCHALL, DANIEL, Performing Work without Doing Jobs, 180-90
Minimum wage, 124, 144
Modernization, 137

National Adult Literacy Survey, 47, 49
National Labor Relations Act (NLRA), 176, 178
National state, breakdown of, 55-56, 138-39
NEW SOCIAL CONTRACT, A, Jeremy Rifkin, 16-26
New Standards Project, 51
Nonprofit sector, see Third Sector

Occupational Safety and Health Administration (OSHA), 176, 178
On-the-job training, 50, 77-78
Organized labor
  Japan, 145, 149-52
  occupational unionism, 180-90
  strength, 21, 37, 56-59, 98, 103, 108, 110, 115, 157, 172-73, 176

PERFORMING WORK WITHOUT DOING JOBS, Daniel Marschall, 180-90
Protectionism, and unemployment, 165

Repetitive strain injury (RSI), 171
Retirement age, see Work life, length of
REWORKING WORK: TOUGH TIMES AHEAD, Joseph F. Coates, 154-66
Richardson, Charley, 12, 14
RICHARDSON, CHARLEY, Computers Don't Kill Jobs, People Do: Technology and Power in the Workplace, 167-79
Rifkin, Jeremy, 9, 14
RIFKIN, JEREMY, A New Social Contract, 16-26
Rosen, Sumner M., 9, 14

INDEX

ROSEN, SUMNER M., Jobs: New Challenges, New Responses, 27-42

Scientific management, 75, 134
Self-employment, 163-64, 187-88
Service sector
  automation in, 115, 155-56
  growth in, 182
  workers in, 68-82, 110
SERVICE WORKERS: HUMAN RESOURCES OR LABOR COSTS? Barbara A. Gutek, 68-82
SHOSTAK, ARTHUR B., Epilogue, 203-5
SHOSTAK, ARTHUR B., Preface, 8-15
Skill, 60-62, 63-65
Skill standards, 186-87
Stockholders, influence on corporate human resource management, 158, 166
Swissair, 130-31
Switzerland, unemployment in, 132-33

Taira, Koji, 12, 14
TAIRO, KOJI and SOLOMON B. LEVINE, Employment Flexibility and Joblessness in Low-Growth Restructured Japan, 140-53
Taxes, and unemployment, 164
Technology
  and collective bargaining, 176, 178
  and harm to workers, 170-71
  and productivity gains, 19
  and workers' power vis-à-vis management, 167-79
Temporary workers, 86, 114, 157, 199
Third Sector, economic role of, 19, 21-26, 164-65
Thurow, Lester, 14
Trade Readjustment Act/Trade Adjustment Assistance (TRA/RAA), 116-18
Transfer payments, 41-42

Underemployment, measurement of, 35

Unemployment
  causes, 35-36, 136-37, 200
  effect on health, 32-33
  immigration, 156-57
  Japan, 141-43, 144-45
  measurement, 33-34, 36-37, 192, 193-94
  permanent unemployment, 191-202
  protectionism, 165
  remedies, 160, 162-66
  structural unemployment, 96-97, 154-66
  Switzerland, 132-33
  taxes, 164
U.S. Conference of Catholic Bishops, position on full employment, 32
Universal basic income, 201
USX Corporation, 113, 117-26

Vocational education, 48-49, 83-94, 183, 185-86
Volkswagen Corporation, 133-36

Wage-productivity relationship, 143-44, 162, 166, 169, 172
Wages, 159, 160, 200
  see also Minimum wage; Wage-productivity relationship
Welfare, 160, 162
Williams Air Force Base, 113, 118-26
Women as skilled workers, 64-65
Work life, length of, 38, 157, 162, 197
Work redistribution, 135-37
Workers
  computer monitoring, 171-72, 173
  decision making, 75-76, 174-75
  knowledge, 71-72
  physical attractiveness, 75
  power vis-à-vis management, 158-60, 167-79
  women as skilled workers, 64-65
Workers Adjustment Retraining Act (WARN), 117-18, 125
Workweek, shortening of, 19-21, 25, 38-39, 133, 134-35, 144, 162, 177, 197

Protection that moves with you, no matter where you go. A simple idea really.

The problem is a familiar one. Switch jobs, and you have to work out a new insurance plan. Well, as a member of AAPSS, you don't have to put up with that.

You see, one of the best AAPSS member benefits is that you can get outstanding insurance that you take with you—to your next job. No getting acquainted with another insurance company. No relearning paperwork and procedures. Our group rates are competitive. And because we understand your lifestyle, we can customize a plan that fits.

To speak with a customer service representative, call 1 800 424-9883, or in Washington, DC (202) 457-6820, between 8:30 a.m. and 5:30 p.m. eastern time. Now that was easy, wasn't it?

AAPSS Insurance
Term Life • Excess Major Medical • In-Hospital
High-Limit Accident • Medicare Supplement Insurance

The term life and high-limit accident plans are underwritten by
the New York Life Insurance Company, 51 Madison Avenue, New York, NY 10010.

The journal that everyone in management is talking about — and reading!

"...the only journal by the side of my bed — because it's interesting enough to keep me awake."
— *Jane Dutton*
University of Michigan

"A breath of fresh air! **JMI** captures many exciting ideas and debates. A wonderful contribution to the field!"
— *Peter Frost*
University of British Columbia

"**JMI** is helping define the cutting edge for the field of organizational behavior and management... if you want to peek into the future of our field, look at **JMI** today."
— *Tim Hall*
Executive Development Roundtable
Boston University

Editor: Thomas G. Cummings,
University of Southern California

The **Journal of Management Inquiry** is a high-quality refereed journal for scholars and professionals in management, organizational behavior, strategy, and human resources. **JMI** goes beyond the traditional, presenting the latest research and practice in a direct and forthright fashion. Each quarterly issue presents provocative and inquisitive scholarship that explores ideas and builds knowledge.

Subscribe Today!
Sage Customer Service: 805-499-9774 • **Sage FaxLine**: 805-499-0871

	1 Year	2 Years	3 Years
Individual	$52	$104	$156
Institutional	$135	$270	$405

SAGE PUBLICATIONS, INC. • 2455 Teller Road • Thousand Oaks, CA 91320

Journal of Management Education

Editor: Joan V. Gallos, *University of Missouri, Kansas City*

The **Journal of Management Education** (formerly the Organizational Behavior Teaching Review) serves as a forum for the improvement of management education in both classroom and corporate settings.

The journal is a lively, thought-provoking and practical compilation of ideas, models, techniques and tools for management and organizational behavior education. The **Journal of Management Education's** insightful analyses are distilled from a blend of new and seasoned teachers and trainers. **JME** examines what teaching methods work, which do not work — and why.

Created nineteen years ago to meet the growing demand for research, analysis and discussion on management and organizational behavior education, the **Journal of Management Education** provides you with information you can use today. **JME** brings you comprehensive coverage of the entire public and private management spectrum, including such diverse areas as:

- Human Resources
- Public Administration
- Government
- Entrepreneurship
- Hospital Administration
- Information Systems
- Organizational Behavior
- Management Consultation
- Organizational Communication
- Industrial and Labor Relations
- Education Administration
- Production/Operations

Subscribe Today!
Sage Customer Service: 805-499-9774 • Sage FaxLine: 805-499-0871

	1 Year	2 Years	3 Years
Individual	$52	$104	$156
Institution	$138	$276	$414

SAGE PUBLICATIONS, INC.
2455 Teller Road
Thousand Oaks, CA 91320

SAGE PUBLICATIONS LTD
6 Bonhill Street
London EC2A 4PU, England

SAGE PUBLICATIONS INDIA PVT. LTD
M-32 Market, Greater Kailash I
New Delhi 110 048, India

Work and Occupations

An International Sociological Journal

Editor: Daniel Cornfield, *Vanderbilt University*

As a major source of current theory and findings on the world of work, **Work and Occupations** is an indispensable resource for practitioners and researchers interested in the interaction of organizations, occupations, and society.

For over twenty years, this preeminent journal has provided an outlet for theoretical contributions, sound research, and original ideas in a variety of fields related to work, such as:
- Employee participation and ownership
- Occupations and professions
- Occupational socialization
- Occupational mobility
- Labor markets
- Effects on organizations and society

Contributors to the journal include anthropologists, management specialists, psychologists, educational researchers, population researchers, government administrators, and business specialists — in addition to sociologists — making the journal a truly interdisciplinary, international collection of critical writing that spans the field of work and occupations.

The Articles, Research Notes, Review Essays, and book reviews combine to make **Work and Occupations** an indispensable source of thought-provoking and informative scholarship. In addition, **Work and Occupations** occasionally publishes Special Issues devoted to a single topic of current concern.

Subscribe Today!
Sage Customer Service: 805-499-9774 • Sage FaxLine: 805-499-0871

	1 Year	2 Years	3 Years
Individual	$56	$112	$168
Institution	$167	$334	$501

SAGE PUBLICATIONS, INC.
2455 Teller Road
Thousand Oaks, CA 91320

SAGE PUBLICATIONS LTD
6 Bonhill Street
London EC2A 4PU, England

SAGE PUBLICATIONS INDIA PVT. LTD
M-32 Market, Greater Kailash I
New Delhi 110 048, India

A Special Issue of Business & Society

NEW PERSPECTIVES ON BUSINESS & SOCIETY

This Special Issue of **Business & Society** adds groundbreaking analysis to the business and society research literature.

To this point, a strong tradition of critical analysis, so prevalent in other disciplines, has not been part of business and society literature. However, the authors of these papers bring newly applied perspectives to the most prevalent relationships in business and society. To further encourage thoughtful discussion at least one commentary is included for each article.

Contents: Missing the Forest for the Trees: A Critique of the Social Responsibility Concept and Debate - *Marc Jones brings a Marxist-structuralist perspective in this critique of the social responsibility concept* / Commentary: Capitalism and Sin: Please Exploit Me for Your Benefit / Commentary: Are We Looking at the Same Forest? / **A Postmodern Feminist Perspective on Organizations in the Natural Environment: Rethinking Ecological Awareness** - *Kelly Strong makes a case for adopting a feminist ecological paradigm* / Commentary: Dualists or Duelists? Feminism, Ecology, and Business / Commentary: Can Feminist Language Change Organizational Behavior? Some Research Questions / **Overcoming the Separation Thesis: The Need for a Reconsideration of Business & Society Research** - *In the final article, Andy Wicks presents three value dichotomies which counter the usual arguments about business and society relationships.* / Commentary: Reconciliation Awaits: Dichotomies in Business & Society Theory

Business & Society
Volume 35, Number 1 / March 1996
Individual $15 / Institution $36

Frequency: March, June, September, December

	Subscribe Today!		
Sage Customer Service: 805-499-9774 • Sage FaxLine: 805-499-0871			
	1 Year	2 Years	3 Years
Individual	$50	$100	$150
Institutional	$132	$264	$396

SAGE PUBLICATIONS, INC.
2455 Teller Road
Thousand Oaks, CA 91320

SAGE PUBLICATIONS LTD
6 Bonhill Street
London EC2A 4PU, England

SAGE PUBLICATIONS INDIA PVT. LTD
M-32 Market, Greater Kailash I
New Delhi 110 048, India

The information you need to make intelligent judgments regarding the issues affecting you... your work... your society... and your world. Subscribe to

THE ANNALS

OF THE AMERICAN ACADEMY OF POLITICAL AND SOCIAL SCIENCE

Subscription Order Form

	Individual			Institution		
	One Year	Two Years	Three Years	One Year	Two Years	Three Years
Hardcover	❏ $74	❏ $148	❏ $222	❏ $229	❏ $458	❏ $687
Softcover	❏ $51	❏ $102	❏ $153	❏ $197	❏ $394	❏ $591

Name / Institution _____

Address _____

_____

City _____ State _____ Zip _____ Country _____

❏ My check or credit card information is enclosed.   ❏ Bill me.

Charge my: ❏ MasterCard   ❏ Visa   Exp. Date _____ Phone _____

Account # _____ Signature _____

Prices effective through August 31, 1996. Institutional checks for personal orders cannot be accepted. Phone number must be included with bill-me and credit card orders. In Canada, add 7% GST (#R129786448). On subscriptions outside the United States, add $12 per year for foreign postage. All foreign orders must be paid in U.S. funds. Make checks payable to:

SAGE Publications, Inc. • P.O. Box 5084 • Thousand Oaks, CA 91359 • (805) 499-0721   **T5686**

The information you need to make intelligent judgments regarding the issues affecting you... your work... your society... and your world. Subscribe to

THE ANNALS

OF THE AMERICAN ACADEMY OF POLITICAL AND SOCIAL SCIENCE

Subscription Order Form

	Individual			Institution		
	One Year	Two Years	Three Years	One Year	Two Years	Three Years
Hardcover	❏ $74	❏ $148	❏ $222	❏ $229	❏ $458	❏ $687
Softcover	❏ $51	❏ $102	❏ $153	❏ $197	❏ $394	❏ $591

Name / Institution _____

Address _____

_____

City _____ State _____ Zip _____ Country _____

❏ My check or credit card information is enclosed.   ❏ Bill me.

Charge my: ❏ MasterCard   ❏ Visa   Exp. Date _____ Phone _____

Account # _____ Signature _____

Prices effective through August 31, 1996. Institutional checks for personal orders cannot be accepted. Phone number must be included with bill-me and credit card orders. In Canada, add 7% GST (#R129786448). On subscriptions outside the United States, add $12 per year for foreign postage. All foreign orders must be paid in U.S. funds. Make checks payable to:

SAGE Publications, Inc. • P.O. Box 5084 • Thousand Oaks, CA 91359 • (805) 499-0721   **T5686**

BUSINESS REPLY CARD

FIRST CLASS MAIL   PERMIT NO. 90   THOUSAND OAKS, CA

POSTAGE WILL BE PAID BY ADDRESSEE

SAGE PUBLICATIONS, INC.
P.O. BOX 5084
THOUSAND OAKS, CA 91359-9924

NO POSTAGE
NECESSARY
IF MAILED
IN THE
UNITED STATES

BUSINESS REPLY CARD

FIRST CLASS MAIL   PERMIT NO. 90   THOUSAND OAKS, CA

POSTAGE WILL BE PAID BY ADDRESSEE

SAGE PUBLICATIONS, INC.
P.O. BOX 5084
THOUSAND OAKS, CA 91359-9924

NO POSTAGE
NECESSARY
IF MAILED
IN THE
UNITED STATES